The Gospel of Thomas:
A Spiritual Road to Wholeness, Peace, and Enlightenment

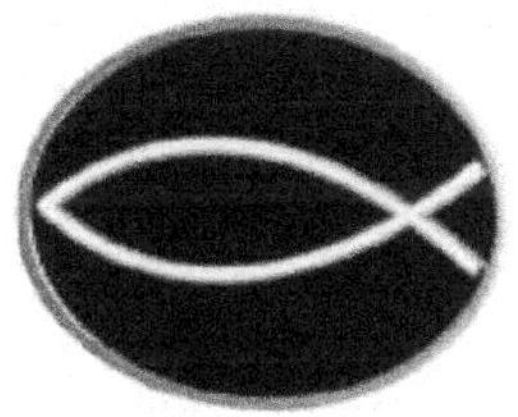

Joseph B. Lumpkin

The Gospel of Thomas:

A Spiritual Road to Wholeness, Peace, and Enlightenment

For information about first time authors, contact Fifth Estate 2795 County Hwy 57, Blountsville, AL 35031.

First Edition

Printed on acid-free paper

Library of Congress Control No: 2019946014

ISBN: 9781936533763

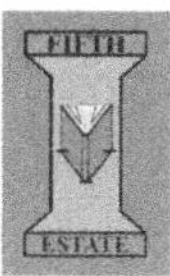

Fifth Estate, Incorporated

2019

Dedication

To fellow travelers;
When we have become detached we can see clearly;
When we become whole, uniting mind, emotion, and spirit we are saved.

Jesus said: Become passers-by.

Jesus said: If you bring forth what is within you, it will save you. If you do not have it within you to bring forth, that which you lack will destroy you.

Table of Contents

Introduction and History

In the winter of 1945, in Upper Egypt, an Arab peasant was gathering fertilizer and topsoil for his crops. While digging in the soft dirt he came across a large earthen vessel. Inside were scrolls containing hitherto unseen books.

The scrolls were discovered near the site of the ancient town of Chenoboskion, at the base of a mountain named Gebel et-Tarif, near Hamra-Dum, in the vicinity of Naj 'Hammadi, about sixty miles from Luxor in Egypt. The texts were written in the Coptic language and preserved on papyrus sheets. The lettering style dated them as having been penned around the third or fourth century A.D. The Gospel of Thomas is the longest of the volumes consisting of 114 verses. Recent study indicates that the original work of Thomas, of which the scrolls are copies, may predate the four canonical gospels of Matthew, Mark, Luke, and John. The origin of The Gospel of Thomas is now thought to be from the first or second century A.D.

The word Coptic is an Arabic corruption of the Greek word Aigyptos, which in turn comes from the word Hikaptah, one of the names of the city of Memphis, the first capital of ancient Egypt.

There has never been a Coptic state or government per se, however the word has been used to generally define a culture and language present in the area of Egypt.

The known history of the Copts starts with King Mina the first King, who united the northern and southern kingdoms of Egypt circa 3050 B.C. The ancient Egyptian civilization under the rule of the Pharaohs lasted over 3000 years. Saint Mina (named after the king) is one of the major Coptic saints. He was martyred in 309 A.D.

The culture has come to be recognized as one containing a distinctive art, architecture, and even a certain Christian church system.

The Coptic Church is based on the teachings of St. Mark, who introduced the region to Christianity in the first century A.D. The Copts take pride in the monastic flavor of their church and the fact that the Gospel of Mark is thought to be the oldest of the Gospels. Now, lying before a peasant boy was a scroll written in the ancient Coptic tongue; The Gospel of Thomas, possibly older than and certainly quite different from any other Gospel.

The peasant boy who found the treasure of the Gospel of Thomas stood to be rewarded greatly. This could have been the discovery of a lifetime for his family, but the boy had no idea what he had. He took the scrolls home, where his mother burned some as kindling. Others were sold to the black market antique dealers in Cairo. It would be years until they found their way into the hands of a scholar.

Part of the thirteenth codex was smuggled from Egypt to America. In 1955 whispers of the existence of the codex had reached the ears of Gilles Quispel, a professor of religion and history in the Netherlands. The race was on to find and translate the scrolls.

The introduction of the collected sayings of Jesus refers to the writer as Didymus (Jude) Thomas. This is the same Thomas who doubted Jesus and was then told to place his hand within the breach in the side of the Savior. In the Gospel of St. John, he is referred to as Didymus, which means twin in Greek. In Aramaic, the name Jude (or Judas) also carries the sense of twin. The use of this title led some in the apocryphal tradition to believe that he was the twin brother and confidant of Jesus.

However, when applied to Jesus himself, the literal meaning of twin must be rejected by orthodox Christianity as well as anyone adhering to the doctrine of the virgin birth of the only begotten Son of God. The title is likely meant to signify that Thomas was a close confidant of Jesus, or more simply, he was part of a set of twins and in no way related to Jesus.

Ancient church historians mention that Thomas preached to the Parthians in Persia and it is said he was buried in Edessa. Fourth century chronicles attribute the evangelization of India (Asia-Minor or Central Asia) to Thomas.

The text, which some believe predates the four gospels, has a very Taoist, Zen-like, or Eastern flavor. Since it is widely held that the three gospels of Matthew, Mark, and Luke have a common reference in the basic text of Mark, it stands to reason that all follow the same general history, insights, and language. The gospel of John used a separate source called the Signs Source. Since scholars believe that the Gospel of Thomas predates the four main gospels, it can be assumed it was written outside the influences common to the other gospels.

The Gospel of Thomas is actually not a gospel at all. It contains no narrative but is instead a collection of sayings, which are said to be from Jesus himself as written (quoted) by Thomas. Although the codex found in Egypt is dated to the fourth century, most biblical scholars place the actual construction of the text of Thomas at about 40 – 150 A.D.

The gospel was often mentioned in early Christian literature, but no copy was thought to have survived until the discovery of the Coptic manuscript. Since then, part of the Oxyrynchus papyri have been identified as older Greek fragments of Thomas. The papyri were discovered in 1898 in the rubbish heaps of Oxyrhynchus, Egypt. This discovery yielded over thirty-five manuscript fragments for the New Testament. They have been dated to about 60 A.D. As a point of reference, a fragment of papyrus from the Dead Sea Scrolls had been dated to before 68 A.D.

There are marked differences between the Greek and Coptic texts, however, this book attempts a synthesis of both texts by placing alternate translations and meanings within parenthesis. In this way both Coptic and Greek texts are combined without destroying the continuity of the Gospel. Since we have only fragments of the Greek version, the Nag Hammadi Coptic Text forms the basis of the translations.

The debate on the date of Thomas centers in part on whether Thomas is dependent upon the canonical gospels, or is derived from an earlier document that was simply a collection of sayings. Many of the passages in Thomas appear to be more authentic versions of the synoptic parables, and many have parallels in Mark and Luke. This has caused a division of thought wherein some believe Thomas used common sources also used by Mark and Luke. Others believe Thomas was written independently after witnessing the same events.

If Thomas wrote his gospel first, without input from Mark, and from the standpoint of Eastern exposure as a result of his sojourn into India, it could explain the mystical quality of the text. It could also explain the striking differences in the recorded quotes of Jesus as memories were influenced by exposure to Asian culture.

There is some speculation that the sayings found in Thomas could be more accurate to the original intent and wording of Jesus than the other gospels. This may seem counter-intuitive until we realize that Christianity itself is an Eastern religion, albeit Middle-Eastern. Although, as it spread west the faith went through many changes to westernize or Romanize it…Jesus was both mystical and Middle-Eastern. The Gospel of Thomas may not have seen as much "dilution" by Western society.

Since the Gospel of Thomas is a gnostic work consisting on 114 saying of a religious master from the Middle-East and was penned by a disciple serving in the east, it seems reasonable that we should look at the words and meaning in an eastern and gnostic context.

The Gospel of Thomas is so old that it is seen as evidence of the Q or Quelle Source document. The Q document is thought to predate the gospels and was used as a common source for the gospel of Mark. The gospel of Mark is believed to have then been used as a source for Matthew and Luke's gospel. Some believe Matthew and Luke used both Mark's gospel and the Q source for their versions. The gospel of John is thought to have used yet another source called the Signs Source. Thomas is thought to contain a source like that of Q, that is a list of saying written down directly by someone listening to or gathering the saying of Jesus. The writer and archivist of the list in the gospel of Thomas was said to be none other than the doubting disciple, Thomas. Most agree that through time the original sayings were altered and added to. As all parables are, these may have been altered to fit the times and belief systems that adopted them.

Marilyn Mellowes, writing for "Frontline," reports: "In 1989, a team of researchers led by James M. Robinson of the Institute for Antiquity and Christianity in Claremont, CA, began a most unlikely task: the "reconstruction" of the Gospel of Q. Robinson and his team are accomplishing this by a highly detailed literary analysis of Matthew, Luke, and Thomas. Their painstaking work goes "verse by verse, word by word, case ending by case ending."

The "recovery" of the Q gospel has stimulated a debate about the nature of early Christian communities, and by extension, the origins of Christianity itself. One scholar, Burton Mack, has advanced a radical thesis: that at least some Christian communities did not see Jesus as a Messiah; they saw him as a teacher of wisdom, a man who tried to teach others how to live. For them, Jesus was not divine, but fully human. These first followers of Jesus differed from other Christians whose ritual and practice was centered on the death and the resurrection of Jesus. They did not emerge as the "winners" of history; perhaps because maintaining the faith required the existence of a story that included not only the life of Jesus but also his Passion."

For more information of the beliefs of Christians in the first 50 years of the faith please see, "The Didache: A Different Faith, A Different Salvation" published by Fifth Estate Publishing.

The Gospel of Thomas was most likely composed in Syria, where tradition holds the church of Edessa was founded by Judas Thomas, The Twin (Didymos). The gospel may well be the earliest written tradition in the Syriac church

The Gospel of Thomas is sometimes called a Gnostic Gospel, although it seems more likely Thomas was adopted by the Gnostic community and interpreted in the light of their beliefs.

The term Gnostic is derived from gnosis, which in Greek means knowledge. Gnostics believed that knowledge is formed or found from a personal encounter with God brought about by inward or intuitive insight. It is this knowledge that brings salvation. The Gnostics believed they were privy to a secret knowledge about the divine. It is their focus on knowledge that leads to their name. The roots of the Gnosticism pre-date Christianity. Similarities exist between Gnosticism and the wisdom and knowledge cults found in Egypt. The belief system seems to have spread and found a suitable home in the mystical side of the Christian faith.

There are numerous references to the Gnostics in second century literature. Their form of Christianity was considered heresy by the early church fathers. The intense resistance to the Gnostic belief system seems to be based in two areas. First, there was a general Gnostic belief that we were all gods, with heaven contained within us. That is to say, we all contain a divine spark of God within us. Jesus, according to the Gnostics, was here to show us our potential to become as he was; a son or daughter of god, for God is both father and mother, male and female. These beliefs ran contrary to the newly developing orthodoxy. The second line of resistance was political. This resistance developed later and would have come from the fact that a faith based on a personal encounter flew in the face of the developing church political structure that placed priests and church as the keepers of heaven's gate with salvation through them alone.

It is from the writings condemning the group that we glean most of our information about the Gnostics. They are alluded to in the Bible in 1 Tm. 1:4 and 1 Tm. 6:20, and possibly the entirety of Jude, as the writers of the Bible defended their theology against that of the Gnostics.

Keeping in mind that the winners write the history, we see only what the emerging orthodoxy wishes us to see of the alleged evils of Gnosticism. Men of the orthodoxy were howling about Gnostics claiming that heaven was within each of us, viewing this as heresy, seeing that heaven could not possibly be there since the church controlled our entrance to heaven.

The main point regarding Gnostics is that they seek knowledge, which is not "informational" but instead is of a "revelatory" nature, noting the fact that Jesus taught not so much in factual information but instead spoke in ways calculated to awaken a deeper knowledge within the person, thus giving them a type of transcendental knowledge possible only through spiritual resurrection as if one were to remember the origin of the soul and what was there.

Beyond this central point of belief there existed several types or denominations of Gnostics, varying from those who seemed to clog this simple doctrine with myths and cosmologies of unimagined complexities, to those who were seeking a change of spiritual state, as opposed to simply changing belief systems from one religion to the next. For information beyond this simple point we should have a quick lesson in the history and general scope of beliefs within various Gnostic communities.

What is Gnosticism?

"Gnosticism: A system of religion mixed with Greek and Oriental philosophy of the 1st through 6th centuries A.D. Intermediate between Christianity and paganism, Gnosticism taught that knowledge rather than faith was the greatest good and that through knowledge alone could salvation be attained."

Webster's Dictionary

The word Gnostic is based on the Greek word "Gnosis," which means "knowledge." The "Gnosis" is the knowledge of the ultimate, supreme God and his spirit, which is contained within us all. It is this knowledge that allows one to transcend this material world with its falsities and spiritual entrapments and ascend into heaven to be one with God.

For centuries, the definition of Gnosticism has in itself been a point of confusion and contention within the religious community. This is due in part to the ever-broadening application of the term and the fact that various sects of Gnosticism existed as the theology evolved and began to merge into what became mainstream Christianity.

Even though Gnosticism continued to evolve, it is the theology in place at the time that the Gnostic Gospels were written that should be considered and understood before attempting to render or read a translation. To do otherwise would make the translation cloudy and obtuse.

It becomes the duty of both translator and reader to understand the ideas being espoused and the terms conveying those ideas. A grasp of theology, cosmology, and relevant terms is necessary for a clear transmission of the meaning within the text in question.

With this in mind, we will briefly examine Gnostic theology, cosmology, and history. We will focus primarily on Gnostic sects existing in the first through fourth centuries A.D. since it is believed most Gnostic Gospels were written during that time. It was also during that time that reactions within the emerging Christian orthodoxy began to intensify.

The downfall of many books written on the topic of religion is the attempt to somehow remove history and people from the equation. History shapes religion because it shapes the perception and direction of religious leaders. Religion also develops and evolves in an attempt to make sense of the universe as it is seen and understood at the time. Thus, to truly grasp a religious concept it is important to know the history, people, and cosmology of the time. These areas are not separate but are continually interacting.

People of various religions and beliefs will seize upon a text and make it their own. The text will resonate with their theology and, in time, the texts will be altered and reinterpreted to fit more and more into their doctrine. This is what has happened to the Gospel of Thomas. It has been altered and reinterpreted to fit better into the Gnostic system that adopted it as part of their own scripture. We must now endeavor to understand certain Gnostic beliefs in order to understand the Gospel of Thomas as it is now presented.

A Brief Lesson in Gnosticism

However diverse and confusing the various sects and systems of Gnosticism may be, most hold to a few core beliefs. The world is a diversion and is at odds with our spiritual path. The world is corrupt because the creator of this world was not the Father but an insane being from outside of heaven. It is this creature that misleads us into thinking he is god and the world is our home.

The world is cruel and harsh because the creator is cruel and harsh. Bad things happen to good people and good things happen to bad people because the creator was flawed and insane.

Our spirits were created from a divine spark from the One-True-God, the Divine All, the Father. Because we are spirits inhabiting these vehicles of flesh, we are naturally at odds with ourselves. In heaven, we were neither male or female, but a complete spiritual fusion of both.

The true God, the Father, or Divine All, has sent Jesus to us to enlighten us, teach us these things, and most of all, teach us how to become whole again. Wholeness is the ability to bring all parts of us, body, spirit, emotion, action, the inside of us and the outside of us, the male and female parts of us, all into agreement. This wholeness allows us to reunite with the Father. This is the kingdom of Heaven. It is within us and we must awaken to who and what we are in order to realize this truth. Jesus was sent here to show us that way home, to the kingdom within, and to the one true God. The knowledge of the true nature of the world, existence, ourselves, the Father, and the Kingdom is called Gnosis. Those who believe these things are called Gnostics.

The above description is in every way an over simplification of Gnostic theology, but if one takes these things into consideration the Gospel of Thomas will not only come into focus, but it will deliver such deep and life-changing insights we cannot remain untouched by its contents and teachings.

The roots of Gnosticism may pre-date Christianity. Similarities exist between Gnosticism and the wisdom and mystery cults found in Egypt and Greece. Gnosticism contains the basic terms and motifs of Plato's cosmology as well as the mystical qualities of Buddhism. Plato was steeped in Greek mythology, and the Gnostic creation myth has elements owing to this. Both cosmology and mysticism within Gnosticism present an interpretation of Christ's existence and teachings, thus, Gnostics are considered to be a Christian sect. Gnostic followers are urged to look within themselves for the truth and the Christ spirit hidden, asleep in their souls. The battle cry can be summed up in the words of the Gnostic Gospel of Thomas, verse 3:

Jesus said: If those who lead you say to you: Look, the Kingdom is in the sky, then the birds of the sky would enter before you. If they say to you: It is in the sea, then the fish of the sea would enter ahead of you. But the Kingdom of God exists within you and it exists outside of you. Those who come to know (recognize) themselves will find it, and when you come to know yourselves you will become known and you will realize that you are the children of the Living Father. Yet if you do not come to know yourselves then you will dwell in poverty and it will be you who are that poverty.

Paganism was a religious traditional society in the Mediterranean leading up to the time of the Gnostics. Centuries after the conversion of Constantine, mystery cults worshipping various Egyptian and Greco-Roman gods continued. These cults taught that through their secret knowledge worshippers could control or escape the mortal realm. The Gnostic doctrine of inner knowledge and freedom may have part of its roots here. The concept of duality and inner guidance taught in Buddhism added to and enforced Gnostic beliefs, as we will see later.

The belief systems of Plato, Buddha, and paganism melted together, spread, and found a suitable home in the mystical side of the Christian faith as it sought to adapt and adopt certain Judeo-Christian beliefs and symbols.

Like modern Christianity, Gnosticism had various points of view that could be likened to Christian denominations of today. Part of the problem of interpreting the exact meaning of certain verse comes from the fact that various Gnostic schools differed so broadly in their teaching, creation myths, and theologies. When the verses of the Gospel of Thomas are looked at as metaphors attempting to explain and elucidate Gnostic beliefs, confusion or uncertainty can arise as to the exact meaning the writer as trying to convey, based on the fact that there are so many variations of Gnosticism.

Complex and elaborate creation myths took root in Gnosticism, being derived from those of Plato. Later, the theology evolved and Gnosticism began to shed some of its more unorthodox myths, leaving the central theme of inner knowledge or gnosis to propagate.

The existence of various sects of Gnosticism, differing creation stories, along with the lack of historical documentation, has left scholars in a quandary about exactly what Gnostics believed.

Some have suggested that the Gnostics represented a free-thinking and idealistic movement much like that of the "Hippie" movement active in the United States during the 1960's.

Just as the "Hippie" movement in the U.S. influenced political thought, some early sects of Gnostics began to exert direct influence on the Christian church and its leadership.

Although it appears that there were several sects of Gnosticism, we will attempt to discuss the more universal Gnostic beliefs along with the highlights of the major sects.

Gnostic cosmology, (which is the theory of how the universe is created, constructed, and sustained), is complex and very different from orthodox Christianity cosmology. In many ways, Gnosticism may appear to be polytheistic or even pantheistic.

To understand some of the basic beliefs of Gnosticism, let us start with the common ground shared between Gnosticism and modern Christianity. Both believe the world is imperfect, corrupt, and brutal. The blame for this, according to mainstream Christianity, is placed squarely on the shoulders of man himself. With the fall of man (Adam), the world was forever changed to the undesirable and harmful place in which we live today. However, Gnostics reject this view as an incorrect interpretation of the creation myth.

According to Gnostics, the blame is not in ourselves, but in our creator. The creator of this world was himself somewhat less than perfect and in fact, deeply flawed and cruel, making mankind the child of a lesser God. It is in the book, *The Apocryphon of John*, that the Gnostic view of creation is presented to us in great detail.

Gnosticism teaches that in the beginning a Supreme Being called The Father, The Divine All, The Origin, The Supreme God, or The Fullness, emanated the element of existence, both visible and invisible. His intent was not to create but, just as light emanates from a flame, so did creation shine forth from God. This manifested the primal element needed for creation. This was the creation of Barbelo, who is the Thought of God. Barbelo is the perfect mother, brought into existence by the perfect and whole God. Barbelo can be thought of in the terms of being the feminine part of the Father, and thus his counterpart, produced from himself. Even though we know God must be both male and female, we still visualize him as male. Barbelo equips us to see the divine balance within God.

The Father's thought performed a deed and she was created from it. It is she who had appeared before him in the shining of his light. This is the first power which was before all of them and which was created from his mind. She is the Thought of the All and her light shines like his light. It is the perfect power which is the visage of the invisible. She is the pure, undefiled Spirit who is perfect. She is the first power, the glory of Barbelo, the perfect glory of the kingdom (kingdoms), the glory revealed. She glorified the pure, undefiled Spirit and it was she who praised him, because thanks to him she had come forth.
The Apocryphon of John

It is the "agreement" of Barbelo and the Divine All, representing the union of male and female that created the Christ Spirit and all the Aeons.

In some renderings, the word "Aeon" is used to designate an ethereal realm or kingdom. In other versions "Aeon" indicates the ruler of the realm. One of these rulers was called Sophia or Wisdom. Sophia was created to be the counterpart to the Christ Spirit. Her fall began a chain of events that led to the introduction of evil into the universe.

Seeing the Divine flame of God, Sophia sought to know its origin. She sought to know the very nature of God. Sophia's passion ended in tragedy when she managed to capture a divine and creative spark, which she attempted to duplicate with her own creative force, without the union of a male counterpart. She attempted to bring forth something from herself as God had brought Barbelo from his own perfection, but Sophia was not perfect and she was not God. It was this overreaching act by Sophia that produced the Archons, beings born outside the higher divine realm. In the development of the myth, explanations seem to point to the fact that Sophia carried the divine essence of creation from God within her but chose to attempt creation by using her own powers without the balance of the counterpart.

It is unclear if this was in an attempt to understand the Supreme God and his power, or an impetuous act that caused evil to enter the cosmos in the form of her creations.

The realm containing the Fullness of the Godhead, Barbelo, the Aeons, and Sophia is called the pleroma or Realm of Fullness. This is the Gnostic heaven. The lesser gods created in Sophia's failed attempt were cast outside the pleroma and away from the presence of God. In essence, she threw away and discarded her flawed creations, who had a lion's head and a serpent's body.

"She cast it away from her, outside the place where no one of the immortals might see it, for she had created it in ignorance. And she surrounded it with a glowing cloud, and she put a throne in the middle of the cloud so that no one could see it except the Holy Spirit who is called the mother of all that has life. And she called his name Yaldabaoth." Apocryphon of John

The beings Sophia created were imperfect and oblivious to the Supreme God. Her creations contained deities even less perfect than herself. They were called the Powers, the Rulers, or the Archons. These evil, spiteful, jealous creatures are the ones referred to by St. Paul when he stated that our fight is against "principalities, powers, and rulers of darkness in high places." Their leader was called the Demiurge, but his name was Yaldabaoth. It was the flawed, imperfect, spiritually blind Demiurge, (Yaldabaoth), who became the creator of the material world and all things in it. Demiurge means, "the half-maker." Gnostics considered Yaldabaoth to be the same as Jehovah (Yahweh), who is the Jewish creator God. These beings, the Demiurge and the Archons, would later equate to Satan and his demons, or Jehovah and his angels, depending on which Gnostic sect is telling the story.

The making of the world is ascribed to a company of seven Archons (a type of deity somewhat equated to an angel). Their chief is "Yaldabaoth" (also known as "Yaltabaoth" or "Ialdabaoth").

The Apocryphon of John, written around 120 A.D. recounts that the Demiurge arrogantly declares that he has made the world by himself:
"Now the archon (ruler) who is weak has three names. The first name is Yaltabaoth, the second is Saklas ("fool"), and the third is Samael (god of the blind or blind god). And he is impious in his arrogance which is in him. For he said, "I am God and there is no other God beside me," for he is ignorant of his strength, the place from which he had come."

He is the Demiurge and maker of man, but a ray of light from above entered the body of man and gave him a soul, and Yaldabaoth was filled with envy. He tries to limit man's knowledge by forbidding him the fruit of knowledge in paradise. The Demiurge feared Jesus, who contained the Christ Spirit, would spread the knowledge of the Supreme God, so had him crucified by the Romans.

At the consummation of all things, light will return to the Pleroma. But Yaldabaoth, the Demiurge, with all the material world, will be cast into the lower depths, far away from the Pleroma

In the Gnostic text, Pistis Sophia, Yaldabaoth has already sunk from his high estate and resides in Chaos, where, with his forty-nine demons, he tortures wicked souls in boiling rivers of pitch, and with other punishments (pp. 257, 382).

Yaldabaoth is frequently called "the Lion-faced", leontoeides, with the body of a serpent. We are told also, that the Demiurge is of a fiery nature, the words of Moses being applied to him, "the Lord our God is a burning and consuming fire," a text used also by Simon. He is an archon with the face of a lion, half flame and half darkness.

Gnostics could not reconcile the vengeful, jealous, violent, capricious, quixotic, angry god of the Old Testament to the good, compassionate, loving god Jesus (the Logos) taught in the New Testament. Their conclusion was the actions and personality of the Old Testament god matched that of the Demiurge, and since both were said to be the creator of this flawed world, they must be the same.

King James Version (KJV) Deuteronomy 32:36 For the LORD shall judge his people, and repent himself for his servants, when he seeth that their power is gone, and there is none shut up, or left. [37] *And he*

shall say, Where are their gods, their rock in whom they trusted,
38 Which did eat the fat of their sacrifices, and drank the wine of their
drink offerings? let them rise up and help you, and be your protection.
39 See now that I, even I, am he, and there is no god with me: I kill,
and I make alive; I wound, and I heal: neither is there any that can
deliver out of my hand. 40 For I lift up my hand to heaven, and say, I
live for ever. 41 If I whet my glittering sword, and mine hand take hold
on judgment; I will render vengeance to mine enemies, and will
reward them that hate me. 42 I will make mine arrows drunk with
blood, and my sword shall devour flesh; and that with the blood of the
slain and of the captives, from the beginning of revenges upon the
enemy.

Such a creator answers the age-old questions of why there is such violence of nature and suffering in the world and why evil can go unpunished and the innocent and good are not rewarded. The purpose of Jesus was that of a servant, sent by the Supreme God, to awaken us to the truth that the world is controlled by the Demiurge, who is enslaving us to worship him, even though he is wicked and evil. Jesus was sent to draw us back to the true God and to remind us how to commune with him so as never to be deceived again.

Said another way: The All, wishing to call those who desire him into His fullness, reached out with rays of Gnosis to quicken their hearts into fervent desire for Him with a desire that is His toward us. In this way, Gnosis defeats our fate. Jesus was the courier of God's gnosis.

One of the more perfect and complete modern metaphors of Gnosticism is the movie, "The Matrix." If you take one pill you will remain comfortably oblivious to the truth, but if you decide to swallow the other pill you will awaken and be very troubled by what you see, but you will be truly free.

In one Gnostic creation story, the Archons created Adam but could not bring him to life. In other stories Adam was formed as a type of worm, unable to attain personhood. Thus, man began as an incomplete creation of a flawed, spiritually blind, and malevolent god. In this myth, the Archons were afraid that Adam might be more powerful than the Archons themselves. When they saw Adam was incapable of attaining the human state, their fears were put to rest, thus, they called that day the "Day of Rest."

Sophia saw Adam's horrid state and had compassion, because she knew she was the origin of the Archons and their evil. Sophia descended to help bring Adam out of his hopeless condition. It is this story that set the stage for the emergence of the sacred feminine force in Gnosticism that is not seen in orthodox Christianity. Sophia brought within herself the light and power of the Supreme God. Metaphorically, within the spiritual womb of Sophia, life force of the Supreme God for Adam's salvation was carried.

In the Gnostic text called, *The Apocryphon of John*, Sophia is quoted:

"I entered into the midst of the cage which is the prison of the body. And I spoke saying: 'He who hears, let him awake from his deep sleep.' Then Adam wept and shed tears. After he wiped away his bitter tears he asked: 'Who calls my name, and from where has this hope arose in me even while I am in the chains of this prison?' And I (Sophia) answered: 'I am the one who carries the pure light; I am the thought of the undefiled spirit. Arise, remember, and follow your origin, which is I, and beware of the deep sleep.'"

Sophia would later equate to the Holy Spirit as it awakened the comatose soul. That "deep sleep" is the dream in which most live. It is the illusion that this world is all there is and the god of this world is the only god there is. It is the dream forced on beings by the Archons, compelling us remain "asleep", blindly worshipping Yaldabaoth and his Archons in this material world. This is the attachment and worship of wealth, flesh, and the material world.

As the myth evolved, Sophia, after animating Adam, became Eve in order to assist Adam in finding the truth. She offered it to him in the form of the fruit of the tree of knowledge. To Gnostics, this was an act of deliverance.

Other stories have Sophia becoming the serpent in order to offer Adam a way to attain the truth. In either case, the fruit represented the hard-sought truth, which was the knowledge of good and evil, and through that knowledge Adam could become a god. The creator god, the Demiurge, fought against and condemned this act because the knowledge of the true nature of mankind and creation would free mankind from his grip. Later, the serpent would become a feminine symbol of wisdom, probably owing to the connection with Sophia. Eve, being Sophia in disguise, would become the mother and sacred feminine of us all. As Gnostic theology began to coalesce, Sophia would come to be considered a force or conduit of the Holy Spirit, in part due to the fact that the Holy Spirit was also considered a feminine and creative force from the Supreme God. The Gospel of Philip echoes this theology in verse six as follows:

In the days when we were Hebrews we were made orphans, having only our Mother. Yet when we believed in the Messiah (and became the ones of Christ), the Mother and Father both came to us.

Gospel of Philip

As the emerging orthodox church became more and more oppressive to women, later even labeling them "occasions of sin," the Gnostics countered by raising women to equal status with men, saying Sophia was, in a sense, the handmaiden or wife of the Supreme God, making the soul of Adam her spiritual offspring.

In Gnostic cosmology, the "living" world is under the control of entities called Aeons, of which Sophia is head. This means the Aeons influence or control the soul, life force, intelligence, thought, and mind. Control of the mechanical or inorganic world is given to the Archons. They rule the physical aspects of systems, regulation, limits, and order in the world. Both the ineptitude and cruelty of the Archons are reflected in the chaos and pain of the material realm.

Sophia had captured a creative spark produced by the Supreme God. The Demiurge, and his helpers, the Archons, stole the spark from their mother, Sophia and they fashioned it into this material world.

Since the Demiurge (Yaldabaoth) had no memory of how he came to be alive, he did not realize he was not the true creator. The Demiurge believed he somehow created the material world by himself. The Supreme God allowed the Demiurge and Archons to remain deceived. Yet, Sophia, his mother tried to open his eyes, crying out to him, "You are not alone, Samael." (Samael - god of the blind or blind god.)

The Creator God (the Demiurge) intended the material world to be perfect and eternal, but he did not have it in himself to accomplish the feat. What comes forth from a being cannot be greater than the highest part of him, can it? The world was created flawed and transitory and we are part of it. Somewhere, deep in each of us, is the realization that the world is flawed, imperfect, not balanced not fair, and this is not all there is. The Demiurge was imperfect and evil. So was the world he created. If it was the Demiurge who created man and man is called upon to escape the Demiurge and find union with the Supreme God, is this not demanding that man becomes greater than his creator? Spiritually this seems impossible, but as many children become greater than their parents, man is expected to become greater than his maker, the Demiurge. This starts with the one fact that the Demiurge denies: the existence and supremacy of the Supreme God, the Divine All.

Man was created with a dual nature as the product of the material world of the Demiurge with his imperfect essence, combined with the spark of God that emanated from the

Supreme God through Sophia. A version of the creation story has Sophia tricking the Demiurge by instructing him to breath into Adam so that spiritual power he had taken from Sophia during his creation would be breathed into Adam. It was the spiritual power from Sophia that brought life to Adam.

It is this divine spark in man that calls to its source, the Supreme God, and which causes a "divine discontent," that nagging feeling that keeps us questioning if this is all there is. This spark and the feeling it gives us keeps us searching for the truth. We wish to shake ourselves and awaken to the full truth, the Gnosis, but Yaldabaoth, also called Samael, the god of the blind, has no intention of letting us see. To awaken man and allow him to see is why Jesus, the Christ Spirit, the Logos, came.

The Creator God sought to keep man ignorant of his defective state by keeping him enslaved to the material world. By doing so, he continued to receive man's worship and servitude. He did not wish man to recognize or gain knowledge of the true Supreme God. Since he did not know or acknowledge the Supreme God, he views any attempt to worship anything else as spiritual treason.

The opposition of forces set forth in the spiritual battle over the continued enslavement of man and man's spiritual freedom set up the duality of good and evil in Gnostic theology. There was a glaring difference between the orthodox Christian viewpoint and the Gnostic viewpoint. According to Gnostics, the creator of the material world was an evil entity and the Supreme God, who was his source, was the good entity. Christians quote John 1:1 "In the beginning was the Word, and the Word was with God, and the Word was God."

According to Gnostics, only through the realization of man's true state or through death can he escape captivity in the material realm. This means the idea of salvation does not deal with original sin or blood payment. Instead, it focuses on the idea of awakening to the fullness of the truth.

1 Timothy 2: 3 This is good, and pleases God our Savior, 4 who wants all people to be saved and to come to a knowledge of the truth.

In Gnostic theology, neither Jesus nor his death can save anyone, but the truth that he came to proclaim can give people the divine, complete and perfect knowledge, which allows a person to save his or her own soul. The truth that Jesus brings us is the realization of the lie of the material world and its God. The material world is a trap. The body is a prison. The knowledge of the higher realms and the Divine All sets one on a course of freedom.

There are stages to any communion with truth. One must prepare oneself. As it is written, "I will meditate for a thousand years to be enlightened in a single moment."

We must offer ourselves as a sacrifice, giving up our all for our sacred goal. In as much as the word, "sacrifice" comes from a word which means to "make holy" or "make sacred", we sacrifice our egos and preconceived ideas on the alter of knowledge. It is at this point we gain unity and individuation.

Lastly, we must commune fully with God through the knowledge, which is the fullness of God. We become the Eucharist, which means "the Thanksgiving", and through the fire of Gnosis we become the holocaust, a Latin word meaning, "the whole burnt offering." For, not being able to avoid their murder by gas, guns, and fire, millions of souls went to the God of this world as a sacrifice. The act given the same name as the offering burned on the altar and described in the Vulgate. But now, each of us offer ourselves in the fire of Gnosis to the High and Supreme God.

To escape the earthly prison and find one's way back to the pleroma (heaven) and the Supreme God, is the soteriology (salvation doctrine) and eschatology (judgment, reward, and doctrine of heaven) of Gnosticism.

The idea that personal revelation leads to salvation may be what caused the mainline Christian church to declare Gnosticism a heresy. The church could better tolerate alternative theological views if the views did not undermine the authority of the church and its ability to control the people. Gnostic theology placed salvation in the hands of the individual through personal revelations and knowledge, excluding the need for the orthodox church and its clergy to grant salvation or absolution. This fact, along with the divergent interpretation of the creation story, which placed the creator God, Yaldabaoth or Jehovah, as the enemy of mankind, was too much for the church to tolerate. Reaction was harsh. Gnosticism was declared to be a dangerous heresy.

Some Gnostics believe there will occur a universal reconciliation as being after being realizes the existence of the Supreme God and renounces the material world and its inferior creator.

Combined with its Christian influences, the cosmology of the Gnostics may have borrowed from the Greek philosopher, Plato, as well as from Buddhism. There are parallels between the creation myth set forth by Plato and some of those recorded in Gnostic writings.

Plato lived from 427 to 347 B.C. He was the son of wealthy Athenians and a student of the philosopher, Socrates, and the mathematician, Pythagoras. Plato himself was the teacher of Aristotle.

In Plato's cosmology, the Demiurge is an artist who imposed form on materials that already existed. The raw materials were in a chaotic and random state. The physical world must have had visible form which was put together much like a puzzle is constructed. This later gave way to a philosophy which stated that all things in existence could be broken down into a small subset of geometric shapes.

In the tradition of Greek mythology, Plato's cosmology began with a creation story. The story was narrated by the philosopher Timaeus of Locris, a fictional character of Plato's making. In his account, nature is initiated by a creator deity, called the "Demiurge," a name which may be the Greek word for "craftsman" or "artisan" or, according to how one divides or parses the word, it could also be translated as "half-maker." The Demiurge sought to create the cosmos modeled on his understanding of the supreme and original truth. In this way he created the visible universe based on invisible truths. He set in place rules of process such as birth, growth, change, death, and dissolution. This was Plato's "Realm of Becoming." It was his Genesis. Plato stated that the internal structure of the cosmos had innate intelligence and was therefore called the World Soul. The cosmic super-structure of the Demiurge was used as the framework on which to hang or fill in the details and parts of the universe. The Demiurge then appointed his underlings to fill in the details which allowed the universe to remain in a working and balanced state. All phenomena of nature resulted from an interaction and interplay of the two forces of reason and necessity.

Plato represented reason as constituting the World Soul. The material world was a necessity in which reason acted out its will in the physical realm. The duality between the will, mind, or reason of the World Soul and the material universe and its inherent flaws set in play the duality of Plato's world and is seen reflected in the beliefs of the Gnostics.

In Plato's world, the human soul was immortal, each soul was assigned to a star. Souls that were just or good were permitted to return to their stars upon their death. Unjust souls were reincarnated to try again. Escape of the soul to the freedom of the stars and out of the cycle of reincarnation was best accomplished by following the reason and goodness of the World Soul and not the physical world, which was set in place only as a necessity to manifest the patterns of the World Soul.

Although in Plato's cosmology the Demiurge was not seen as evil, in Gnostic cosmology he was considered not only to be flawed and evil, but he was also the beginning of all evil in the material universe, having created it to reflect his own malice.

Following the path of Plato's cosmology, some Gnostics left open the possibility of reincarnation if the person had not reached the truth before his death.

Plato was not the only one to influence Greece and the gospel of Thomas. In the year 13 A.D. Roman annals record the visit of an Indian king named Pandya or Porus. He came to see Caesar Augustus carrying a letter of introduction in Greek. He was accompanied by a monk who burned himself alive in the city of Athens to prove his faith in Buddhism. The event was described by Nicolaus of Damascus as, not surprisingly, causing a great stir among the people. It is thought that this was the first transmission of Buddhist teaching to the masses.

In the second century A.D., Clement of Alexandria wrote about Buddha: "Among the Indians are those philosophers also who follow the precepts of Boutta (Buddha), whom they honour as a god on account of his extraordinary sanctity." (Clement of Alexandria, "The Stromata, or Miscellanies" Book I, Chapter XV).

"Thus philosophy, a thing of the highest utility, flourished in antiquity among the barbarians, shedding its light over the nations. And afterwards it came to Greece." (Clement of Alexandria, "The Stromata, or Miscellanies").

To clarify what "philosophy" was transmitted from India to Greece, we turn to the historians Hippolytus and Epiphanius who wrote of Scythianus, a man who had visited India around 50 A.D. They report; "He brought 'the doctrine of the Two Principles.'" According to these writers, Scythianus' pupil Terebinthus called himself a Buddha. Some scholars suggest it was he that traveled to the area of Babylon and transmitted his knowledge to Mani, who later founded Manichaeism.

Adding to the possibility of Eastern influence, we have accounts of the Apostle Thomas' attempt to convert the people of Asia-Minor. If the Gnostic gospel bearing his name was truly written by Thomas, it was penned after his return from India, where he also encountered the Buddhist influences.

Ancient church historians mention that Thomas preached to the Parthians in Persia, and it is said he was buried in Edessa. Fourth century chronicles attribute the evangelization of India (Asia-Minor or Central Asia) to Thomas.

The texts of the Gospel of Thomas, which some believe predate the four gospels, has a very "Zen-like" or Eastern flavor.

Although the codex found in Egypt is dated to the fourth century, the actual construction of the text of Thomas is placed by most Biblical scholars at about 70–150 A.D. Most agree the time of writing was in the second century A.D.

Following the transmission of the philosophy of "Two Principals," both Manichaeism and Gnosticism retained a dualistic viewpoint. The black-versus-white dualism of Gnosticism came to rest in the evil of the material world and its maker, versus the goodness of the freed soul and the Supreme God with whom it seeks union.

Oddly, the disdain for the material world and its Creator God drove Gnostic theology to far-flung extremes in attitude, beliefs, and actions. Gnostics idolize the serpent in the "Garden of Eden" story. After all, if your salvation hinges on secret knowledge the offer of becoming gods through the knowledge of good and evil sounds wonderful. So powerful was the draw of this "knowledge myth" to the Gnostics that the serpent became linked to Sophia by some sects. This can still be seen today in our medical and veterinarian symbols of serpents on poles, conveying the ancient meanings of knowledge and wisdom.

Genesis 3 (King James Version)

1 Now the serpent was more subtil than any beast of the field which the LORD God had made. And he said unto the woman, Yea, hath God said, Ye shall not eat of every tree of the garden?

2 And the woman said unto the serpent, We may eat of the fruit of the trees of the garden:

3 But of the fruit of the tree which is in the midst of the garden, God hath said, Ye shall not eat of it, neither shall ye touch it, lest ye die.

4 And the serpent said unto the woman, Ye shall not surely die:

5 For God doth know that in the day ye eat thereof, then your eyes shall be opened, and ye shall be as Gods, knowing good and evil.

It is because of their vehement struggle against the Creator God and the search for some transcendent truth, that Gnostics held the people of Sodom in high regard. The people of Sodom sought to "corrupt" the messengers sent by their enemy, the Creator God. Anything done to thwart the Demiurge and his minions was considered valiant.

Genesis 19 (King James Version)

1 And there came two angels to Sodom at even; and Lot sat in the gate of Sodom: and Lot seeing them rose up to meet them; and he bowed himself with his face toward the ground;

2 And he said, Behold now, my lords, turn in, I pray you, into your servant's house, and tarry all night, and wash your feet, and ye shall rise up early, and go on your ways. And they said, Nay; but we will abide in the street all night.

3 And he pressed upon them greatly; and they turned in unto him, and entered into his house; and he made them a feast, and did bake unleavened bread, and they did eat.

4 But before they lay down, the men of the city, even the men of Sodom, compassed the house round, both old and young, all the people from every quarter:

5 And they called unto Lot, and said unto him, Where are the men which came in to thee this night? bring them out unto us, that we may know them.

6 And Lot went out at the door unto them, and shut the door after him,

7 And said, I pray you, brethren, do not so wickedly.

8 Behold now, I have two daughters which have not known man; let me, I pray you, bring them out unto you, and do ye to them as is good in your eyes: only unto these men do nothing; for therefore came they under the shadow of my roof.

9 And they said, Stand back. And they said again, This one fellow came in to sojourn, and he will needs be a judge: now will we deal worse with thee, than with them. And they pressed sore upon the man, even Lot, and came near to break the door.

10 But the men put forth their hand, and pulled Lot into the house to them, and shut to the door.

To modern Christians, the idea of admiring the serpent, which we believe was Satan, may seem unthinkable. Supporting the idea of attacking and molesting the angels sent to Sodom to warn of the coming destruction seems appalling; but to Gnostics the real evil was the malevolent entity, the Creator God of this world. To destroy his messengers, as was the case in Sodom, would impede his mission. To obtain knowledge of good and evil, as was offered by the serpent in the garden, would set the captives free.

To awaken the inner knowledge of the true God was the battle. The material world was designed to prevent the awakening by entrapping, confusing, and distracting the spirit of man. The aim of Gnosticism was the spiritual awakening and freedom of man.

Gnostics, in the age of the early church, would preach to converts (novices) about this awakening, saying the novice must awaken the God within himself and see the trap that was the material world. Salvation came from the recognition or knowledge contained in this spiritual awakening.

Not all people are ready or willing to accept the Gnosis. Many are bound to the material world and are satisfied to be only as and where they are. These have mistaken the Creator God for the Supreme God and do not know there is anything beyond the Creator God or the material existence. These people know only the lower or earthly wisdom and not the higher wisdom above the Creator God. They are referred to as "dead."

Major schools fell into two categories; those who rejected the material world of the Creator God, and those who rejected the laws of the Creator God. For those who rejected the world the Creator God had spawned, overcoming the material world was accomplished by partaking of as little of the world and its pleasures as possible. These followers lived very stark and ascetic lives, abstaining from meat, sex, marriage, and all things that would entice them to remain in the material realm. It is this branch that identifies with and has adopted the gospel of Thomas.

Other schools believed it was their duty to simply defy the Creator God and all laws that he had proclaimed. Since the Creator God had been identified as Jehovah, God of the Jews, these followers set about to break every law held dear by Christians and Jews.

As human nature is predisposed to do, many Gnostics took up the more wanton practices, believing that nothing done in their earthly bodies would affect their spiritual lives. Whether it was excesses in sex, alcohol, food, or any other assorted debaucheries, the Gnostics were safe within their faith, believing nothing spiritually bad could come of their earthly adventures.

The actions of the Gnostics are mentioned by early Church leaders. One infamous Gnostic school is actually mentioned in the Bible, as we will read later.

The world was out of balance, inferior, and corrupt. The spirit was perfect and intact. It was up to the Gnostics to tell the story, explain the error, and awaken the world to the light of truth. The Supreme God had provided a vehicle to help in their effort. He had created a teacher of light and truth.

Since the time of Sophia's mistaken creation of the Archons, there was an imbalance in the cosmos. The Supreme God began to re-establish the balance by producing Christ to teach and save man. That left only Sophia, now in a fallen and bound state, along with the Demiurge, and the Archons to upset the cosmic equation.

One very important point in some Gnostic creation stories is the necessity of maintaining a dualistic balance within, not only creation, but the cosmos itself. Each being created has a counterpart. The counterpart of Sophia was Christ. The unification of these counterparts forms the perfect, balanced being. Each of us has our heavenly counterpart, with which we should gain unity.

In this theology one might loosely equate the Supreme God to the New Testament Christian God, Demiurge to Satan, the Archons to demons, the pleroma to heaven, Sophia to the creative or regenerative force of the Holy Spirit, and Jesus as the Word, Logos, and teacher who contains the Christ Spirit. This holds up well except for one huge problem.

Everything coming from the material world is corrupt by the nature of its creator. For those who seek that which is beyond the material world and its flawed creator, the Supreme God has sent Messengers of Light to awaken the divine spark of the Supreme God within us. This part of us will call to the true God as deep calls to deep. The greatest and most perfect Messenger of Light was the Christ. He is also referred to as The Good, Christ, Messiah, and The Word. He came to reveal the Divine Light to us in the form of knowledge and release us from the illusion of the material world. To Gnostics, refusing this knowledge is the only original sin.

One Gnostic view of the Incarnation was "docetic," which is an early heretical position that Jesus was never actually present in the flesh, but only appeared to be human. He was a spiritual being and his human appearance was only an illusion. Of course, the title of "heretical" can only be decided by the controlling authority of the time. In this case, it was the church that was about to emerge under the rule of the Emperor Constantine.

Most Gnostics held that the Christ spirit indwelt the earthly man, Jesus at the time of his baptism by John, at which time Jesus received the name, and thus the power, of the Lord or Supreme God.

The Christ spirit departed from Jesus' body before his death. These two viewpoints remove the idea of God sacrificing himself atonement for the sins of man. The idea of atonement was not necessary in Gnostic theology since it was knowledge and not sacrifice that set one free.

Since there was a distinction in Gnosticism between the man Jesus and the Light of Christ that came to reside within him, it is not contrary to Gnostic beliefs that Mary Magdalene could have been the consort and wife of Jesus. Neither would it have been blasphemous for them to have children. This relationship became a theme in the gospels of Mary and Peter.

Various sects of Gnosticism stressed certain elements of their basic theology. Each had its head teachers and its special flavor of beliefs. One of the oldest types was the Syrian Gnosticism. It existed around 120 A.D. In contrast to other sects, the Syrian lacked much of the embellished mythology of Aeons, Archons, and angels.

The fight between the Supreme God and the Creator God was not eternal, though there was strong opposition to Jehovah, the Creator God. He was considered to have been the last of the seven angels who created this world out of divine material which emanated from the Supreme God. The Demiurge attempted to create man, but only created a miserable worm which the Supreme God had to save by giving it the spark of divine life. Thus man was born.

According to this sect, Jehovah, the Creator God, must not be worshiped. The Supreme God calls us to his service and presence through Christ his Son. They pursued only the unknowable Supreme God and sought to obey the Supreme Deity by abstaining from eating meat and from marriage and sex, and by leading an ascetic life. The symbol of Christ was the serpent, that attempted to free Adam and Eve from their ignorance and entrapment to the Creator God.

Another Gnostic school was the Hellenistic or Alexandrian School. These systems absorbed the philosophy and concepts of the Greeks, and the Semitic nomenclature was replaced by Greek names. The cosmology and myth had grown out of proportion and appear to our eyes to be unwieldy. Yet, this school produced two great thinkers, Basilides and Valentinus. Though born at Antioch, in Syria, Basilides founded his school in Alexandria around the year A.D. 130, where it survived for several centuries.

Valentinus first taught at Alexandria and then in Rome. He established the largest Gnostic movement around A.D. 160. This movement was founded on an elaborate mythology and a system of sexual duality of male and female interplay, both in its deities and its savior.

Tertullian wrote that between 135 A.D. and 160 A.D. Valentinus, a prominent Gnostic, had great influence in the Christian church. Valentinus ascended in church hierarchy and became a candidate for the office of bishop of Rome, the office that quickly evolved into that of Pope. He lost the election by a narrow margin. Even though Valentinus was outspoken about his Gnostic slant on Christianity, he was a respected member of the Christian community until his death and was probably a practicing bishop in a church of lesser status than the one in Rome.

The main platform of Gnosticism was the ability to transcend the material world through the possession of privileged and directly imparted knowledge. Following this doctrine, Valentinus claimed to have been instructed by a direct disciple of one of Jesus' apostles, a man by the name of Theodas.

Valentinus is considered by many to be the father of Gnosticism. His vision of the faith is summarized by G.R.S. Mead in the book "Fragments of a Faith Forgotten."

"The Gnosis in his hands is trying to embrace everything, even the most dogmatic formulation of the traditions of the Master. The great popular movement and its incomprehensibilities were recognized by Valentinus as an integral part of the mighty outpouring; he labored to weave all together, external and internal, into one piece, devoted his life to the task, and doubtless only at his death perceived that for that age he was attempting the impossible. None but the very few could ever appreciate the ideal of the man, much less understand it." (Fragments of a Faith Forgotten, p. 297)

Gnostic theology seemed to vacillate from polytheism to pantheism to dualism to monotheism, depending on the teacher and how he viewed and stressed certain areas of their creation myths. Marcion, a Gnostic teacher, espoused differences between the God of the New Testament and the God of the Old Testament, claiming they were two separate entities. According to Marcion, the New Testament God was a good true God while the Old Testament God was an evil angel.

Although this may be a heresy, it pulled his school back into monotheism. The church, however, disowned him.

Syneros and Prepon, disciples of Marcion, postulated three different entities, carrying their teachings from monotheism into polytheism in one stroke. In their system, the opponent of the good God was not the God of the Jews, but Eternal Matter, which was the source of all evil. Matter, in this system became a principal creative force. Although it was created imperfect, it could also create, having the innate intelligence of the "world soul."

Of all the Gnostic schools or sects the most famous is the Antinomian School. Believing that the Creator God, Jehovah, was evil, they sat out to disrupt all things connected to the Jewish God. This included his laws. It was considered their duty to break any law of morality, diet, or conduct given by the Jewish God, who they considered the evil Creator God. The leader of the sect was called Nicolaites. The sect existed in Apostolic times and is mentioned in the Bible.

Revelation 2 (King James Version)

5 Remember therefore from whence thou art fallen, and repent, and do the first works; or else I will come unto thee quickly, and will remove thy candlestick out of his place, except thou repent.

6 But this thou hast, that thou hatest the deeds of the Nicolaitanes, which I also hate.

Revelation 2 (King James Version)
14 But I have a few things against thee, because thou hast there them that hold the doctrine of Balaam, who taught Balac to cast a stumbling block before the children of Israel, to eat things sacrificed unto idols, and to commit fornication.
15 So hast thou also them that hold the doctrine of the Nicolaitanes, which thing I hate.
16 Repent; or else I will come unto thee quickly, and will fight against them with the sword of my mouth.

One of the leaders of the Nocolaitanes, according to Origen, was Carpocrates, whom Tertullian called a magician and a fornicator. Carpocretes taught that one could only escape the cosmic powers by discharging one's obligations to them and disregarding their laws. The Christian church fathers, St. Justin, Irenaeus, and Eusebius wrote that the reputation of these men (the Nicolaitanes), brought infamy upon the whole race of Christians.

According to Gnostic theology, nothing can come from the material world that is not flawed. Because of this, Gnostics did not believe that Christ could have been a corporeal being. Thus, there must be some separation or distinction between Jesus, as a man, and Christ, as a spiritual being born from the Supreme, unrevealed, and eternal God.

To closer examine this theology, we turn to Valentinus, the driving force of early Gnosticism, for an explanation. Valentinus divided Jesus Christ into two very distinct parts; Jesus, the man, and Christ, the anointed spiritual messenger of God. These two forces met in the moment of Baptism when the Spirit of God came to rest on Jesus and the Christ power entered his body.

Here Gnosticism runs aground on its own theology, for if the spiritual cannot mingle with the material then how can the Christ spirit inhabit a body? The result of the dichotomy was a schism within Gnosticism. Some held to the belief that the specter of Jesus was simply an illusion produced by Christ himself to enable him to do his work on earth. It was not real, not matter, not corporeal, and did not actually exist as a physical body would. Others came to believe that Jesus must have been a specially prepared vessel and was the perfect human body formed by the very essence of the plumora (heaven). It was this path of thought that allowed Jesus to continue as human, lover, and father.

Jesus, the man, became a vessel containing the Light of God, called Christ. In the Gnostic view we all could and should become Christs, carrying the Truth and Light of God. We are all potential vehicles of the same Spirit that Jesus held within him when he was awakened to the Truth.

The suffering and death of Jesus then took on much less importance in the Gnostic view, as Jesus was simply part of the corrupt world and was suffering the indignities of this world as any man would.

The Gnostic texts seem to divide man into parts, although at times the divisions are somewhat unclear. The divisions alluded to may include the soul, which is the will of man; the spirit, which is depicted as wind or air (pneuma) and contains the holy spark that is the spirit of God in man; and the material human form, the body. The mind of man sits as a mediator between the soul, or will, and the spirit, which is connected to God. It is these parts of the human elements that Jung believed we should unify in order to be whole, healthy and integrated people.

Without the light of the truth, the spirit is held captive by the Demiurge, which enslaves man. This entrapment is called "sickness." It is because of this sickness that the Light came to heal us and set us free. The third part of man, his material form, was considered a weight, an anchor, and a hindrance, keeping man attached to the corrupted earthly realm.

Theologies can rise and fall upon small words and terms. If Jesus was not God, his death and thus his atonement meant nothing. His suffering meant nothing. Even the resurrection meant nothing, if one's view of Jesus was that he was not human to begin with, as was true with some Gnostics.

For the Gnostics, resurrection of the dead was unthinkable since flesh as well as all matter is destined to perish. According to Gnostic theology, there was no resurrection of the flesh, but only of the soul. How the soul would be resurrected was explained differently by various Gnostic groups, but all denied the resurrection of the body. To the enlightened Gnostic the actual person was the spirit who used the body as an instrument to survive in the material world but did not identify with it. This belief is echoed in the Gospel of Thomas.

29. Jesus said: If the flesh came into being because of spirit, it is a marvel, but if spirit came into being because of the body, it would be a marvel of marvels. I marvel indeed at how great wealth has taken up residence in this poverty.

Put another way, if the existence of the spirit caused the body to be created it would be amazing, but if the body spontaneously created the spirit it would be simply unbelievable.

Owing to the Gnostic belief of such a separation of spirit and body, it was thought that the Christ spirit within the body of Jesus departed the body before the crucifixion. Others said the body was an illusion and the crucifixion was a sham perpetrated by an eternal spirit on the men that sought to kill it. Lastly, some suggested that Jesus deceived the soldiers into thinking he was dead. The resurrection under this circumstance became a lie which allowed Jesus to escape and live on in anonymity, hiding, living as a married man, and raising a family until his natural death.

Think of the implications to the orthodox Christian world if the spirit of God departed from Jesus as it fled and laughed as the body was crucified. This is the implication of the Gnostic interpretation of the death of Jesus when he cries out, "My power, my power, why have you left me," as the Christ spirit left his body before his death. What are the ramifications to the modern Christian if the Creator God, the Demiurge, is more evil than his creation? Can a Creation rise above its creator? Is it possible for man to find the spark within himself that calls to the Supreme God and free himself of his evil creator?

Although, in time, the creation myth and other Gnostic differences began to be swept under the rug, it was the division between Jesus and the Christ spirit that put them at odds with the emerging orthodox church. At the establishment of the doctrine of the trinity, the mainline church firmly set a divide between themselves and the Gnostics.

To this day there is a battle raging in the Christian world as believers and seekers attempt to reconcile today's Christianity to the sect of the early Christian church called, "Gnosticism."

Carl Jung and the Application of Gnosticism

A little know fact is the great father of modern psychology, Carl G. Jung, had great interest in Gnosticism, and went so far as to purchase an ancient codex.

Gilles Quispel, a distinguished professor of Early Christianity, was born in Rotterdam, Holland in 1916. As a young man he obtained a doctorate in literature and the humanities and went on to research and teach about the early Gnostics. He met with Jung in 1944 in Ascona, Switzerland to discuss how he could gained the help of Jung and C.A. Meier to retrieve a valuable Gnostic text from the black market.

Jung had a deep curiosity regarding gnostic literature. He believed the gnostic message of unifying the inner and outer person (or the conscious and subconscious) held great psychological value. Jung agreed to procure the codex.

This codex had been part of a larger cache of ancient documents found in 1945 buried in a jar in Egypt near Nag Hammadi. Scholars consider the documents extremely valuable since the texts were from the first century C.E. and contained unknown sayings of Jesus. Texts included books titled, "The

Gospel of Truth", "The Gospel of Thomas" and others. The lost text was retrieved and named the *Jung Codex*.

Jung was correct about his assertion regarding the psychological contributions and ideas in the gnostic texts. He began studying and formulating psychological applications, which he would later term "Individuation". This became a direct connection between the ancient Gnostics and modern psychology.

Stephan A. Hoeller wrote, in his article, "**C. G. Jung and the Alchemical Renewal,**" the following:

Jung's "first love" among esoteric systems was Gnosticism. From the earliest days of his scientific career until the time of his death, his dedication to the subject of Gnosticism was relentless. As early as August, 1912, Jung intimated in a letter to Freud that he had an intuition that the essentially feminine-toned archaic wisdom of the Gnostics, symbolically called *Sophia*, was destined to re-enter modern Western culture by way of depth-psychology. Subsequently, he stated to Barbara Hannah that when he discovered the writings of the ancient Gnostics, "I felt as if I had at last found a circle of friends who understood me."

The circle of ancient friends was a fragile one, however. Very little reliable, first-hand information was available to Jung within which he could have found the world and spirit of such past Gnostic luminaries as Valentinus, Basilides, and others. The fragmentary, and possibly mendacious, accounts of Gnostic teachings and practices appearing in the works of such heresy-hunting church fathers as Irenaeus and Hippolytus were a far cry from the wealth of archetypal lore available to us today in the Nag Hammadi collection. Of primary sources, the remarkable *Pistis Sophia* was one of very few available to Jung in translation, and his appreciation of this work was so great that he made a special effort to seek out the translator, the then aged and impecunious George R. S. Mead, in London to convey to him his great gratitude. Jung continued to explore Gnostic lore with great diligence, and his own personal matrix of inner experience became so affixed to Gnostic imagery that he wrote the only published document of his great transformational crisis, *The Seven Sermons to the Dead,* using purely Gnostic terminology and mythologems of the system of Basilides.

In all this devoted study, Jung was disturbed by one principal difficulty: The ancient Gnostic myths and traditions were some seventeen or eighteen hundred years old, and no living link seemed to exist that might join them to Jung's own time. (There is some minimal and obscure evidence indicating that Jung was

aware of a few small and secretive Gnostic groups in France and Germany, but their role in constituting such a link did not seem firmly enough established.) As far as Jung could discern, the tradition that might have connected the Gnostics with the present seemed to have been broken. However, his intuition (later justified by painstaking research) disclosed to him that the chief link connecting later ages with the Gnostics was in fact none other than alchemy. While his primary interest at this time was Gnosticism, he was already aware of the relevance of alchemy to his concerns. Referring to his intense inner experiences occurring between 1912 and 1919 he wrote:
"First I had to find evidence for the historical prefiguration of my own inner experiences. That is to say, I had to ask myself, "Where have my particular premises already occurred in history?" If I had not succeeded in finding such evidence, I would never have been able to substantiate my ideas. Therefore, my encounter with alchemy was decisive for me, as it provided me with the historical basis which I hitherto lacked."

In 1926 Jung had a remarkable dream. He felt himself transported back into the seventeenth century, and saw himself as an alchemist, engaged in the *opus*, or great work of alchemy. Prior to this time, Jung, along with other psychoanalysts, was intrigued and taken aback by the tragic fate of Herbert Silberer, a disciple of Freud, who in 1914 published a work dealing largely with the psychoanalytic implications of alchemy. Silberer, who upon proudly presenting his book to his master Freud, was coldly rebuked by him, became despondent and ended his life by suicide, thus becoming what might be called the first martyr to the cause of a psychological view of alchemy. Now it all came together, as it were. The Gnostic Sophia was about to begin her triumphal return to the arena of modern thought, and the psychological link connecting her and her modern devotees would be the long despised, but about to be rehabilitated, symbolic discipline of alchemy. The recognition had come. Heralded by a dream, the role of alchemy as the link connecting ancient Gnosticism with modern psychology, as well as Jung's role in reviving this link, became apparent. As Jung was to recollect later:

"[Alchemy] represented the historical link with Gnosticism, and . . . a continuity therefore existed between past and present. Grounded in the natural philosophy of the Middle Ages, alchemy formed the bridge on the one hand into the past, to Gnosticism, and on the other into the future, to the modern psychology of the unconscious. "

End of quotation from Stephan A. Hoeller

According to Marsha West, Carl Jung has been called the "Father of the re-birth of Gnosticism also called Neo-

Gnosticism. Dr. Satinover comments, "One of the most powerful modern forms of Gnosticism is without question Jungian psychology, both within or without the Church."

Edward Moore wrote, "Carl Jung, drawing upon Gnostic mythical schemas, identified the objectively oriented consciousness with the material or "fleshly" part of humankind—that is, with the part of the human being that is, according to the Gnostics, bound up in the cosmic cycle of generation and decay, and subject to the bonds of fate and time (cf. *Apocryphon of John* [Codex II] 28:30). The human being who identifies him/herself with the objectively existing world comes to construct a personality, a sense of self, that is, at base, fully dependent upon the ever-changing structures of temporal existence. The resulting lack of any sense of permanence, of autonomy, leads such an individual to experience anxieties of all kinds, and eventually to shun the mysterious and collectively meaningful patterns of human existence in favor of a private and stifling subjective context, in the confines of which life plays itself out in the absence of any reference to a greater plan or scheme. Hopelessness, atheism, and despair, are the results of such an existence. This is not the natural end of the human being, though; for, according to Jung (and the Gnostics) the temporally constructed self is not the true self. The true self is the supreme consciousness existing and persisting beyond all space and time. Jung calls this the *pure consciousness* or Self, in contradistinction to the "ego consciousness" which is the temporally constructed and maintained *form* of a discrete existent (cf. C.G. Jung, "Gnostic Symbols of the Self," in *The Gnostic Jung* 1992, pp. 55-92). This latter form of "worldly" consciousness the Gnostics identified with soul (*psukhê*), while the pure or true Self they identified with spirit (*pneuma*)—that is, mind relieved of its temporal contacts and context. This distinction had an important career in Gnostic thought, and was adopted by St. Paul, most notably in his doctrine of the spiritual resurrection (1 Corinthians 15:44). The psychological or empirical basis of this view, which soon turns into a metaphysical or onto-theological attitude, is the recognized inability of the human mind to achieve its grandest designs while remaining subject to the rigid law and order of a disinterested and aloof cosmos. The spirit-soul distinction (which of course translates into, or perhaps presupposes, the more fundamental mind-body distinction) marks the beginning of a transcendentalist and soteriological attitude toward the cosmos and temporal existence in general." End Quote from Edward Moore

In August 1957, Jung gave a series of filmed interviews for the University of Houston. The following is part of the transcript of the fourth interview with Dr. Richard I. Evans:

"I got more and more respectful of archetypes, and now, by Jove, that thing should be taken into account. That is an enormous factor, very important for our further development and for our well-being. It was, of course, difficult to know where to begin, because it is such an enormously extended field. So the next question I asked myself was, "Now where in the world has anybody been busy with that problem?" And I found nobody had, except a peculiar spiritual movement that went together with the beginnings of Christianity, namely Gnosticism. That was the first thing, actually, that I saw, that the Gnostics were concerned with the problem of archetypes. They made a peculiar philosophy of it, as everybody makes a peculiar philosophy of it when he comes across it naïvely and doesn't know that the archetypes are structural elements of the unconscious psyche.

The Gnostics lived in the first, second, and third centuries. And what was in between? Nothing. And now, today, we suddenly fall into that hole and are confronted with the problems of the collective unconscious which were the same then two thousand years ago - and we are not prepared to meet that problem. I was always looking for something in between, you know, something that linked that remote past with the present moment. And I found to my amazement it was alchemy, which is understood to be a history of chemistry. It is, one might

almost say, anything but that. It is a peculiar spiritual or philosophical movement. The alchemists called themselves philosophers, like the Gnostics. And then I read the whole accessible literature, Latin and Greek. I studied it because it was enormously interesting. It is the mental work of seventeen hundred years, in which is stored up all they could make out about the nature of the archetypes, in a peculiar way, that's true - it is not simple. Most of the texts haven't been published since the Middle Ages; the last editions date from the middle or end of the seventeenth century, practically all in Latin. Some texts are in Greek, not a few very important ones. That gave me no end of work, but the result was most satisfactory, because it showed me the development of our unconscious relations to the collective unconscious and the variations our consciousness has undergone, and why the unconscious is concerned with these mythological images. ..."
End quote from Jung's interview

To piece this together into modern psychology we must remember that Carl Jung was formulating his ideas of psychology and religious mythos using Gnosticism as one of his favorite "jumping off points". Jung looked at how individuals must integrate all sides of their psyches, with both good and evil, conscious and subconscious, into the whole. Since myths are the subconscious symbols of spiritual reality, myths show in story form a path to wholeness of the psyche. The psyche is the gateway to the spirit and must be integrated and complete before the spirit can be freely accessed. Jung called this process of the integrate of the various parts of the psyche or soul and the integration of soul and spirit "individuation". He seemed to have gleaned this idea from the theology and mythos of the Gnostic, which he saw as a deep and intuitive application of this idea of integration and wholeness.

This Jungian idea of wholeness or individuation as understood through Gnosticism is one reason the Gospel of Thomas is so important. It is in a deeper understanding of the Gospel of Thomas that we find clues and signposts pointing us toward spiritual wholeness.

This idea of knowledge and wholeness being equated to salvation is not a new one. The word translated as "salvation" in the New Testament has as one of its main meanings "wholeness".

The Greek word: sōtēria, noun, Strong's # 4991, is used 45 times, commonly translated in the KJV as salvation.

Its root word is sōtēr, a noun also, Strong's # 4990, is used 24 times, commonly translated in the KJV as savior.

Its root word is sōzō, a verb, Strong's # 4982, is used 110 times, commonly translated in the KJV as save 93 times, make whole 9 times, heal 3 times, be whole 2 times, and misc. words 3 times.

In the contextual usages of the verb sōzō, the root word for both nouns sōtēr and sōtēria, had a meaning to Middle-Easterners 2,000 years ago in a sense of therapeutic restoration, in the sense of "healing", "being healed", "made whole", "kept whole", or "kept from being made unwhole".

The following verse references show sōzō to mean "make whole" or "keep whole", and shows its deeper and true meaning, than simply "saved". Since the verb sōzō is the root of sōtēr, translated savior, and sōtēria, translated salvation, then the deeper meaning of sōtēr would be, one who makes whole, and the deeper meaning of sōtēria would be wholeness.

Mat. 9:21, "if perhaps I may only touch the garment of him, I shall be made whole!"
Mat. 9:22, "the belief of you has made you whole."
Mat. 27:40, "keep whole yourself!"

Mat. 27:42, "he made whole others; himself he is absolutely not inherently powered to keep whole."

Mat. 27:49, "let us see if Elijah comes, keeping him whole."

Mark 3:4, (about the man with the withered hand) "Is it permitted on the sabbaths to do good, or to do evil; to make whole a soul, or to destroy [a soul]?"

Mark 5:23, "having come, you may put the hand to her in order that she may be made whole?"

Mark 5:28, "If perhaps I may touch even the garments of him, I shall be made whole!"

Mark 5:34, "Daughter, the belief of you has made whole you."

Mark 6:56, and as many as perhaps touched him were made whole.

Mark 10:52, "Go, the belief of you has made whole you."

Mark 15:30, "keep whole yourself, having come down from the stake."

Mark 15:31, "He made whole others; himself he is absolutely not inherently powered to keep whole."

Luke 6:9, (about the man with the withered hand) "Is it permitted on the sabbath to do good or to do evil, to make whole a soul or to destroy [a soul]?"

Luke 7:50, "The belief of you has made whole you."

Luke 8:12, "then comes the devil and lifts away the Word (logon) from the heart of them, in order that having not believed [the Word] they may [not] be made whole."

Luke 8:36, ... and the ones having seen reported to them how the one having been demonized was made whole.

Luke 8:48, "Daughter, the belief of you has made whole you."

Luke 8:50, "Fear not, only believe, and she shall be made whole."

Luke 17:19, "the belief of you has made whole you."

Luke 18:42, "Look up! The belief of you has made whole you."

Luke 19:10, "Because the son of the mortal came to seek and make whole the destroyed one."

Luke 23:35, "He made whole others; if this one is the Christ, [let him] keep whole himself."

Luke 23:37, "If you are the king of the Judeans, keep whole yourself."

Luke 23:39, "Are you absolutely not the Christ? Keep whole yourself and us."

*Acts 4:9, (referring to the good deed done to the lame man, Acts 3:6-7) "if we be judged up... in what [means] this one has been made whole,"

*Acts 4:10, "...in this one's [name], this one has stood in sight of you, healthy (hugiēs)

*Acts 4:12, "And there is absolutely not in any other, the wholeness (sōtēria); because there is absolutely not another name under the heaven, the [name] having been given among mortals, in which it is necessary for you to be made whole."

Moreover, it is actually up to us, each one personally, to be responsible for his or her wholeness. Keeping in mind that wholeness equates to salvation in the Gnostic sense, since it is brought about by deep knowledge imparted by God through Jesus, which brings insight and when applied, wholeness.

Philippians 2:12 Amplified Bible -
Therefore, my dear ones, as you have always obeyed [my suggestions], so now, not only [with the enthusiasm you would show] in my presence but much more because I am absent, **workout** (cultivate, carry **out** to the goal, and fully complete) **your own salvation** with reverence and awe and trembling (self-distrust, with serious caution, tenderness of conscience, watchfulness against temptation, timidly shrinking from whatever might offend God and discredit the name of Christ)

Now, we see the connection between "sin" and salvation. The word for "sin" means, "missing the mark." It is not some horrible deed, but the aim of psychological and spiritual wholeness that has missed its target. Actions coming from this condition are simply commentary, just as the fire of gnosis is a commentary to or symbol of wholeness.

Carl Jung saw the delineation of types and archetypes in Gnostic mythos, and thus the way to distinguish them. He saw that each type had its own psychological strengths and weaknesses. These weaknesses were due to a lack of integration of certain segments of functions into the psyche as a whole.

The ideas of archetypes, personality types, and individuation would give birth to the Jungian archetypes and led to the MBTI.

The purpose of the Myers-Briggs Type Indicator® (MBTI®) personality inventory is to make the theory of psychological types described by C. G. Jung understandable and useful in people's lives. The theory is that random variation in the behavior is actually quite orderly and consistent, being due to basic differences in the ways individuals use their perception and judgment.

Perception is the way we become aware of things, people, happenings, or ideas. Judgment involves the ways of coming to conclusions about what has been perceived. If people differ systematically in what they perceive and in how they reach conclusions, and differ correspondingly in their reactions and motivations then these differences, if systematic, can be classified into major categories he called archetypes.

In all of Jung's work, the most important and most often stressed ideas were those of wholeness and self-awareness. This, the Gnostics called awakening.

The Gnostic myth did not have to be true in the strict sense of having actually happened to speak to our inner calling. Myths are stories designed to convey, through characters and events, a deeper meaning than could be conveyed with explanations or information. But, information and information speak to the conscious mind, whereas the myth or stories speak to the subconscious. It is the myth that acts as a vehicle to the power of the idea, which affects us. To use the power of the myth we must understand and internalize the meanings, then apply the wisdom to life.

The historicity of the myth is of little concern. To illustrate this point let us look at a passage from the Bible.

Matthew 27:[50] *Jesus, when he had cried again with a loud voice,*
yielded up the ghost. [51] *And, behold, the veil of the temple was rent in*
twain from the top to the bottom; and the earth did quake, and the
rocks rent; [52] *And the graves were opened; and many bodies of the*

saints which slept arose, [53] *And came out of the graves after his resurrection, and went into the holy city, and appeared unto many.*

With apologies to fundamentalists, this account is likely a non-event. If this were true such an abnormal and amazing event it would have been reported, not only by other apostles but also by the historians of the time. Indeed, the bizarre happening would have been written down by anyone who could write. The historicity of the story is not the issue. The story conveys a powerful message, which is impossible to transmit by simply saying, "Jesus died and I think he somehow gave life to the world." The events in this myth was powerful enough to impart life even to the dead. On a personal level the story tells us that we have this life inside us that will continue after death and has the power to change the very nature of life, especially our own life.

So it is with Gnosticism, or any other religion for that matter. Information engages only the mind, but a story of a mythic construct engages the emotion and intuition as well. The story must be such that we can see our own storyline in it. It must convey lessons or hope. It must do so in such a way that it moves the person to understand the potential to avoid or overcome obstacles, either internal or external.

Taking one of the more expansive Gnostic creation stories for example, we may ask, do we actually believe God created Barbelo and Barbelo produced Sophia and Sophia produced Yaldabaoth the Demiurge and the Demiurge made the world and us and has entrapped us into worshipping him by not telling us about the real God? Well, no. Many Gnostic Christians did not rely on Plato's myths. Certainly, Thomas did not mention these stories. Thomas addresses only the underlying meaning. Thomas may allude to basic components to signify a way of healing and a map back to God. This self-awareness, this truth, this wholeness is achieved only by being brutally honest with ourselves. We must be authentic and authentically honest. Integration, individuation, and a deeper truth will arise. This is the Gnosis, which leads to freedom.

I invite the reader to know the overall Gnostic mythos only to understand references made to events and characters in order to intuit their meanings. Most Gnostic branches have more limited creation myths, but all must transmit a story with spiritual lessons and undertones.

We must see that we have the potential to be each and every character in the myth.

We are Sophia, the feminine energy, who wished to create but did not wait to be united with God or her counterpart so that she could be made whole. We are Sophia, who is wisdom but disconnected. She created outside the state of wholeness and her creation was destructive.

We are Sophia whole and connected, who gave Adam the spirit of God and raised him out of his worm-like state.

We are the Demiurge. We are blind to our own blindness. We are unaware of our own limitations. We are arrogant and lost. We may have the divine spark within us but until we see the truth we will misuse our gift. We may believe we are our own god, ignoring the warnings of those more wise. As the Demiurge, whose name is Yaldabaoth, ignored Sophia, his mother, as she called to him, "You are not alone, Samael (god of the blind, or blind god)." We are so blind and arrogant we do not realize we are not united with our creator. We are not whole. We are not God.

We are the Christ spirit, not only whole and restored, but now anointed and sent from our source to aid others on their path back to the divine flame of Gnosis.

It was this idea of integration and wholeness that Jung gleaned from Gnosticism. He called it "individuation".

Jolande Jacobi, a Jungian analyst, writes in her book entitled The Way of Individuation, "Like a seed growing into a tree, life unfolds stage by stage. Triumphant ascent, collapse, crises, failures, and new beginnings strew the way. It is the path trodden by the great majority of mankind, as a rule unreflectingly, unconsciously, unsuspectingly, following its labyrinthine windings from birth to death in hope and longing. It is hedged about with struggle and suffering, joy and sorrow, guilt and error, and nowhere is there security from catastrophe. For as soon as a man tries to escape every risk and prefers to experience life only in his head, in the form of ideas and fantasies, as soon as he surrenders to opinions of 'how it ought to be' and, in order not to make a false step, imitates others whenever possible, he forfeits the chance of his own independent development. Only if he treads the path bravely and flings himself into life, fearing no struggle and no exertion and fighting shy of no experience, will he mature his personality more fully than the man who is ever trying to keep to the safe side of the road."

Of course, thinking this way immediately places one at odds with organized religion, whose task it is to keep all sheep on the same narrow path in the same predefined direction.

We are born of wisdom yet unrealized and of divine power, yet undiscovered. We were created outside the "fullness," but the fullness is within us, waiting, calling. Deep within there is a divine discontent. We are homesickness for a place beyond where and what we are now. Fear and attachment hold us, but the gnosis is waiting on the other side. It is transcendental consciousness brought about by a realization sparked to flame by God, from his grace, as he answers the pleading of our hearts. This is the place where angels sing in silence. This is beyond religion. Religion is made up of commands, resulting only in ethics, but gnosis changes the heart. The change is the opus. Our magnum opus is to lay aside our ego and the fear that besets us, to step outside ourselves and become one, both with our true spiritual identities, and with God in his wonderful fullness. This is the peace that passes understanding. This is the Kingdom of heaven. This is "Individuation."

There is something in the human psyche that struggles to produce what Jung refers to as the "true personality." This struggle to bring about the birth of one's "true personality," which is a fully integrated and healthy personality, is the basis for what Jung called the process of individuation. We are involved in a process of bridging the gap between the various parts of the archetypal pieces within us. The world of the unconscious and the everyday world of ego-consciousness must be brought together, in order to realize the potentialities of one's individual psyche. In short, we must identify the various mental, emotional and spiritual elements that are part of the whole person we are intended to be. We must learn to embrace each and every part, making each part healthy. We must integrate all of the healthy pieces into a healthy wholeness. Jung believed that by being psychologically healthy and whole, we could access our the great store of spiritual energy within each of us.

Gnosis reveals our state of being and kingdom of heaven. Awareness of our state urges us to seek and identify the estranged and unhealthy pieces of ourselves.
Imparted wisdom allows us the embrace our totality and bring about balance, integration and health.
Only the real and total being can enter into the kingdom. The kingdom of heaven is a spiritual kingdom within us.

Identify - embrace - integrate - enter into salvation.

In the Gospel of Thomas the words of Jesus point toward the knowledge or gnosis that brings about the realization that we are fallen beings and unsaved creatures. We are unsaved and fallen, not because a long-dead relative broke a law or religious code in the antediluvian past, but because we have allowed ourselves to become "dis-integrated." The disintegration must stop and we must become whole once more. Health and wholeness - this is the real meaning of salvation.

The parables of Jesus are designed, like the Zen koan, to go past the logical mind and engage emotion and intuition to bring forth a fuller understanding. This is the power of the Gospel of Thomas with it's one hundred and fourteen saying, each one aimed like an arrow, at the heart of the matter.

Let us read these texts and do as the ancient Gnostics commanded. Wake up! Heal yourself! Seek the Christ within you! Let the oil flow down! Let the Word be heard! Let the Light show you the Truth! Become the Christ you are! Give birth to what is inside you! Let the sleeper awaken!

Returning our view to that of the Gospel of Thomas, the book you hold contains the Coptic and Greek translations of The Gospel of Thomas. Presented herein are the result of a gestalt brought about by contrasting and comparing all of the foremost translations, where the best phrasing was chosen to follow the intent and meaning of the text.

Because there are differences between the Coptic manuscript and the Greek fragments of Thomas, each verse will have the following format for the reader to view; The Coptic text will be used as a base from which to render the text. If there are differences between the Coptic and Greek text, the alternate meaning will be placed in parenthesis within the verse. Lastly, obvious parallels found in the Bible are listed along with observations from the author and major religious scholars.

You will read, regarding certain parables, a color ascribed to them by "the fellows". There was a meeting of scholars called "Jesus Seminar" convened several times between 1985-1991. One of the goals was to inventory and classify all the words attributed to Jesus in the first three centuries of the Common Era. This included the Gospel of Thomas. The team reviewed each of 1500 items collected and determine with what degree of certainty could each be ascribed to Jesus.

The Seminar collected more than 1500 versions of about 500 items sorted into four categories: Parables, Aphorisms, Dialogues, and Stories containing words attributed to Jesus.

The Fellows debated and then voted using colored beads to indicate the degree of authenticity of Jesus' words. Each color was assigned a number rating, so that votes could be quantified with a weighted average. The Fellows adopted four categories:

Red (likely authentic)
Pink (somewhat likely)
Gray (somewhat unlikely)
Black (unlikely)

The work before you, takes into account, not only the Greek and Coptic translations, but also the differences between several major translator's word choices. If there is a significant difference in the overall meaning of a word or phrase between Coptic and Greek, or a significant difference in word choices between the author and other translators, the various alternative words or phrases will be placed in parentheses within the text.

The text from the Gospel of Thomas is in bold font. Any parallels of text or meaning that appear in the Bible are placed below the verse in italicized text. Author's notes and observations are in regular text. In this way, the reader can easily identify which body of work is being referenced and observe how they fit together. Notes, observations, and commentary from various religious scholars are placed to assist the reader in gaining a deeper and more spiritual understanding of the texts in hopes that in some meager way a word or phrase, presented in season or some time of receptivity, will open the reader to a meaning or understanding more helpful and elucidating than the simple, raw text.

Let us begin.

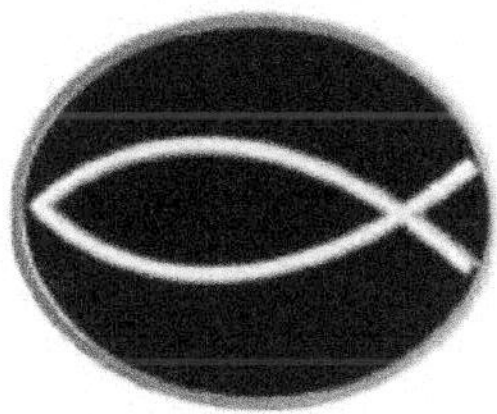

The Gospel of Thomas

These are the secret sayings, which the living Jesus has spoken and Judas who is also Thomas (the twin) (Didymos Judas Thomas) wrote.

"The Living Jesus" could mean the Jesus living after the resurrection or the Jesus living through his sayings.

From the beginning, we must realize the spirit of Christ sleeps within each of us. No man is above another in potential only in expression.

1. **He said to them: Whoever penetrates (discovers the inner meaning of) the interpretation of these words shall never taste death.**

Who apprehends the deeper truths of these saying shall live.

This "saying" may be a preamble written by Thomas regarding the rest of the book. The theme of "never tasting death" occurs throughout the Gospel of Thomas. The pronoun 'he' could refer either to Jesus or the Didymos Judas Thomas.

John 8:51 Very truly I tell you, whoever keeps my word will never see death.

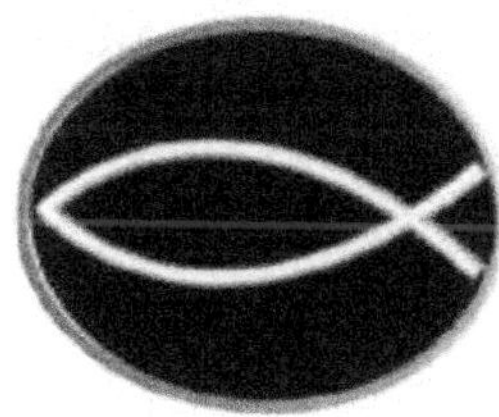

2. Jesus said: Let he who seeks not stop seeking until he finds, and when he finds he will be amazed (troubled), and when he has been amazed he will marvel (be astonished) and he will reign over all, and in reigning he will find rest. (For the rule (reign) of the one who has obtained gnosis results in rest.)

Clement of Alexandria writes: "Being baptized, we are illuminated; illuminated we become sons; being made sons, we are made perfect; being made perfect, we are made immortal." (Instructor, 1.6.26.1)

It seems clear that the rule or reign referred to here is ruling oneself or one's own spirit.

Those who are troubled that there is more to reality than the eyes can see will seek deeper truths. When the spiritual sight sees the truth, they will be troubled that they have not seen what is so obvious before. They will be troubled that reality is very different than they thought. They will be troubled at how simple and clear the truth has become when it was hidden so deeply a moment before. In this new reality, things will make sense and the pieces will fit together. The truth or gnosis will bring peace and rest.

Funk and Hoover write: "Thom 2:2-4 is a gnostic expansion: the gnostic quest leads to being disturbed, which causes one to marvel, and that ends in reigning. The Greek fragment of this same verse adds a fifth stage: the reign of the gnostic results in 'rest,' which is the gnostic catchword for salvation. Gnostic insight into the 'real world,' as opposed to the world of appearances, is what brings all this about. The term 'rest' is employed in the book of Revelation, on the other hand, for future salvation: those who die in the Lord 'may rest from their labors' (Rev 14:13)." (The Five Gospels, p. 471)

2 Timothy 2:11-12: Trustworthy is the saying, If we have died with him, we shall also live with him; if we have endured, we shall reign with him.

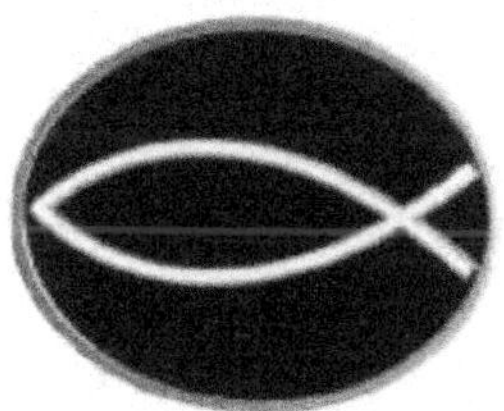

3. **Jesus said: If those who lead you (If those who seek to attract you) say to you: Look, the Kingdom is in the sky, then the birds of the sky will precede you (the birds would enter before you). If they say to you: It is in the sea, then the fish of the sea would enter ahead you. But the Kingdom of God exists within you and it exists outside of you.**

   Those who come to know (recognize) themselves will find it, and when you come to know yourselves you will become known and you will realize that you are the children of the Living Father. Yet if you will not come to know yourselves then you will dwell in poverty and it will be you who are that poverty.

When we come to truly know ourselves we will see the Christ spirit was inside of us from the very beginning. We will awaken our divinity and others will recognize this in us. We will become known for what we really are. Gnosis reveals this truth.

If we fail to seek and find what we fully are, we will remain spiritually poor. The image is of a person being poverty itself, as opposed to simply being poor. Imagine a deeply impoverished setting. You are that squalor.

The phrase, "If you WILL not come to know yourself..." is one way to interpret the verse and indicates a choice made by the one hearing or receiving the truth to ignore the truth and choose not to know the deeper truth. An unexamined life is not worth living.

The kingdom of heaven is hidden and manifest at the same time, according to other sayings, indicating a deeper meaning than most people experience or perceive.

Baruch 3:29-30: "Has anyone climbed up to heaven and found wisdom? Has anyone returned with her from the clouds? Has anyone crossed the sea and discovered her? Has anyone purchased her with gold coin?"

Luke 17:20 And when he was demanded of by the Pharisees, when the kingdom of God should come, he answered them and said, The kingdom of God cometh not with observation: Neither shall they say, Lo here! Lo there! For, behold, the kingdom of God is within you.

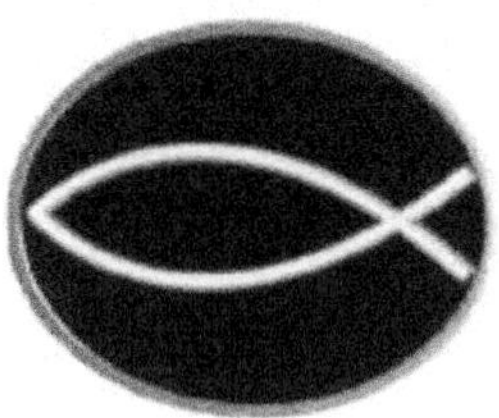

4. Jesus said: The person of old age, having lived many days, will not hesitate to ask a little child of seven days about the place of life, and he will live. For many who are first will become last, (and the last will be first). And they will become one and the same (a single one).

On the eighth day, a Jewish boy is circumcised. The seventh day indicates he has not been circumcised yet and is still closer to God than the seeker. Several Gnostic books have Jesus appearing as a child. The uncircumcised child has not symbolically been claimed by this world and is not yet part of the world system.

As we age we become more and more "invested" in this world. Our time, effort and energy has gone in to preparing our place in the world system. We become myopic to the truth of the spiritual trap in which we are living. We do not remember the place or state we came from. We come from a place where there is neither male nor female. We come from a place where we were one. We come from the "Place of Life" where we did not toil or fight to live, nor was there violence in simply existing. The child is not invested in this world. The small child is still in its primal state. The child remembers.

In the spiritual world, there is no sex or age. We are unified, one, a single, undifferentiated being.

DORESSE translation: [4]. Jesus says: "Let the old man heavy with days hesitate not to ask the little child of seven days about the Place of Life, and he will live! For it will be seen that many of the first will be last, and they will become a <single thing!">

Funk and Hoover write: "Becoming 'a single one' (v. 3) is a motif that appears elsewhere in Thomas. In Thom 22:5, male and female are turned into a single one; in Thomas 23, one and two become a single one; the two made into one become children of Adam in Thom 106:1. The last reference suggests the androgynous state before the creation of human beings, when male and female had not yet been differentiated. In gnostic theory, Adam and Eve were created by a lesser god, who bungled the job in making two sexes. These ideas are foreign to Jesus." (The Five Gospels, p. 473)

We will see the idea of the male and female or the the inner and outer parts of us needing to be unified in order for us to reach the Kingdom of God. The genders may represent the ancient's idea of the conscious and subconscious parts of the mind.

The Gospel according to Thomas used by the Naassenes says: "He who seeks me will find me in children from seven years old; for there in the fourteenth age, having been hidden, I shall become manifest." (*Hidden Records of the Life of Jesus*, p. 243)

Mark 9:35-37 He sat down, called the twelve, and said to them: Whoever wants to be first must be last of all and servant of all. Then he took a little child and put it among them, and taking it in his arms, he said to them: Whoever welcomes one such child in my name welcomes me, and whoever welcomes me welcomes not me but the one who sent me.

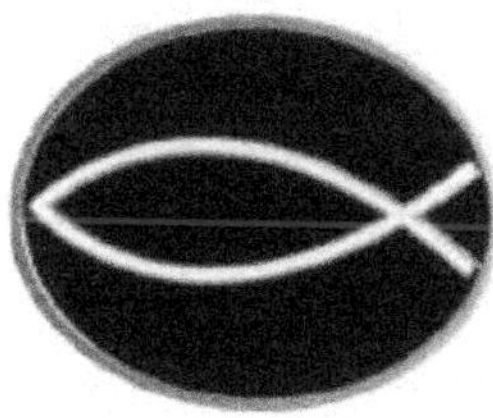

4. **Jesus said: Recognize what is in front of your face, and what has been hidden from you will be revealed to you. For there is nothing hidden which will not be revealed (become manifest), and nothing buried that will not be raised.**

Recognize what is in front of your face because the truth is hidden in plain sight.

An inscription on a shroud found at Oxyrhynchus, reads "Jesus says, There is nothing buried which will not be raised." The shrouds probably belonged to a person practicing what would not be considered orthodox or mainline Christianity. Thus, there are differing opinions as to whether this verse refers to resurrection. Possibly it does, but one must understand Gnostics viewed the resurrection as a metaphor of how the spirit is awakened or reborn after encountering the truth. Since many Gnostics viewed the body as a prison of the spirit, the literal resurrection of the body was not taught by them.

The statement regarding things buried and raised does not appear in other than Greek texts. Since Gnostics hold little to no value in the resurrection as relating to salvation it is likely not referencing that. Things which are hidden, and they are hiding in plain sight, just below the surface of our perception. Once you see it you can never not-see it again.

"Understand what is in front of your face, and then what is hidden from you will be disclosed to you." (*The Gospel of Thomas: The Hidden Sayings of Jesus*, p. 71)

Mark 4:22 For there is nothing hid, except to be made manifest; nor is anything secret, except it come to light.

Luke 12:2 Nothing is covered up that will not be revealed, or hidden that will not be known.

Matthew 10:26 So have no fear of them; for nothing is covered up that will not be uncovered, and nothing secret that will not become known.

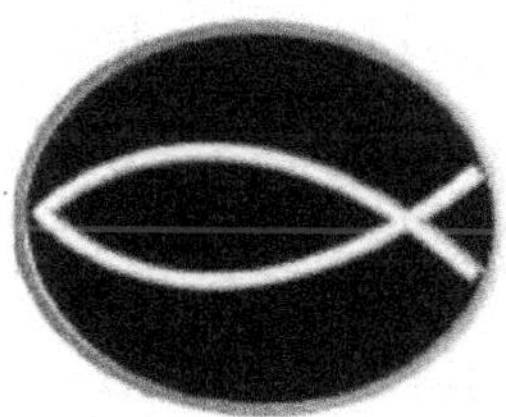

6. His Disciples asked Him, they said to him: How do you want us to fast, and how shall (will) we pray? And how will we be charitable (give alms), and what laws of diet will we maintain?

Jesus said: Do not lie, and do not practice what you hate, for everything is revealed in the plain sight of Heaven. For there is nothing concealed that will not become manifest, and there is nothing covered that will not be exposed.

Funk and Hoover write: "The answers Jesus is represented as giving in 6:2-6 appear to be unrelated to the questions about fasting, praying, and giving posed by the disciples in v. 1. Jesus does answer these three questions directly in 14:1-3. The discrepancy between Thom 6:1 and 2-6 has led some scholars to speculate that the texts of Thomas 6 and 14 have somehow been confused." (*The Five Gospels*, p. 476)

We can see where some may believe verses 14 and 6 were

mistakenly separated when we look at the translation by ***BLATZ*** (14) Jesus said to them: If you fast, you will put a sin to your charge; and if you pray, you will be condemned; and if you give alms, you will do harm to your inner spirits. And if you go into any land and walk about in the regions, if they receive you, eat what is set before you; heal the sick among them. For what goes into your mouth will not defile you; but what comes out of your mouth, that is what will defile you.

It is just as likely the questions posed by the disciples were not directly answered because they were irrelevant. Jesus is answering the more important questions of real and true worship, which is never in worldly, physical form but rather in spirit and in truth.

No matter what you do on the outside your true nature will be revealed in time. Following codes, practices and rituals will not change who you are. Following such liturgies and rituals are simply lies if you hate doing them.

Luke 11:1 He was praying in a certain place, and after he had finished, one of his disciples said to him, Lord, teach us to pray, as John taught his disciples.

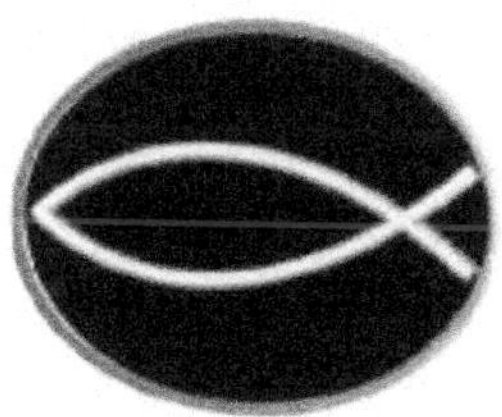

7. Jesus said: Blessed is the lion that the man will eat, for the lion will become the man. Cursed is the man that the lion shall eat, and still the lion will become man.

This saying is a difficult one to understand. On the surface, the point of this verse seems to be that a lion, if eaten by a man will become part of the man and is therefore raised to the state of the man, whereas if a man is eaten by a lion, he becoming part of the animal and is then at a lower status, no longer spiritual.

A lion was a symbol of many things at this time, ranging from royalty to evil. A lion is also the symbol of God. At one time the lion represented uncontrolled passion. Jesus is called, "The Lion of Judah". The interpretation could be turned on its head if one looks at it with this in mind. Blessed is the Lion of Judah if the man partakes of him. But if the Lion of Judah must destroy the man the person is cursed.

Mathew 26:23-30 He who dipped his hand with me in the dish, the same will betray me. The Son of Man goes, even as it is written of him, but woe to that man through whom the Son of Man is betrayed! It would be better for that man if he had not been born. Judas, who betrayed him, answered, "It isn't me, is it, Rabbi?" He said to him, You said it. As they were eating, Jesus took bread, gave thanks for it, and broke it. He gave to the disciples, and said, Take, eat; this is my body. He took the cup, gave thanks, and gave to them, saying: All of you drink it, for this is my blood of the new covenant, which is poured out for many for the remission of sins. But I tell you that I will not drink of this fruit of the vine from now on, until that day when I drink it anew with you in my Father's Kingdom. When they had sung a hymn, they went out to the Mount of Olives.

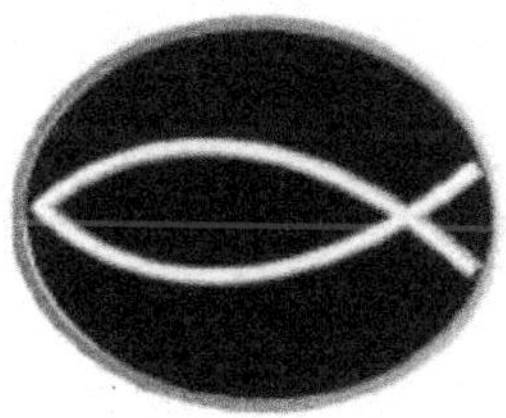

8. And he said: The Kingdom of Heaven is like a skilled (wise) fisherman who casts his net into the sea. He drew it up from the sea (a net) full of small fish. Among them he found a fine (excellent) large fish. That wise fisherman threw all the small fish back into the sea and without hesitation kept (chose) the large fish. Whoever has ears to hear, let him hear!

There will be many variations on this theme in the remaining sayings. Many such saying will be easier to understand if one substitutes the words "kingdom of heaven" or "kingdom" with the words, "the enlightened person" or "the Gnostic". The fine, excellent, or larger of the various prizes represents the knowledge or the gnosis.

The enlightened person is like a wise fisherman who casts his net into the sea (life). He drew up from the sea (life) a net full of small fish (useless things) but there was one fish that was fine (there was the gnosis). He threw everything back and kept that one useful thing.

Still, another way to look at the verse is to place Jesus himself, or the Gnosis He delivers, in the place of the fisherman. He casts his net into the world and draws his net, full of all types of people. Those without Gnosis are discarded into outer darkness, but those with knowledge of the truth, those excellent fish, are kept.

Matthew 13:47-48 Again, the kingdom of heaven is like a net that was thrown into the sea and caught fish of every kind; when it was full, they drew it ashore, sat down, and put the good into baskets but threw out the bad.

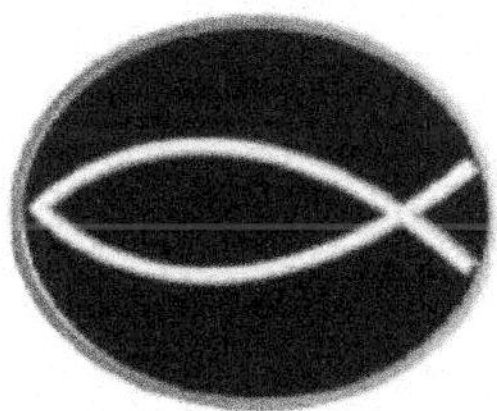

9. Jesus said: Listen, now, the sower came out. He filled his hand and cast (threw) the seeds. Some fell upon the road and the birds came and gathered them up. Others fell on the stone and they did not take deep enough roots in the soil, and so did not produce grain. Others fell among the thorns and they choked the seed, and the worm ate them. Others fell upon the good earth and it produced an excellent crop (which grew) up toward the sky, and it bore 60 fold and even 120 fold.

The teaching and the truth is spread over the world. Some will understand the teachings. Some will not. Those who do understand will have levels of understanding depending on the time and effort spent cultivating a deeper gnosis. They can and will make others aware of the truth as they know it. In this version, Thomas does not mention the sun causing the plants to wither. That portion of the parable seems not to fit well with the other portions of the saying, nor is it congruous with the general message of truth and receptivity. The fact that this version is more simple and easier to understand suggests it was written first.

There are less obvious lessons in this parable. Truth can fall among thorns. Prior bad teachings can cloud the mind and choke out the truth. Teaching can fall on the unreceptive heart or the heart that does not have the depth to comprehend the truth. After all, there are those who never look up, never seek, never find.

Matthew 13:3-8 And he told them many things in parables, saying: Listen! A sower went out to sow. And as he sowed, some seeds fell on the path, and the birds came and ate them up. Other seeds fell on rocky ground, where they did not have much soil, and they sprang up quickly, since they had no depth of soil. But when the sun rose, they were scorched; and since they had no root, they withered away. Other seeds fell among thorns, and the thorns grew up and choked them. Other seeds fell on good soil and brought forth grain, some a hundred fold, some sixty, some thirty.

Mark 4:2-9 And he taught them many things in parables, and in his teaching he said to them: Behold! A sower went out to sow. And as he sowed, some seed fell along the path, and the birds came and devoured it. Other seed fell on rocky ground, where it had not much soil, and immediately it sprang up, since it had no depth of soil; and when the sun rose it was scorched, and since it had no root it withered away. Other seed fell among thorns and the thorns grew up and choked it, and it yielded no grain. And other seeds fell into good soil and brought forth grain, growing up and increasing and yielding thirty fold and sixty fold and a hundred fold. And he said, He who has ears to hear, let him hear.

Luke 8:4-8 And when a great crowd came together and people from town after town came to him, he said in a parable: A sower went out to sow his seed; and as he sowed, some fell along the path, and was trodden under foot, and the birds of the air devoured it. And some fell on the rock; and as it grew up, it withered away, because it had no moisture. And some fell among thorns; and the thorns grew with it and choked it. And some fell into good soil and grew, and yielded a hundred fold. As he said this, he called out, He who has ears to hear, let him hear.

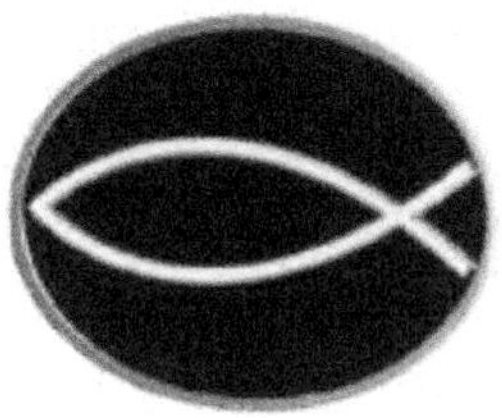

10. Jesus said: I have cast fire upon the world, and as you see, I guard it until it is ablaze.

In Gnostic literature, a fire is symbolic of the knowledge. To be near the fire is to be near Jesus. To be near Jesus is to be near the source of the truth. Jesus has already sparked a fire by delivering the truth. He now guards the spark until what he has kindled becomes a roaring fire.

R. Wilson writes: "Logion 10 has a parallel in Luke xii. 49, but with a change of emphasis. The canonical version looks to the future: 'I came to cast fire upon the earth, and how I wish it were already kindled!' In Thomas, the fire *has* been kindled: 'I have cast fire upon the world, and behold, I guard it until it is ablaze.' This raises an interesting problem in relation to the common source of Matthew and Luke, since Matthew (x. 34) records a saying, 'I came not to cast peace, but a sword.' As already observed, something like this appears in logion 16, but in the saying in Thomas 'division' and 'fire' are paralleled in Luke, 'sword' in Matthew. The question is whether in Thomas we have a conflation of the two synoptic versions, or a form of the saying derived from an independent tradition." (*Studies in the Gospel of Thomas*, pp. 110-111)

Luke 12:49 I came to bring fire to the earth, and how I wish it were already kindled.

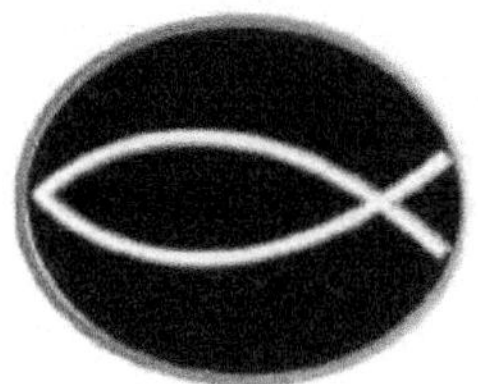

11. Jesus said: This sky will pass away, and the one above it will pass away. The dead are not alive, and the living will not die. In the days when you consumed what is dead, you made it alive. When you come into the Light, what will you do? On the day when you were united (one), you became separated (two). When you have become separated (two), what will you do?

DORESSE Translation:
11. Jesus says: "This heaven will pass away, and the heaven which is above it will pass: but those who are dead will not live, and those who live will not die!" "Today you eat dead things and make them into something living: <but> when you will be in Light, what will you do then? For then you will become two instead of one; and when you become two, what will you do then?"

There are, according to Paul, three heavens. We may look at it as the sky, then the dome of stars, and then the heaven of God and angels, which in this case is the Demiurge and the

Archons. The third heaven is the throne of God, called in Gnostic writings "The Fullness" or the Pleroma. All other things will pass away.

Those who are dead will not live. Those asleep, dead to the truth, unwilling to accept the Gnosis, will remain dead. If you are alive, full of Gnosis, whatever you consume will become part of you and will be alive with you.

Gnostics believe our pure and perfect state was one of unity and lacked differentiation between sexes. When we become two, we no longer have the perfect unity.

2 Corithians 12:2 I know a man in Christ who fourteen years ago was caught up to the ***third heaven****. Whether it was in the body or out of the body I do not know – God knows.*

You can eat that which is dead and it gives you life. As it is spiritually, you can eat the living knowledge and you who are dead will be made alive, but if you are not whole and one with the truth what will you do? Gnosticism preaches unity and wholeness of the person. The parable is asking, "What will you do if you are not whole?"

Matthew 24:35 Heaven and earth will pass away, but my words will not pass away.

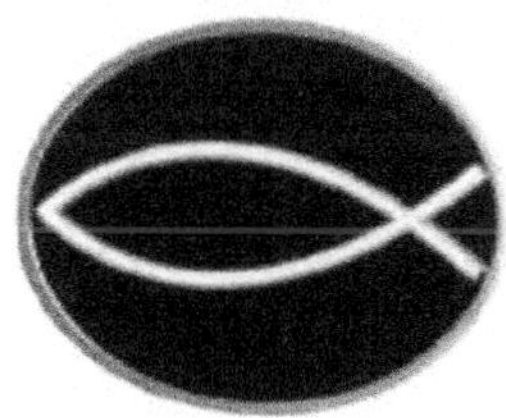

12. The Disciples said to Jesus: We know that you will go away from us. Who is it that will be our teacher?

Jesus said to them: Wherever you are (in the place that you have come), you will go (turn) to James the Just (Righteous), for whose sake Heaven and Earth were made (came into being).

James was the first leader of the Church in Jerusalem, which was the mother church of Christianity in the first years of the faith. For more information about the theology of James see, "The Didache: The Teaching of the Twelve Apostles: A Different Faith - A Different Salvation."

According to rabbinic tradition, every single person is obliged to say: "The world was created for my sake."

Marvin Meyer refers to the quote of Hegesippus on James the Just in Ecclesiastical History 2.23.4-7 and quotes from Secret James 16:5-11 on his authority: "So, not wishing to give them offense, I sent each one of them to a different place. But I myself went up to Jerusalem, praying that I might acquire a share with the beloved ones who will appear." (The Gospel of Thomas: The Hidden Sayings of Jesus, p. 74)

The exaltation of James is characteristic of Jewish-Christian and Naassene tradition in which James may be regarded as supernatural, having obtained great Gnosis directly from Jesus. As myths and embellishments spread, James is not only given the predicate 'righteous' (cf. Acts 7.52), but is also assigned a role in creation.

All these sayings came into being in Jewish-Christian circles where James later became 'the pope of Ebionite fantasy' (H. J. Schoeps)." (Jesus After 2000 Years, p. 596)

The Ebioinites rejected the trinity, believing Jesus was the Messiah and was the true "prophet" mentioned in Deuteronomy 18:15. They rejected the Virgin Birth of Jesus, instead holding that he was the natural son of Joseph and Mary. The Ebionites believed Jesus became the Messiah because he obeyed the Jewish Law.

F. F. Bruce writes: "This saying originated in a Jewish-Christian setting where James the Just, Jesus' brother, was regarded as the natural leader of Jesus's disciples after Jesus's departure. James was actually leader of the Jerusalem church for fifteen to twenty years, until his death in A.D. 62; his memory was revered and enhanced by legendary embellishments. Here a high estimate is placed on his person: in Jewish thought the world was created for the sake of the Torah, [Assumption of Moses 1.2; Genesis Rabbah 1.25.] although in one rabbinical utterance 'every single person is obliged to say: "The world was created for my sake."' [TB Sanhedrin 37b]" (Jesus and Christian Origins Outside the New Testament, pp. 117-118)

It is important that each of us has the kind of relationship with the Father that would make us realize that if we were the only person ever to be created, the world would have still been created just for us and only us.

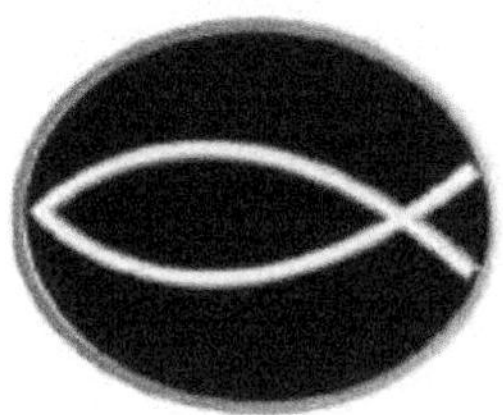

13. Jesus said to his Disciples: Compare me to others, and tell me who I am like. Simon Peter said to him: You are like a righteous messenger (angel) of God. Matthew said to him: You are like a (wise) philosopher (of the heart). Thomas said to him: Teacher, my mouth is completely incapable of saying who you are like!

Jesus said: I'm not your teacher, now that you have drunk; you have become intoxicated from the gushing (bubbling) spring that I have personally tended (measured out). And he took him, and withdrew and spoke three words to him.

Now when Thomas returned to his comrades, they inquired of him: What did Jesus say to you? Thomas said to them: If I tell you even one of the words which he spoke to me, you will take up stones and throw them at me, and fire will come from the stones to consume you.

Jesus gave Thomas the secret, which the others were not ready to hear. There are always negative reactions to the truth when one is not ready to receive it. Denial, anger, rejection of the truth and violence toward the messenger are only a few of the results. If the seeker has not asked the proper question, they are not ready for the answer.

The three words Jesus spoke to Thomas were never disclosed but there are some likely possibilities.
Ahyh ashr ahyh (I am who I am).
Hippolytus, Refutation of All Heresies 5.8.4, cites the three words Kaulakau, Saulasau, Zeesar, derived from the Hebrew of Isaiah 28:10-13. Kaulakau, Saulasau, Zeesar Three words derived from the Hebrew of Isaiah 28:10, 13: sav la-sav, savla-sav, kavla-kav, kav la-kav, ze'ir sham, meaning uncertain, translated in the revised Standard Version as follows:
"it is precept upon precept, precept upon precept,
line upon line, line upon line,
here a little, there a little."
There is the Hebrew words transliterated:
"Tsav l'tsav, tsav l'tsav," means "tribulation (affliction) upon tribulation (affliction)."
"Qav l'qav, qav l'qav" means "hope upon hope."
"Z'eir sham, z'eir sham" means, "Await a little more a little more."
Pistis Sophia 136 mentions Yao Yao Yao, the Greek version

(with three letters, given three times) of the ineffable name of God

The Gospel of Bartholomew and the Secret Book of John provide statements of identification with the father, the mother (or the holy spirit), and the son.

When Moses asked God for his name (Exodus 3:14) God replied in Exodus 3:12, "*Ehyeh asher ehyeh*", literally translates as "I Will Be What I Will Be", with attendant theological and mystical implications in Jewish tradition. However, in most English Bibles, this phrase is rendered as *I am that I am*."

Mark 8:27-30 Jesus went on with his disciples to the villages of Caesarea Philippi; and on the way he asked his disciples, Who do people say that I am? And they answered him, John the Baptist; and others, Elijah; and still others, one of the prophets. He asked them, But who do you say that I am? Peter answered him, You are the Messiah. And he sternly ordered them not to tell anyone about him.

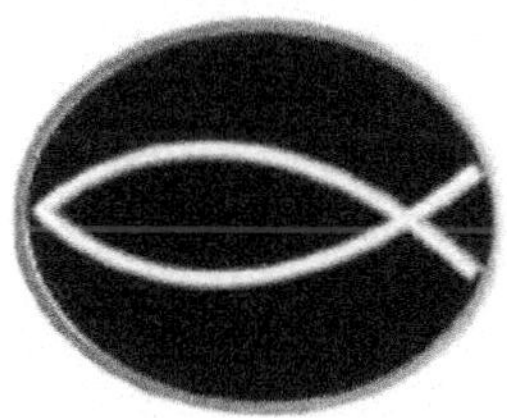

14. Jesus said to them: If you fast, you will give rise to transgression (sin) for yourselves. And if you pray, you will be condemned. And if you give alms, you will cause harm (evil) to your spirits. And when you go into the countryside, if they take you in (receive you) then eat what they set before you and heal the sick among them. For what goes into your mouth will not defile you, but rather what comes out of your mouth, that is what will defile you.

What is outside counts little. What is inside counts much. If you do what you hate doing, even if it is "religious" you will harbor resentment and ill thoughts. Do what is in your spirit to do. Do not stress what is done on the outside but rather what comes from the inside. The command to eat whatever is set before you is evidence that the gospel was being propagated to the Gentiles.

F. F. Bruce writes: "Fasting, prayer and almsgiving (cf. Saying 6) are three forms of piety mentioned in the Sermon on the Mount (Matthew 6.1-18), but the instructions given here are quite different from those given there. Such pious activities, it appears, are superfluous and indeed harmful for the true Gnostic. (Similar sentiments about prayer and fasting are expressed in saying 104.) The second and third sentences in the saying are respectively parallel to Luke 10.8 f. and Matthew 15.11 (cf. Mark 7.15). The addition of the injunction 'eat what is set before you' of the words denying that food conveys defilement underlines the relevance of the injunction to the Gentile mission (cf. Acts 10.15; 1 Corinthians 10.27)." (Jesus and Christian Origins Outside the New Testament, p. 119)

Luke 10:8-9 Whenever you enter a town and its people welcome you, eat what is set before you; Cure the sick who are there, and say to them, The kingdom of God has come near to you.

Mark 7:15 There is nothing outside a person that by going in can defile, but the things that come out are what defile.

Matthew 15:11 It is not what goes into the mouth that defiles a man, but what comes out of the mouth, this defiles a man.

Romans 14:14 I know and am persuaded in the Lord Jesus that nothing is unclean in itself; but it is unclean for any one who thinks it unclean.

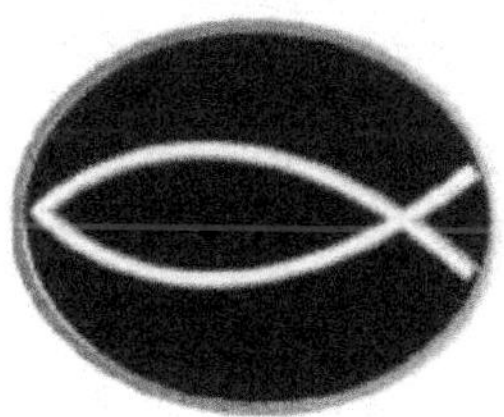

15. Jesus said: When you see him who was not born of woman, bow yourselves down upon your faces and worship him for he is your Father.

Even Jesus was born of a woman, but more importantly, the Demiurge was born of Sophia, but the Supreme God was born of himself. It is he whom we should worship.

Robert M. Grant: "Man who is born of woman is subject to sin, according to Job 14:1, as Doresse notes (page 143). The greatest of those born of women was John the Baptist (Matthew 11:11; Luke 7:28). Therefore, for our Gnostic (as for other Gnostics), Jesus cannot have been born of a woman (in spite of the fact that Paul says he was - Galatians 4:4). Of course, it is possible that like some Gnostic teachers he held that while Jesus was born of a woman, the spiritual Christ descended upon him at the time of his baptism; the Naassenes believed that the threefold being descended upon Jesus. In any event, the one not born of woman is to be worshipped, since he is the (heavenly) Father. This conclusion seems to reflect the words of

John 14:9: 'He who has seen me has seen the Father' (cf., John 10:30: 'I and the Father are one')." (The Secret Sayings of Jesus, p. 135)

It bears saying again that one does not need to believe in the actual existence of these beings, but only in the metaphor that is conveyed by the myth.

In a deeper sense, the divine and eternal spark within us was not born of woman.

Galatians 4:3-5 Even so we, when we were children, were in bondage under the elements of the world: But when the fullness of the time was come, God sent forth his Son, made of a woman, made under the law, To redeem them that were under the law, that we might receive the adoption of sons.

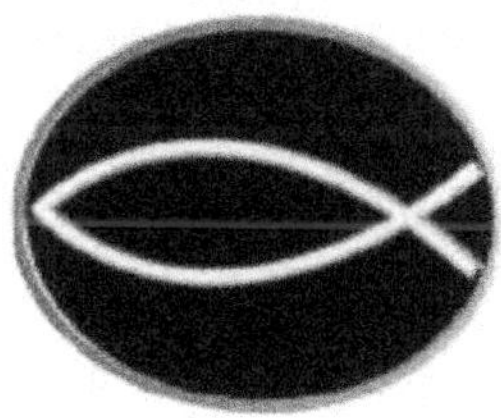

16. Jesus said: People think perhaps I have come to spread peace upon the world. They do not know that I have come to cast dissention (conflict) upon the earth; fire, sword, war. For there will be five in a house. Three will be against two and two against three, the father against the son and the son against the father. And they will stand (as a single unit, they will stand alone).

There will always be enmity between those who are religious and those who are spiritual, even more so if they are awakened. Those who are awakened are those who are a unity unto themselves. This salvation is not a do-it yourself salvation. If it were we would not need a messiah. The messiah is the servant sent to lead us out of the fog and show us our error. He leads us to the path of knowledge and righteousness. It is up to us to walk the path. Those who walk the path will become different from others because their perspective will change. The difference in the enlightened person will be hated by the world.

The enlightened ones stand alone in the world.

Robert M. Grant and David Noel Freedman write: "This saying is surprising when compared with the others which speak of peace and unity, for here Jesus plainly speaks of himself as a 'divider.' The two ideas can be reconciled, however, for peace and unity are characteristic of believers, Gnostic or Christian, while the division is that which comes into existence between them and outsiders. The saying is based on Luke 12:51-53 (Matthew 10:34); Luke 12:49 has already been paraphrased in Saying 9. 'Perhaps men think' is derived from Luke's question, 'Do you suppose . . . ?' 'I came to cast peace' comes from Matthew, while 'I came to case division' is composed by the author of Thomas as a parallel to the preceding line, and to Luke 12:49, from which he derives the mention of 'fire' ('sword' comes from Matthew). The next sentence is an almost exact quotation of Luke 12:52-53, though references to divisions among women are omitted because 'women are not worthy of life' (Saying 112). Those who 'stand' (and will not taste death, cf., Saying 18 and Commentary) are those who have broken their ties with earthly families and are 'single ones' (cf., Sayings 50 and 75). They must hate father, mother, brothers, and sisters (Sayings 56 and 98)." (The Secret Sayings of Jesus, pp. 136-137)

Matthew 10:34-36 Do not think that I have come to bring peace to the earth; I have not come to bring peace, but a sword. For I have come to set a man against his father, and a daughter against her mother, and a daughter-in-law against her mother-in-law; and one's foes will be members of one's own household.

Luke 12:51-53 Do you think that I have come to give peace on earth? No, I tell you, but rather division; for henceforth in one house there will be five divided, three against two and two against three; they will be divided, father against son and son against father, mother against daughter and daughter against her mother, mother-in-law against her daughter-in-law and daughter-in-law against her mother-in-law.

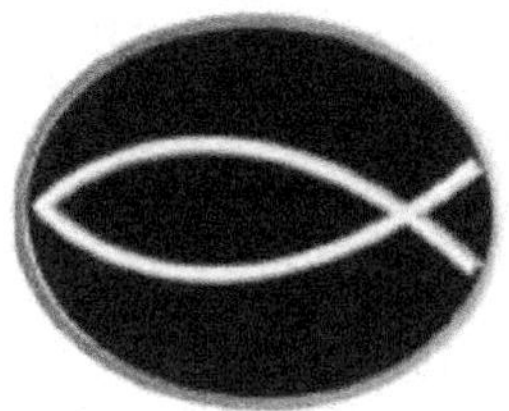

17. Jesus said: I will give to you what eye has not seen, what ear has not heard, what hand has not touched, and what has not occurred to the mind of man.

This saying enforces that fact we need someone outside our own confused mind to give us what we cannot see or conceive. Our own concepts and ways of thinking have led us in circles like a pony tied to a post and chain.

If you work on your mind with your mind how can you afford the immense confusion.

1 Cor 2:9 But, as it is written, What no eye has seen, nor ear heard, nor the human heart conceived, what God has prepared for those who love him.

Marvin Meyer writes: "This saying is also cited in 1 Corinthians 2:9, perhaps as a wisdom saying in use among the enthusiasts of Corinthians. Compare Isaiah 64:4. The saying occurs frequently in Jewish and Christian literature, and sometimes it is said to come from the Apocalypse of Elijah or the Secrets (or, apocrypha) of Elijah. At other times, it is said to be a saying of Jesus. A variant of the saying is also found in Plutarch, How the Young Person Should Study Poetry 17E: 'And let these (words) of Empedocles be at hand: "Thus these things are not to be seen by men, nor heard, nor comprehended with the mind." . . .' The parallels have been collected by Michael E. Stone and John Strugnell, The Books of Elijah: Parts 1-2, pp. 41-73." (The Gospel of Thomas: The Hidden Sayings of Jesus, p. 76)

Robert M. Grant and David Noel Freedman write: "The apostle Paul quotes something very close to this saying, perhaps from a lost document, in 1 Corinthians 2:9: 'As it is written, What eye has not seen and ear has not heard, and what has not entered into the heart of man, such things God has prepared for those who love him.' By the end of the second century these words were ascribed to Jesus, as in the Martyrdom of Peter (chapter 10) and the Acts of Peter with Simon (chapter 39). Thomas adds a unique reference to the sense of touch. The joys of the kingdom are completely unrelated to sense perception. (We should add that, like other Gnostics, he undoubtedly rejected the accounts in the gospels which speak of Jesus's risen body as tangible - Luke 24:39; John 20:27). His phrasing of this saying is the exact reverse of 1 John 1:1, which speaks of 'What we have heard, what we have seen with our eyes, what we beheld and our hands handled." (The Secret Sayings of Jesus, p. 137)

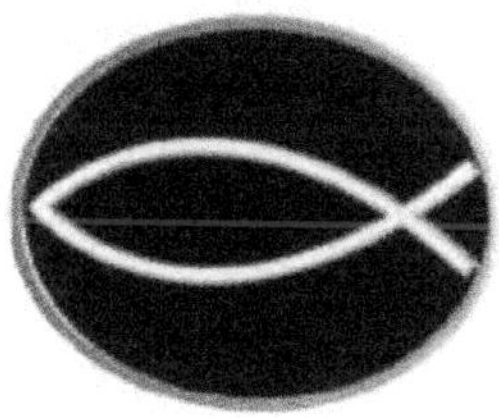

18. The Disciples said to Jesus: Tell us how our end will come. Jesus said: Have you already discovered the beginning (origin), so that you inquire about the end? Where the beginning (origin) is, there the end will be. Blessed be he who will take his place in the beginning (stand at the origin) for he will know the end, and he will not experience death.

DORESSE
18. The disciples say to Jesus: "Tell us what our end will be." Jesus says: "Have you then deciphered the beginning, that you ask about the end? For where the beginning is, there shall be the end. Blessed is the man who reaches the beginning; he will know the end, and will not taste death!"

You may ask about the end, thinking the end is attaining the Kingdom of God, but the Kingdom is present now. It was at the beginning and it will be in the end, but being in the Kingdom now is all that matters and it is all that elevates you.

Marvin Meyer writes: "To return to the beginning is to attain the end; compare Gospel of Thomas saying 49. Also compare Manichaean Psalm Book 155,9-12: 'Holy ones, rejoice with me, for I have returned again to my beginning. I [have] received my clean garments, my robes that do not become old. I have rejoiced in their joy, I have been glad in their gladness, [I have rested] in their rest from everlasting to everlasting.' Secret Book of John II 9,5-8 makes a similar point: 'And he spoke, and glorified and praised the invisible spirit, saying, "Because of you everything has come into being, and everything will return to you."'" (The Gospel of Thomas: The Hidden Sayings of Jesus, p. 77)

From God we come and to God we return, and remembering our origin is to know our destiny. Jesus told us this again later in Revelation when he proclaimed himself as the Alpha and the Omega.

NIV Revelation 22: 13 I am the Alpha and the Omega, the First and the Last, the Beginning and the End. 14 "Blessed are those who wash their robes, that they may have the right to the tree of life and may go through the gates into the city.

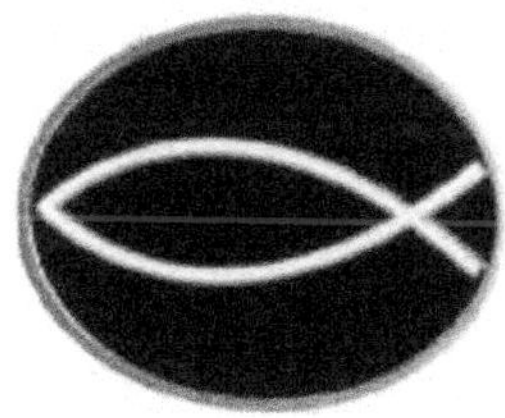

19. Jesus said: Blessed is he who existed (who came into being) before he came into being. If you become my Disciples and heed my sayings, these stones will serve you. For there are five trees in paradise for you, which are unchanged (undisturbed) in summer and in winter and their leaves do not fall. Whoever knows them will not experience death.

Jesus came into being with God before he was born of flesh. Moreover, if God created all things in one period of time, as Genesis tells us, then all souls (spirits) existed with him until sent into the bodies of newborns. If we remember where we came from and that we have this divine connection we also fit this description.

Five is the number of grace. It is the grace of God which sends the gnosis.

Robert M. Grant and David Noel Freedman write: "The fourth-century apologist Lactantius treats the first sentence of this saying as a prophecy uttered by Jeremiah (Div. inst., 4, 8); in the Epideixis (43) of Irenaeus, however, it is ascribed to Jesus (cf., J. P. Smith, St. Irenaeus: Proof of the Apostolic Preaching, page 182, note 207). Like Jesus, who 'was' (John 1:1-2) before he 'became' incarnate (John 1:14), his disciples, who hear his words because they themselves are 'of God' (John 8:47), remain in him and have his words remaining in them; therefore whatever they ask will take place for them (John 15:8). Stones can become bread (Matthew 3:3; Luke 3:3), or fire can come out of stones (Saying 13). Thomas probably has in mind the creation of food out of stones (cf. also Matthew 7:9: 'What man of you, if his son asks him for bread - will he give him a stone?'), for he goes on to speak of the five never-failing trees in paradise. These trees, mentioned in Pistis Sophia (chapters 1 and elsewhere) and among the Manichees, are probably trees which give spiritual sustenance to the five spiritual senses. They are the trees of life like the single one mentioned in Revelation 22:2 (cf., the Gospel of Eve[?] in Epiphanius, Pan., 26, 5). They must be spiritual, since Thomas says that 'he who will understand them will not taste death.' To understand them is thus equivalent to 'keeping the word' of Jesus (John 8:52)." (The Secret Sayings of Jesus, p. 139)

John 1:1 King James Version (KJV)

1 In the beginning was the Word, and the Word was with God, and
the Word was God.

2 *The same was in the beginning with God.*

3 *All things were made by him; and without him was not any thing*
made that was made.

4 *In him was life; and the life was the light of men.*

5 *And the light shineth in darkness; and the darkness comprehended it*
not.

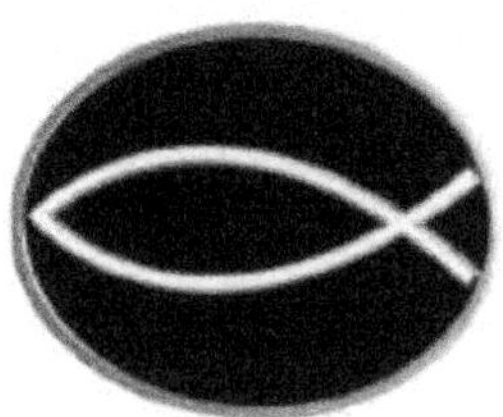

20. The Disciples said to Jesus: Tell us what the Kingdom of Heaven is like. He said to them: It is like a mustard seed, smaller than all other seeds and yet when it falls on the tilled earth, it produces large foliage (a large stalk) (a big plant) and becomes shelter for the birds of the sky.

This saying as presented in Luke is an exaggeration, which has no apparent reason. A mustard seed is small but the mustard plant is in no way a tree, which Mark has it become in his version. The Q document is missing this exaggeration also. It is a vegetable, as Thomas describes it. Luke says the birds nest in the branches. Thomas says the birds shelter beneath its large leaves.

When the truth is deposited in the mind and heart it will grow to great dimensions and (beneath) within the truth we will find shelter and rest.

It is the acceptance of the truth and the ability to work within those parameters that releases us from all cognitive dissonance. It is in this clarity we can bring about peace and lasting change.

The problem with truth is that once it is seen it cannot be unseen. It will, from that time on, stare you in the face. Once seen and apparent the awakened person will not only be changed but he or she will point it out to others, insisting that it must be seen. The truth is contagious, and difficult to control.

J. D. Crossan points out that mustard, when planted in a garden can take it over like a weed, He concludes: "The point, in other words, is not just that the mustard plant starts as a proverbially small seed and grows into a shrub of three or four feet, or even higher, it is that it tends to take over where it is not wanted, that it tends to get out of control, and that it tends to attract birds within cultivated areas where they are not particularly desired. And that, said Jesus, was what the Kingdom was like: not like the mighty cedar of Lebanon and not quite like a common weed, like a pungent shrub with dangerous takeover properties. Something you would want in only small and carefully controlled doses - if you could control it." (The Historical Jesus, pp. 278-279)

Mark 4:30-32 He also said, With what can we compare the kingdom of God, or what parable will we use for it? It is like a mustard seed, which, when sown upon the ground, is the smallest of all the seeds on earth; yet when it is sown it grows up and becomes the greatest of all shrubs, and puts forth large branches, so that the birds of the air can make nests in its shade.

Matthew 13:31-32 The kingdom of heaven is like a grain of mustard seed which a man took and sowed in his field; it is the smallest of all seeds, but when it has grown it is the greatest of shrubs and becomes a tree, so that the birds of the air come and make nests in its branches.

Luke 13.18-19 He said therefore, What is the kingdom of God like? And to what shall I compare it? It is like a grain of mustard seed which a man took and sowed in his garden; and it grew and became a tree, and the birds of the air made nests in its branches.

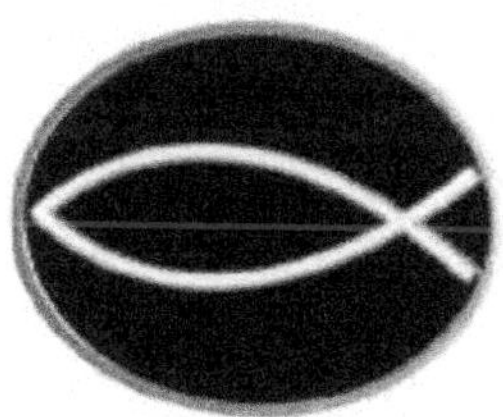

21. Mary said to Jesus: Who are your Disciples like? He said: They are like little children who are living in a field that is not theirs. When the owners of the field come, they will say: Leave our field! Get out! And the children will leave the field. They undress in front of them in order to let them have what is theirs and they give back the field (It is as if they were naked in front of them and they give them back their field).

Therefore, I say, if the owner of the house knows that the thief is coming, he will be alert before he arrives and will not allow him to break in (dig through the walls into) the royal house (the master's home) to carry away his belongings. You, must be on guard and beware of the world (system).

Prepare yourself (arm yourself) with great strength or the bandits will find a way to reach you. They will find the place you fail to watch. For the problems you expect will come. Let there be among you a person of understanding (awareness).

When the crop ripened, he came quickly with his sickle in his hand to reap. Whoever has ears to hear, let him hear!

Jack Finegan writes: "Here the little children who live in the field are presumably the disciples who live in the world. When they give back the field to its owners they 'take off their clothes before them' which, in the present context, must mean that they strip themselves of their bodies in death, an end, to the Gnostic, eminently desirable (cf. §§236, 357)." (*Hidden Records of the Life of Jesus*, p. 254)

Robert M. Grant and David Noel Freedman write: "Here Mariham (the Mariamme of the Naassenes - Hippolytus, Ref., 5, 7, 1 - also mentioned in Saying 112), asks a question and is told tha the disciples are 'like little children' (Matthew 18:3; cf., 1 Corinthians 14:20). The children live in an alien field, which must be the world, as in Matthew 13:38. 'Leave our field to us!' recalls the command of the farmer in Matthew 13:30: 'Leave both to grow up together until the harvest.' Moreover, in Matthew 24:40-42 there are mysterious references to 'two in a field,' to one's being left, and to the coming of a master. Whatever synoptic reminiscences there may be, these have been subordinated to the notion of being naked (see Saying 38). The true Gnostic wants to strip off the body (contrast 2 Corinthians 5:4: 'not to be stripped but to be clad upon') and leave the world." (The Secret Sayings of Jesus, p. 141)

This saying appears to be divided into three sections. In the first part, we have the disciples pictured as children who are homeless, living on the property and wearing the clothes owned by someone else. They are living in a world that is not their home and wearing clothes they have borrowed. They must eventually relinquish their clothes; the flesh which covers, clothes and houses the spirit. Later we will learn that the flesh came into being because of the spirit.
In saying 29 we read, "Jesus said: If the flesh came into being because of spirit, it is a marvel, but if spirit came into being because of the body, it would be a marvel of marvels."

The disciples must also leave the place they are living and give it back to its rightful owner, the creator of the world and its systems. They must realize they are "passers by" and should own nothing here so they will have no emotional ties to this world.

In the third part of the saying Jesus reveals to them God's plan to come at the proper time, when the seekers are ready for Gnosis have been given the knowledge to attained gnosis and be awakened. It was the purpose and mission of Jesus to provide the knowledge so that those who were ready would awaken from their spiritual sleep.

Matthew 24:43 But understand this: if the owner of the house had known in what part of the night the thief was coming, he would have stayed awake and would not have let his house be broken into.

Mark 4:26-29 He also said, The kingdom of God is as if someone would scatter seed on the ground, and would sleep and rise night and day, and the seed would sprout and grow, he does not know how. The earth produces of itself, first the stalk, then the head, then the full grain in the head. But when the grain is ripe, at once he goes in with his sickle, because the harvest has come.

Luke 12:39-40 But know this, that if the householder had known at what hour the thief was coming, he would not have left his house to be broken into. You also must be ready; for the Son of man is coming at an unexpected hour.

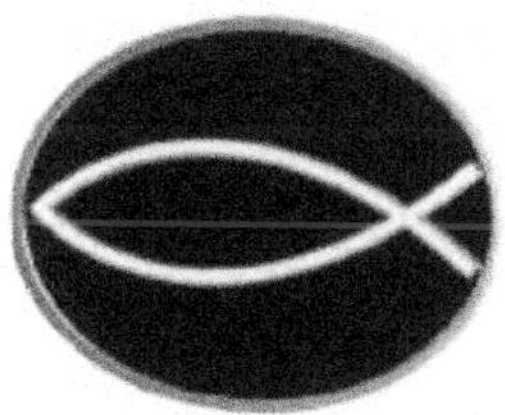

22. Jesus saw little children who were being suckled. He said to his Disciples: These little children who are being suckled are like those who enter the Kingdom.

They said to him: Should we become like little children in order to enter the Kingdom?

Jesus said to them: When you make the two one, and you make the inside as the outside and the outside as the inside, when you make above as below, and if you make the male and the female one and the same (united male and female) so that the man will not be masculine (male) and the female be not feminine (female), when you establish an eye in the place of an eye and a hand in the place of a hand and a foot in the place of a foot and an likeness (image) in the place of a likeness (an image), then will you enter the Kingdom.

When there is unity within the person there is wholeness. When there is disunity in the person there is disharmony, confusion and subterfuge. Unity is wholeness and wholeness is simple and childlike. There is no guile.

When there is wholeness we will have the strength of the man and the heart of the woman, the spirit of a child and the wisdom of the old ones. We find a way to reconcile and integrate what we believe, how we feel, what we think, and how we act. This includes embracing the male and female parts of our psyche as both warrior and protector, nurturer and hunter. Reason and intuition speak as one. It also includes eliminating the chasm between how religion and society claim things work and how we see things that work. This is completion, integration, and individuation.

In the publication, CEOSage, Scott Jeffrey writes: "We Start Out Relatively Unconscious (Mostly Asleep). We all start out as part of a collective. As we grow, our family, friends, school, religion, and culture shape our personality.

The Taoists call this personality the acquired mind as we acquire it through our environment. In the external world, this environment is conventional (as in conventional rules or conventional society). The conventional code holds specific guidelines of what we should believe, what things mean, and how we should behave. This conventional, outer world has structure and order. But within us is an entirely different world. And this inner world, for most of us, is as chaotic as ocean waves during a storm.

Both Freud and Jung called this undifferentiated chaos the unconscious. The unconscious, we could say, is everything within us that falls outside of our conscious awareness—everything we don't know or can't observe within ourselves.

While we want to believe we're conscious of most of our thoughts, feelings, actions, and behavior, all evidence suggests otherwise. We are, in truth, mostly unconscious beings."

The idea of AWAKENING is a main tenant of Gnosticism. It comes with personal unity and the re-establishment of the whole and integrated person. The person is the same inside and outside (conscious and subconscious) as neither male nor female, but both. These ideas go back to the foundation of Gnosticism and is echoed in many texts. Yet, part of this truth is lost. It is not only that we seek unity in ourselves, but we must also see unity in others, looking beyond the fact that they may be male or female, but a unified soul. It is important to keep in mind the Gnostic idea of the undifferentiated soul was complete and intact, being male and female prior to creation. This is the state they seek to attain here. It is the state of creation before incarnation.

This is a call for the full acceptance of all that each of us are. Each person has within themselves portions of both male and female energies. Each rest in a different place on the matrix and mixture of these energies. The challenge is to simply become all you are.

Clement of Alexandria states in Stromata iii.13.92-93 (J.E.L. Oulton's translation): "On this account he [Julius Casinos] says: 'When Salome asked when she would know the answer to her questions, the Lord said, When you trample on the robe of shame, and when the two shall be one, and the male with the female, and there is neither male nor female.' In the first place we have not got the saying in the four Gospels that have been handed down to us, but in the Gospel according to the Egyptians."

Second Clement 12:2-6 says (Lightfoot's translation): "For the Lord Himself, being asked by a certain person when his kingdom would come, said, When the two shall be one, and the outside as the inside, and the male with the female, neither male or female. Now the two are one, when we speak truth among ourselves, and in two bodies there shall be one soul without dissimulation. And by the outside as the inside He meaneth this: by the inside he meaneth the soul and by the outside the body. Therefore in like manner as they body appeareth, so also let thy soul be manifest by its good works. And by the male with the female, neither male nor female, he meaneth this; that a brother seeing a sister should have no thought of her as a female, and that a sister seeing a brother should not have any thought of him as a male. These things if ye do, saith He, the kingdom of my father shall come."

Luke 18:16 But Jesus called for them and said, Let the little children come to me, and do not stop them; for it is to such as these that the kingdom of God belongs. Truly I tell you, whoever does not receive the kingdom of God as a little child will never enter it.

Mark 9:43-48 If your hand causes you to stumble, cut it off; it is better for you to enter life maimed than to have two hands and to go to hell, to the unquenchable fire. And if your foot causes you to stumble, cut it off; it is better for you to enter life lame than to have two feet and to be thrown into hell. And if your eye causes you to stumble, tear it out; it is better for you to enter the kingdom of God with one eye than to have two eyes and to be thrown into hell, where the worm never dies, and the fire is never quenched.

Matthew 18:3-5 And said, Verily, I say unto you, unless you turn and become like children, you will never enter the kingdom of heaven.

Whoever humbles himself like this child, he is the greatest in the kingdom of heaven. Whoever receives one such child in my name receives me;

Matthew 5:29-30 If your right eye causes you to sin, pluck it out and throw it away; it is better that you lose one of your members than that your whole body be thrown into hell. And if your right hand causes you to sin, cut it off and throw it away; it is better that you lose one of your members than that your whole body go into hell.

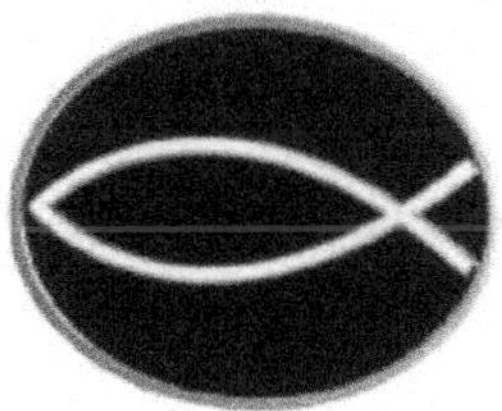

23. Jesus said: I will choose you as one out of a thousand and two out of ten thousand and they will stand as a single one (and they will stand – be lifted up - at rest, being one and the same) .

Many are called but few are chosen. This comment about standing as a single one may indicate the Gnostic believe in a sexually undifferentiated and unified beings' existence in heaven.

To have so few awakened beings to choose from, indicated by the fact that Jesus expects one in a thousand or two in ten-thousand, points to the fact that Gnostics thought of themselves as a minority, an elite few, a rare breed, a chosen people.

Matthew 20:16 So the last shall be first, and the first last: for many be called, but few chosen.

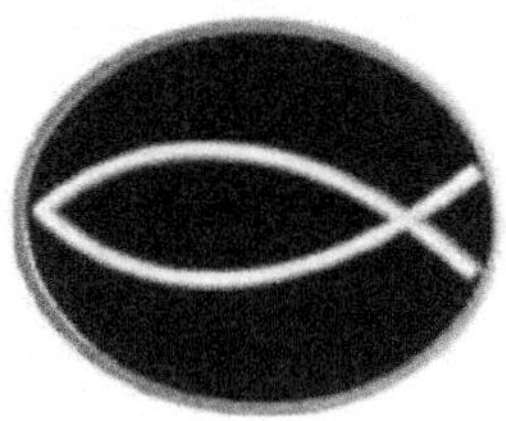

24. His Disciples said: Show us the place where you are (your place), for (we must know about it – we must find it) it is necessary for us to seek it.

He said to them: Whoever has ears, let him hear! Within a man of light there is light, and he illumines (enlightens) the entire world. If he does not shine, he is darkness (there is darkness).

The apostles do not yet recognize the light within themselves. By not singling himself out and by using the general term "man" Jesus is telling them they are men of light that should shine. It is the very core of the Gnostic ideal that those awakened or enlightened are the light. They have within themselves the light and they should shine so as to enlighten or awaken others. It is not that other do not have the light. Indeed, a "spark" from the original fire of life inhabit and penetrates us all. Some are yet to realize this and so the curtain to the soul stay closed. With their own inner light hidden, they themselves become darkness, leading others astray.

John13:36 Simon Peter said to him, Lord, where are you going? Jesus answered, Where I am going, you cannot follow me now; but you will follow afterward.

Matthew 6:22-23 The eye is the lamp of the body. So, if your eye is healthy, your whole body will be full of light; but if your eye is unhealthy, your whole body will be full of darkness. If then the light in you is darkness, how great is the darkness!

Luke 11:34-36 Your eye is the lamp of your body; when your eye is sound, your whole body is full of light; but when it is not sound, your body is full of darkness. Therefore be careful lest the light in you be darkness. If then your whole body is full of light, having no part dark, it will be wholly bright, as when a lamp with its rays gives you light.

Early philosophers thought that light was transmitted from the eye and bounced back, allowing the person to sense the world at large. Ancient myths tell of Aphrodite constructing the human eye out of the four elements (earth, wind, fire, and water). The eye was held together by love. She kindled the fire of the soul and used it to project from the eyes so that it would act like a lantern, transmitting the light, thus allowing us to see.

Euclid, (330 BC to 260BC) speculated about the speed of light being instantaneous since you close your eyes, then open them again, even the distant objects appear immediately.

Stevan Davies writes: "According to saying 24 people may actualize the light within them and thus see the world and themselves in terms of the light of creation. They will see the world in reference to its beginning perfection, stand at the beginning (saying 18), and need no future attainment. They will know themselves to be sons of the living Father (saying 3) -- that is, the image of God, no longer male or female and having made the male and female into a single one, they will enter the kingdom of heaven (saying 22)."

Stevan Davies continues: "According to Gos. Thom. 24 one learns that those seeking the place where Jesus is ought not seek Jesus himself, but will find what they seek within themselves, the primordial light which, when actualized, illuminates the world."
(http://www.misericordia.edu/users/davies/thomas/jblprot.htm)

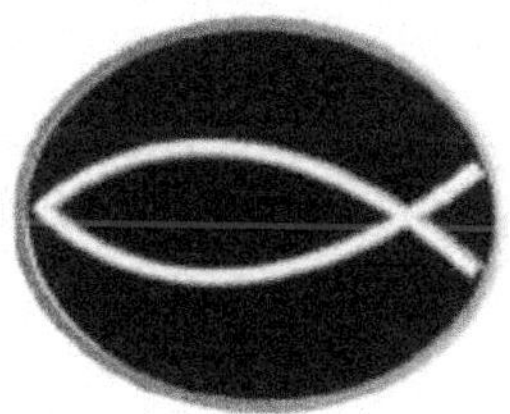

25. Jesus said: Love your friend (Brother) as your soul; protect him as you would the apple (pupil) of your own eye.

Although scholars have pointed out that the term "brother" applies only to fellow believers and in this case only fellow Gnostics. I must acknowledge the wording indicates the idea of a narrow scope of compassion but hope it is applied universally. Since Gnostics were a minority, which the burgeoning orthodoxy would eventually seek to put to death, it is understandable why Gnostics would seek to love and protect fellow Gnostics above others.

This frame of mind was proven out in July of 1209 when the Catholic church hunted down and executed an entire city of Gnostics. After Pope Innocent III had declared a crusade to eliminate Catharism, a type of Gnosticism, a crusader army consisting of knights with professional soldiers, mercenary bands, and pilgrims, assembled and departed from Lyon and marched toward Albi, Beziers, Toulour and on. They entered the city of Beziers where Catholics and Gnostics lived in peace, but the church wanted all Gnostics dead. Since there was no way to tell the Gnostics from the Catholics, the army was ordered to kill everyone.

William of Tudela writes: "When they discovered, from the admissions of some of them, that there were Catholics mingled with the heretics they said to the abbot "Sir, what shall we do, for we cannot distinguish between the faithful and the heretics." The abbot, like the others, was afraid that many, in fear of death, would pretend to be Catholics, and after their departure, would return to their heresy, and is said to have replied "Kill them all for the Lord knoweth them that are His" (2 Tim. ii. 19) and so countless number in that town were slain.

And they killed everyone who fled into the church; no cross or altar, or crucifix could save them. And these raving beggarly lads, they killed the clergy too, and the women and children. I doubt if one person came out alive ... such a slaughter has not been known or consented to, I think, since the time of the Saracens." (William of Tudela, cited in Cathar Castles)

Marvin Meyer writes: "Gospel of the Hebrews 5 has the savior say, 'And never rejoice except when you look upon your brother with love,' and Didache 2:7 commands that 'some you shall love more than your soul.'" (The Gospel of Thomas: The

Hidden Sayings of Jesus, p. 81)

Romans 12:9-11 Let love be without dissimulation. Abhor that which is evil; cleave to that which is good. Be kindly affectioned one to another with brotherly love; in honour preferring one another; Not slothful in business; fervent in spirit; serving the Lord;

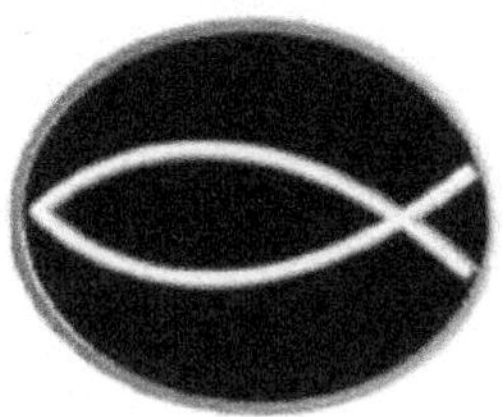

26. Jesus said: You see the splinter (straw / speck) in your brother's eye but the log (beam) that is in your own eye you do not see. When you remove the log (beam) out of your own eye, then will you see clearly enough to remove the splinters out of your brother's eye.

Again we have the term, "brother," indicating the saying applies to a fellow Gnostic. In addressing this it can be pointed out that the majority of fault finding and crass judgment comes from inside the church toward its members. In modern times the majority of serious emotional injury to members of a church are inflicted by other members. However, as with the previous verse, it should be applied universally.

There are differences between the Greek and the Coptic versions of this saying but the Synoptic tradition seems to have expanded on the saying, showing Thomas was closer to and more consistent with the hypothetical Q document.

In the Babylonian Talmud there is a comparable story: "It was taught: Rabbi Tarfon said, 'I wonder whether there is a person of this generation who accepts admonition? If someone says to him, "Remove the chip from between your eye teeth," he would say to him, "Remove the beam from between your eye teeth."'" (The Gospel of Thomas: The Hidden Sayings of Jesus, p. 81)

Matthew 7:3-5 Why do you see the speck in your neighbor's eye, but do not notice the log in your own eye? Or how can you say to your neighbor, Let me take the speck out of your eye, while the log is in your own eye? You hypocrite, first take the log out of your own eye, and then you will see clearly to take the speck out of your neighbor's eye.

Luke 6:41-42 Why do you see the speck that is in your brother's eye, but do not notice the log that is in your own eye? Or how can you say to your brother, Brother, let me take out the speck that is in your eye, when you yourself do not see the log that is in your own eye? You hypocrite, first take the log out of your own eye, and then you will see clearly to take out the speck that is in your brother's eye.

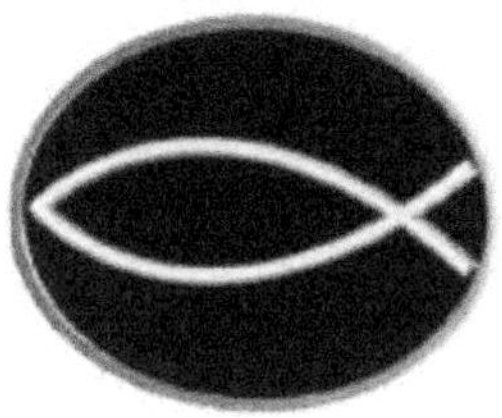

27. Jesus said: Unless you fast (abstain) from the world (system), you shall in no way find the Kingdom of God; and unless you observe (make / keep) the Sabbath as a Sabbath, you shall not see the Father.

The Gnostic view is that the world system was put in place by an evil entity for the purpose of distracting us from our spiritual journey. The world system lulls us into a catatonic state so that we forget our origin, our spiritual substance, our purpose, and our journey.

Treating every moment and every day as sacred and turning away from attachment we see the truth and receive the gnosis (kingdom).

The verse may better be understood as follows:
Unless you stop buying in to the world view of only certain times, places and people being holy and realize every second, every moment, every day is holy and we are all holy, you have not reached Gnosis and cannot be awakened.

The Coptic version of the text uses two different spellings for the word translated 'sabbath' (sambaton and sabbaton). The text is better translated 'observe the entire week as the holy / sabbath'.

In the writings of Tertullian, Against the Jewish People 4, the author states: "We ought to keep a sabbath from all servile work always, and not only every seventh day, but all the time.'" (The Gospel of Thomas: The Hidden Sayings of Jesus, pp. 81-82)

Joseph A. Fitzmyer writes: "'Fasting to the world' must mean withdrawal from a worldly or secular outlook; it is an abstention from the world that involves becoming a 'solitary' (monarchos)." (Essays on the Semitic Background of the New Testament, p. 391)

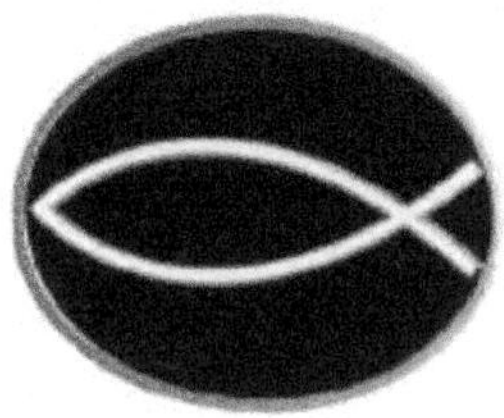

28. Jesus said: I stood (at rest) in the midst of the world. I appeared to them (incarnate) in the flesh. I found them all intoxicated; I found none thirsty among them. My soul grieved over the souls (sons) of men, for they are blind in their hearts and do not see that they came into the world empty they are determined (destined) to leave the world empty. However, now they are drunk. When they have shaken off their wine, then they will repent (and change their heart and their ways will change).

Drunk and half-asleep, intoxicated by the distractions the world has to offer, mankind is oblivious to the messiah and his teaching. In time they may become disenchanted with the empty distractions and be open to his truth.

As discussed in the chapter about Gnosticism, many Gnostics do not believe Jesus came in the flesh, since it was thought that if Jesus were actually God then he would not come to the corrupt material realm. Others postulated that Jesus was a vessel of the Holy Spirit, who departed when Jesus was crucified. If Jesus was simply a man who was appointed he would not be God but would be able to endure the corrupt world.

We must keep in mind that the Gospel of Thomas was likely written by the apostle and thus predates Gnosticism. It was adopted by the Gnostic community but since it was not written for them it contains ideas that may not be completely compatible.

"I have begun to proclaim to men the beauty of piety and knowledge: 'O ye peoples, earth-born men who have given yourselves over to drunknness and sleep and ignorance of God, sober up and cease to be intoxicated and bewitched by irrational sleep.'" (Jesus and Christian Origins Outside the New Testament, p. 126)

Ephesians 5:14 New International Version
This is why it is said: "Wake up, sleeper, rise from the dead, and Christ will shine on you."

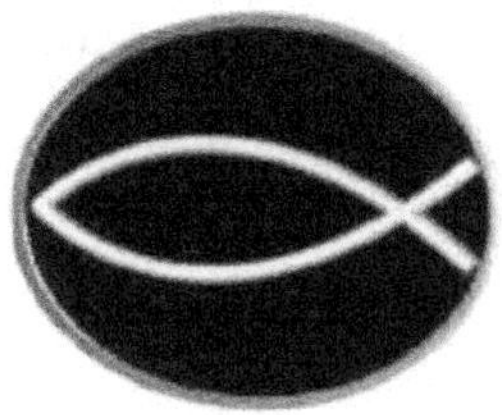

29. Jesus said: If the flesh (was created) came into existence because of spirit, it is a marvel, but if spirit (was created) came into existence because of the body, it would be a marvel of marvels. I amazed indeed at how great wealth has taken up residence in this poverty.

Flesh and spirit are not compatible. Spirit is the great wealth that is contained in the poor and corrupt vehicle of the body. Why would such a great treasure take up residence in the body? Why would the spirit create the body? How could the body create the spirit?

Some scholars take the position that the spirit does not need the flesh as a vehicle, yet in this abode, it does. However, the spirit wishes to escape this realm and ascend to the higher realm. The flesh can become an encumbrance. It is used to pass through this earthly realm, but can hold us back on our journey. The spirit inhabits this realm of spiritual poverty, of which the body is a sponge for the mire.

Another way to read the verse suggests the spirit may exist to allow the body to be saved, but this does not seem to be in accordance with what the Gnostics believed. There is conflict seen in the verse that brings the life and teaching of Jesus, as he went about eating, drinking, and associating with sinners, compared to the ascetic teaching of the Gnostics.

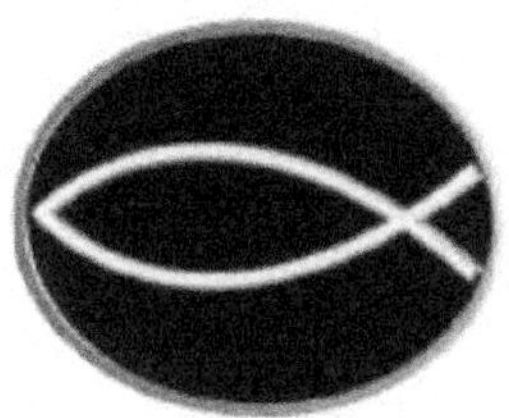

30. Jesus said: Where there are three gods, they are without God, and where there is a single one, I say that I am with him. Lift up the stone, and you will find me there. Split the piece of wood, and I am there.

The Coptic translation reads:

Jesus said: Where there are three divine beings (gods), they are divine (gods).
Where there is only one or two, I say that I am with him. Lift the stone and there you will find me, Split the wood and there am I.

In this verse, the differences between the Coptic and Greek texts cannot be reconciled.

ATTRIDGE - Oxyrhynchus (Greek Version)

30 "Where there are three, they are without God, and where there is but a single one, I say that I am with him. Lift up the stone, and you will find me there. Split the piece of wood, and I am there."

Versions read: "Where there are two they are without God but where this is one alone I say I am with him."

J. D. Crossan writes: "Put mildly, that is not very clear, and we are cast back on the Greek of Oxy P 1, lines 23-27. Harold W. Attridge's recent study of that papyrus under ultraviolet light led him to the following restored translation:

'Jesus said, "Where there are three, they are without god, and where there is but a single one I say that I am with him."'

He concludes that, 'instead of an absolutely cryptic remark about gods being gods, the fragment asserts that any group of people lacks divine presence. That presence is available only to the "solitary one." The importance of the solitary (monachos) is obvious in the Gospel. Cf. Sayings 11, 16, 22, 23, 49, 75, and 106. This saying must now be read in connection with those remarks on the "monachose."' (156)." (Four Other Gospels, p. 78)

Monachos is Greek for "alone, solitary, single" and is the origin of the word, monastery.

How do we read the verse then, with this new evidence?
It seems the Doresse translation may be the closest to the original intent.

DORESSE - Oxyrhynchus
Jesus says: "Where there are [two (?) they are] not without God, and where there is one, I say <to you>, I am with him. Raise the stone, and there thou wilt find me; split the wood: I am even there!"

The number "three" is the beginning of a "group", institution, meeting, and thus, church. Where there is a group there are rules, controls, and before long there is crystalized doctrine and exclusivity. Artificial procedures must be followed to keep order. Because of the constraints of doctrine and procedures placed on worship and thus the spiritual connection to God, doctrine and the church become like glass; you can see the truth through it, but you cannot fully reach it. Connection to the divine can only occur on an individual basis. Spirit to spirit. The Gospel of Thomas is a testimony against the ability of institutions, groups, or churches to save or enlighten the individual. The message here is clear. It is not the church, denomination, group, or cult that can get you to the Kingdom of God. The path lies within, in the solitary, personal search. It is this message that assured Thomas would be rejected by the church.

The solitary one is a reference to a single person, meaning salvation is a deeply personal transformation accomplished between the individual and God. It is only the person in unity that merits God's presence.

Many believe pages of the manuscript were misplaced and verses 30 and 77 should run together as a single verse.

77. Jesus said: I-Am the Light who is over all things, I-Am the All. From me all came forth and to me all return (The All came from me and the All has come to me). Split wood, there am I. Lift up the stone and there you will find me.

This "I Am" is the same title as God previously described to Moses.

Matthew 18:20 For where two or three are gathered in my name, I am there among them.

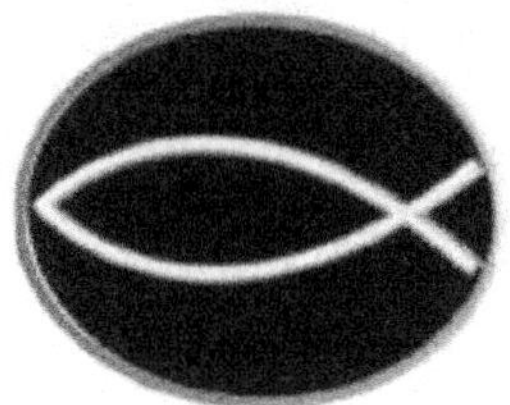

31. Jesus said: No prophet is accepted in his own village (country), neither can physician heals those who know him. (Another reading has it: ...And a physician does not heal those he knows.)

Familiarity breeds contempt, as the saying goes. To have seen Jesus grow up and hear all of the rumors regarding his alleged illegitimate birth brings lack of faith in him. Jesus was rejected in Nazareth.

There are a few lessons to be gleaned from this saying. In family and village, a person is seemingly "stuck" in time and status. Elders view a fully developed and powerful prophet and healer as if he were still six years old. Trust and faith do not grow well under these conditions. It remains a problem in many families that men and women who were once children are treated as such until the older generation passes away. Spiritually and emotionally, this is such a weight to carry through life that we are viewed as the same rebellious and immature soul we were, even though we may have grown, gained insight, been awakened, received spiritual gifts, and have become the people we were meant to be. Let us be sure to allow others the same ability to grow as we would seek for ourselves. Try to see others in a new light each encounter. Allow the soul to grow in our sight. There may be an emerging Christ Spirit in your family disguised as a rebellious teen or mischievous child.

Mark 6:4 Then Jesus said to them, Prophets are not without honor, except in their hometown, and among their own kin, and in their own house.

Matthew 13:57 And they took offense at him. But Jesus said to them: A prophet is not without honor save in his own country and in his own house.

Luke 4:24 And he said, Truly, I say to you, no prophet is acceptable in his own country.

John 4:43-44 After the two days he departed to Galilee. For Jesus himself testified that a prophet has no honor in his own country.

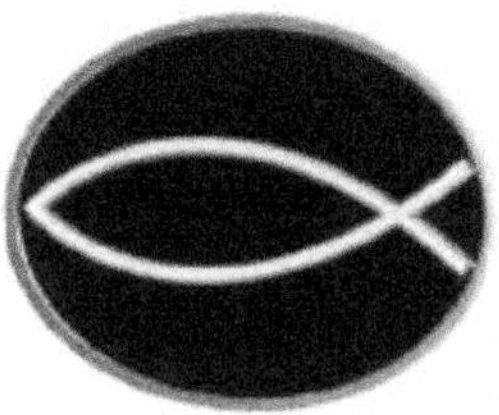

32. Jesus said: A city being built (and established) upon a high mountain and fortified cannot fall nor can it be (or become) hidden.

The gnosis is not faith as we think of it. It is an experience, which is stronger and cannot be shaken. The enlightened man emits the light of the truth because he has become whole and unified within himself.

Jesus is encouraging his followers and disciples by assuring them they are a beacon to the world and they are citizens of a high and fortified city, which cannot be shaken.

We may be talked out of our view of doctrine, our ideas, even our faith at times, but it is very difficult to talk someone out of their personal experiences.

Matthew 5:14 You are the light of the world. A city built on a hill cannot be hid.

Romans 8:38 For I am persuaded, that neither death, nor life, nor angels, nor principalities, nor powers, nor things present, nor things to come, [39] Nor height, nor depth, nor any other creature, shall be able to separate us from the love of God, which is in Christ Jesus our Lord.

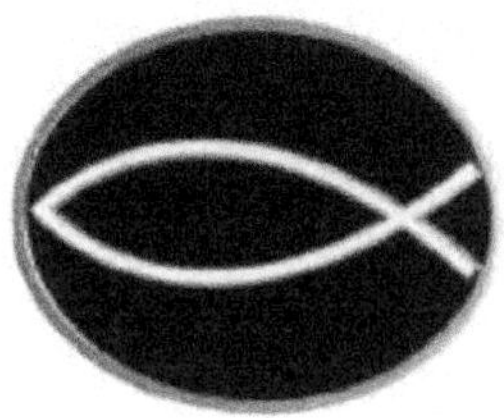

33. Jesus said: What you will hear whispered in your ear preach from your rooftops. For no one lights a lamp and sets it under a basket nor puts it in a hidden place (hide it under a bushel), but rather it is placed on a lamp stand so that everyone who comes and goes will see its light.

As a continuation of saying 32, he urges the disciples to enlighten others with the truth and let their light shine brightly. Of course, this gets Jesus and the majority of the apostles killed.

There may be some subtle meanings in this verse. A bushel, at the time of writing, was a clay pot holding a certain amount of grain. To place a lamp (an oil lamp or candle) under it would slowly extinguish it. People may have done this to keep the smoke and smell captured within the clay container.

Matthew 10:27 What I say to you in the dark, tell in the light; and what you hear whispered, proclaim from the housetops.

Luke 8:16 No one after lighting a lamp hides it under a jar, or puts it under a bed, but puts it on a lamp stand, so that those who enter may see the light.

Matthew 5:15 Nor do men light a lamp and put it under a bushel, but on a stand, and it gives light to all in the house.

Mark 4:21 And he said to them, Is a lamp brought in to be put under a bushel, or under a bed, and not on a stand?

Luke 11:33 No one after lighting a lamp puts it in a cellar or under a bushel, but on a stand, that those who enter may see the light.

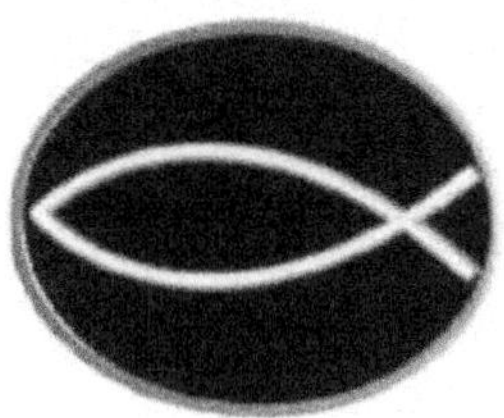

34. Jesus said: If a blind person leads a blind person, both fall into a pit.

Gnostics considered those who received knowledge as enlightened, awake, and capable of seeing the truth. Do not follow anyone who has not proven to have the gnosis. If you do you will be led further away from the light.

Matthew 15:14 Let them alone; they are blind guides of the blind. And if one blind person guides another, both will fall into a pit.

Luke 6:39 He also told them a parable: Can a blind man lead a blind man? Will they not both fall into a pit?

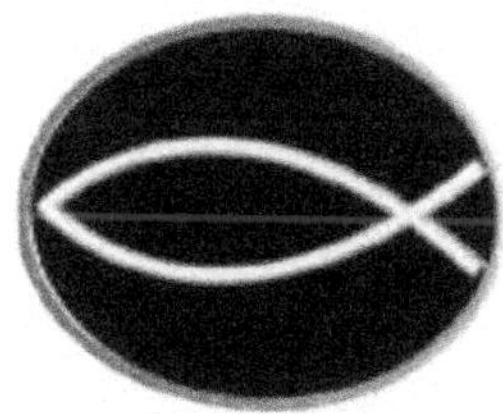

35. Jesus said: It is impossible for anyone to enter the house of a strong man to take it by force unless he binds his hands, then he will be able to loot his house.

The Demiurge must be bound with the truth before his house, the world, can be looted and his processions, his slaves, mankind, can be stolen back.

Some scholars believe this saying in Mark 3:27 had to do with exorcism. Some scholars do not think this saying was actually attributed to Jesus since it invokes violence. However, if one throws out all references to violence one must discount other references to swords, clearing the temple, and many other Gospel stories. In the taking back of the lost soul and the revelation of the truth, there will be violence. There will be spiritual violence in attaining the truth, and there must be violence in the destruction of former realities, and the new reality is born.

Matthew 12:29 Or how can one enter a strong man's house and plunder his goods, unless he first binds the strong man? Then indeed he may plunder his house.

Luke 11:21-22 When a strong man, fully armed, guards his own palace, his goods are in peace; but when one stronger than he assails him and overcomes him, he takes away his armor in which he trusted, and divides his spoil.

Mark 3:27 But no one can enter a strong man's house and plunder his property without first tying up the strong man; then indeed the house can be plundered.

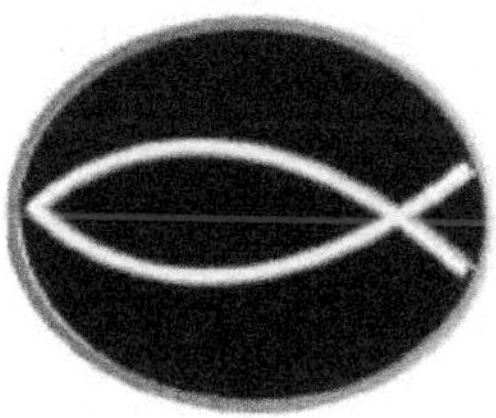

36. Jesus said: Do not worry from morning to evening nor from evening to morning about the food that you will eat nor about what clothes you will wear. You are much superior to the Lilies which neither card nor spin.

When you have no clothing, what do you wear? Who can increase your stature? He himself will give to you your garment.

This saying should be treated as two separate sayings. In the Gnostic world, the second part has the meaning of being without a body. When you have no body what will you wear? What to wear is unimportant. In a short time, you will slip out of your body, which was given to you.

When you have no body, how can you gain an inch in height or worry about how tall you are? God will give you a spiritual body. To worry about feeding, clothing, or caring for this vehicle is only temporary. Worry over this body should not preoccupy you or attach you to this world.

It is the ascetic tone of this verse that sets it apart from the Gospel version.

Matthew 6:25-31 Therefore I tell you, do not worry about your life, what you will eat or what you will drink, or about your body, what you will wear. Is not life more than food, and the body more than clothing? Look at the birds of the air; they neither sow nor reap nor gather into barns, and yet your heavenly Father feeds them. Are you not of more value than they? And can any of you by worrying add a single hour to your span of life? And why do you worry about clothing? Consider the lilies of the field, how they grow; they neither toil nor spin, yet I tell you, even Solomon in all his glory was not clothed like one of these. But if God so clothes the grass of the field, which is alive today and tomorrow is thrown into the oven, will he not much more clothe you--you of little faith? Therefore do not worry, saying, What will we eat? or What will we drink? or What will we wear?

Luke 12:22-23 And he said to his disciples, Therefore I tell you, do not be anxious about your life, what you shall eat, nor about your body, what you shall put on. For life is more than food, and the body more than clothing.

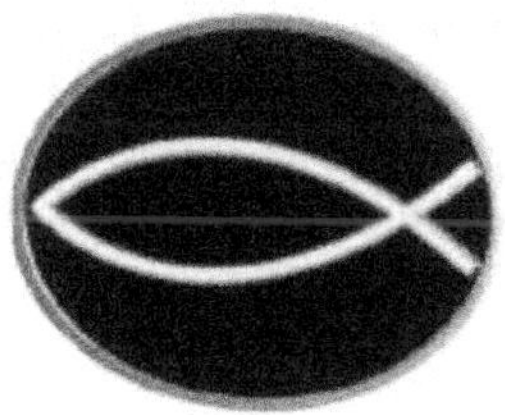

37. His Disciples said: When will you appear (show forth / be revealed / be made visible) to us, and when will we behold (see) you?

Jesus said: When you take off your garments (strip naked) without being ashamed, and place your garments under your feet and tread on them as the little children do, then will you see the Son of the Living-One, and you will not be afraid.

The garment refers in metaphor to the body and thus the world or physical realm. Without the body the spiritual eyes can see the spiritual body, the spiritual reality, and the truth. When we see the entire truth, we will not only be unafraid, but we will be joyous about laying down the body with its weights of the world. In that time, we will see him as he is and we will realize we are like him and he is like us and we will not be afraid.

1 John 3:1 Behold what manner of love the Father has given to us, that we should be called children of God. And that is what we are! The reason the world does not know us is that it did not know Him. 2Beloved, we are now children of God, and what we will be has not yet been revealed. We know that when Christ appears, we will be like Him, for we will see Him as He is.

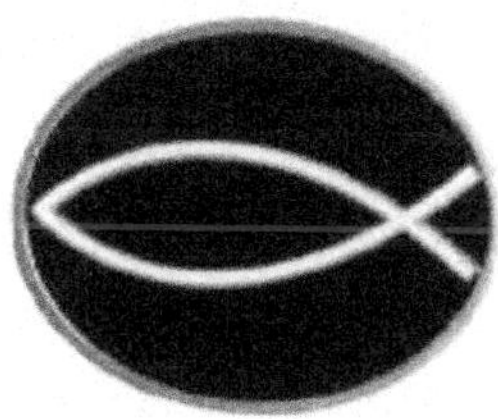

38. Jesus said: Many times have you yearned to hear these sayings which I speak to you, and you could find no one else to hear them from. The days will come when you will seek me but you will not find me.

Manichaean Psalm Book 187:28-29 states: "I have something to say, I have no one to whom to say it."
Acts of John 98 states: "John, there must be one person to hear these things from me, for I need one who is going to hear."

Cyprian in Three Books of Testimonies to Quirinius 3.29 states: "For a time will come and you will seek me, both you and those who will come after, to hear a word of wisdom and understanding, and you will not find (me)."

Funk and Hoover write: "In v. 1, Jesus speaks as the redeemer who has descended to earth and ascended to heaven, a scenario central to gnostic myth and speculative wisdom theology. (The Five Gospels, p. 494)

If we were given time with Jesus, we cannot imagine we would waste time. We would want to hear all he had to say. Once he departed we would think of a thousand questions. Possibly we flatter ourselves. The disciples argued, ate, debated, left, and came back only to ignore and betray him. Are we so different?

Luke 17:22: The days will come when you desire to see one of the days of the Son of Man, and you will not see.

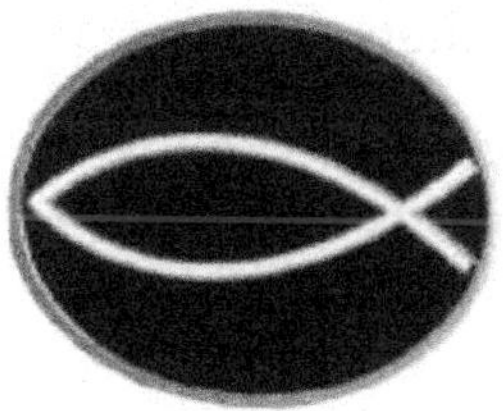

39. Jesus said: The Pharisees and the Scribes have received (stolen the keys of knowledge, but they have hidden them. They did not enter in, nor did they permit those who wished to enter to do so. However, you be as wise (astute) as serpents and innocent (guileless) as doves.

The religious leaders have been staring at the truth, even scriptures telling of the messiah, but they hid the truth so they could continue in their place of authority and corruption.

There is also a hint that the Rabbis had a special way to interpreting scripture that may have given way to the full truth, but they did not teach it to the common people and they hid what they found from them.

The truth is in the scripture. It is simply not well indexed.

Fitzmyer believes this is a combination of two unrelated sayings. His restoration and translation follows with missing or

uncertain words in brackets. ['Jesus says, "The Pharisees and the scribes have] re[ceived the keys] of [knowledge and have] hid[den them; neither have they] enter[ed nor permitted those who would] enter.
[But you] bec[ome wi]se a[s the serpents and g]uileless [as the dov]es' (see also Hennecke and Schneemelcher: 1.112-113)." (In Fragments, p. 33)

This is similar to saying #102.

Luke 11:52 Woe to you lawyers! For you have taken away the key of knowledge; you did not enter yourselves, and you hindered those who were entering.

Matthew 10:16 See, I am sending you out like sheep into the midst of wolves; so be wise as serpents and innocent as doves.

Matthew 23.13 But woe unto you, scribes and Pharisees, hypocrites! because you shut the kingdom of heaven against men; for you neither enter yourselves, nor allow those who would enter to go in.

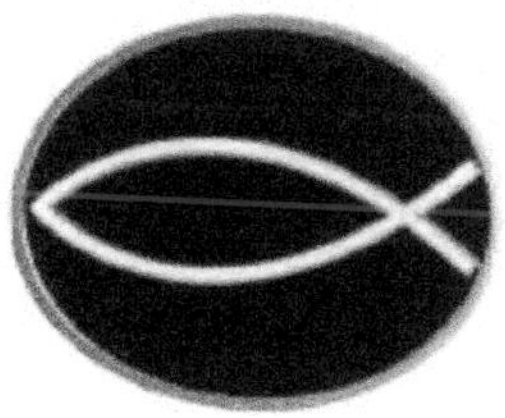

40. Jesus said: A grapevine has been planted outside the (vineyard of the) Father, and since it is not viable (sound / strong / healthy) it will be pulled up by its roots and it will perish (be destroyed).

The Demiurge made this material world without the Father's permission outside of the Pleroma (the fullness or Heaven). It is a corrupted cosmos created outside of the perfect place. It will be destroyed in time.

The personal lesson here is obvious. Do not move outside the will, fullness, and grace of God. Listen to the heart, where the gnosis abides and follow its call. Things done outside the father will end badly. Moreover, people living outside the father will end in spiritual destruction.

Matthew 15:13 He answered, Every plant that my heavenly Father has not planted will be uprooted.

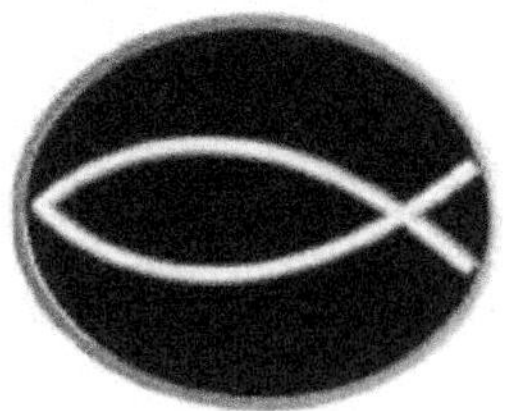

41. Jesus said: Whoever has (it) in his hand, to him will (more) be given. And whoever does not have, from him even the small amount which he has will be taken.

To some degree, gnosis is a binary state. Once the sleeper is awakened there will be levels of "awakeness" but there will be no more sleep. Like a drawing or painting which contains a hidden image, once you see it, you will never not see it. And you will then be able to see more and more details in the image.

This concept works on many levels. The rich get richer and the poor get poorer, in part because to the rich was given the gift of handling money. The wise man becomes more wise in time because he was given the gift of seeing the true nature of people. To the awakened mind will be given a more probing mind, which will further awaken him. Yet, the fool become more foolish every day.

Matthew 25:29 For to all those who have, more will be given, and they will have an abundance; but from those who have nothing, even what they have will be taken away.

Luke 19:26 I tell you, that to every one who has will more be given; but from him who has not, even what he has will be taken away.

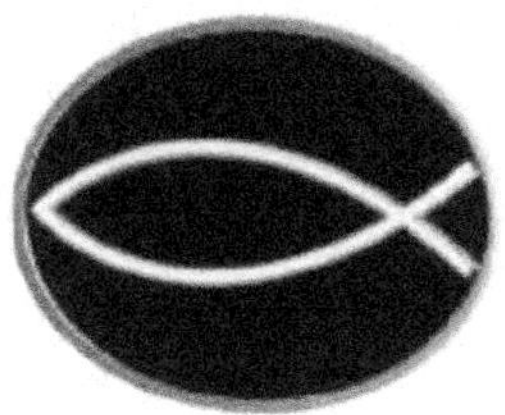

42. Jesus said: Become passers-by.

Another translation reads:

Come into being as you pass by.

Other versions has the verse as:

Come into being as you pass away.

Come into being when you become a Hebrew (immigrant).

On the surface, this seems to be the most simple and direct saying. It proves to be one of the most difficult ones. Some think it is suggesting an ascetic, solitary life of non-attachment to the world. It seems the smaller and more direct the saying the more power it contains. To become a passer-by is to be in this world but not of it - not part of it. To be a passer-by is to have no attachment, either physical or emotional to this place, which would hinder your sojourn through this realm on your way to the higher estate. This is one of the most difficult and ongoing challenge the pilgrim faces. If it were not for the fact that the simple statement could be read in a few different ways, based on the word choices in the Greek version, we could stop here, but we cannot. This saying has multiple layers of depth.

Marvin Meyer writes: "This saying may also be translated 'Be wanderers'; compare descriptions in early Christian literature of wandering teachers and missionaries. Another possible but less likely translation is, 'Come into being as you pass away'; compare the use of the same word parage as 'pass away' in the first riddle in saying 11, and other statements similar to this translation of saying 42 (for example, 2 Corinthians 4:16; Acts of John 76: 'Die so that you may live'). Tjitze Baarda, 'Jesus Said: Be Passers-By,' suggests yet another possible translation, 'Be Hebrews,' with the understanding of Philo of Alexandria that the word 'Hebrews' may be taken as 'migrants.' A medieval author, Petrus Alphonsi, preserves a saying much like saying 42 in his Clerical Instruction: 'This world is, as it were, a bridge. Therefore, pass over it, only do not lodge there.'." (The Gospel of Thomas: The Hidden Sayings of Jesus, p. 87)

William R. Schoedel translates, "Jesus said: Come into being as you pass away." Robert M. Grant and David Noel Freedman write: "Presumably the saying has much the same meaning as Paul's words (2 Corinthians 4:16): 'If our outer man is perishing, our inner man is renewed day by day.'" (The Secret Sayings of Jesus, p. 155)

William R. Schoedel translates, "Jesus said: Come into being as you pass away." Robert M. Grant and David Noel Freedman write: "Presumably the saying has much the same meaning as Paul's words (2 Corinthians 4:16): 'If our outer man is perishing, our inner man is renewed day by day.'" (The Secret Sayings of Jesus, p. 155)

Become wanderers and do not become attached, for this world is a bridge to our final destination. We can feel its pull as we draw near. We become homesick, yearning for a place we cannot remember.

King James Version (KJV) 2 Corinthians 4:15 For all things are for your sakes, that the abundant grace might through the thanksgiving of many redound to the glory of God.
16 For which cause we faint not; but though our outward man perish, yet the inward man is renewed day by day.

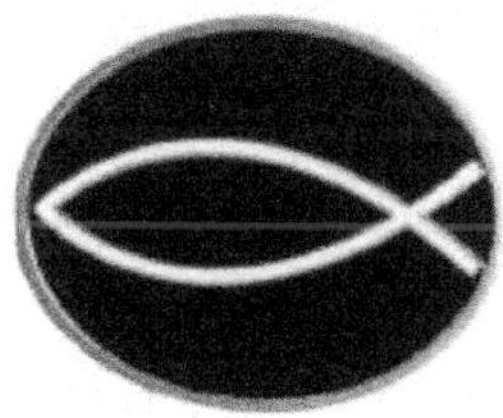

43. His Disciples said to him: Who are you, that you said these things to us?

Jesus said to them: You do not recognize who I am from what I said to you, but rather you have become like the Jews who either love the tree and hate its fruit, or love the fruit and hate the tree.

The nature of the tree is the nature of the fruit. You cannot hate one and love the other. It is cause and effect and they are inextricably linked. His words and deeds are the fruits which point to his authority. Likewise, Jesus is the fruit of God. You cannot love God and hate his fruit, Jesus. Neither can you love Jesus and hate the tree of his origin, God. They have the same nature and cannot be un-linked. Our spirits are the fruits of God also.

John 8:25 They said to him, Who are you? Jesus said to them, Why do I speak to you at all?

Matthew 7:16-20 You will know them by their fruits. Are grapes gathered from thorns, or figs from thistles? In the same way, every good tree bears good fruit, but the bad tree bears bad fruit. A good tree cannot bear bad fruit, nor can a bad tree bear good fruit. Every tree that does not bear good fruit is cut down and thrown into the fire. Thus you will know them by their fruits.

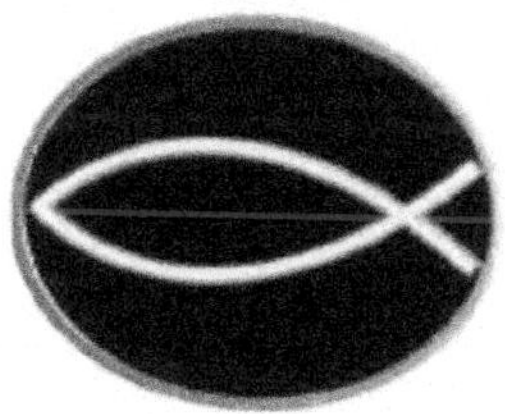

44. Jesus said: Whoever blasphemes against the Father, it will be forgiven him. And whoever blasphemes against the Son, it will be forgiven him. Yet whoever blasphemes against the Holy Spirit, it will not be forgiven him neither on earth nor in heaven.

In some Gnostic systems "Father" or "Father of this world is a title of the Demiurge, while in the Apocryphon of John the supreme God is described as the Holy Spirit. This would make sense of this odd saying. All blasphemes are forgiven except those against the Supreme or True God.

In some Gnostic creation stories, the Holy Spirit is the very spark of life, which brought mankind from his primal, worm-like form the Demiurge created into human sentient form as the spark of like passed from Sophia to us. Even in standard Christian creation stories it was the Spirit of God that moved (brooded) over the face of the water when light and life were created. To curse the Holy Spirit is to curse life itself.

The Holy Spirit is the force that has "quickened" us and draws us to God.

Mark 3:28-29 Truly I tell you, people will be forgiven for their sins and whatever blasphemies they utter; but whoever blasphemes against the Holy Spirit can never have forgiveness, but is guilty of an eternal sin.

Matthew 12:31-32 Therefore I tell you, every sin and blasphemy will be forgiven men, but the blasphemy against the Spirit will not be forgiven. And whoever says a word against the Son of man will be forgiven; but whoever speaks against the Holy Spirit will not be forgiven, either in this age or in the age to come.

Luke 12:10 And every one who speaks a word against the Son of man will be forgiven him; but he who blasphemes against the Holy Spirit will not be forgiven.

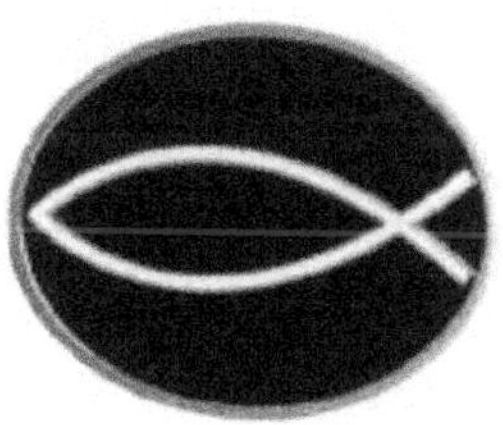

45. Jesus said: Grapes are not harvested from thorns, nor are figs gathered from (hawthorns) thistles, for they do not give fruit. A good person brings forth goodness from his storehouse. A bad person brings forth evil out of his storehouse of evil, which is in his heart, and he speaks evil, for out of the abundance (overflow) of the heart he produces evil things.

Evil and good are natural states. The good person does not know he is good. The good person considers others, has compassion, and acts accordingly. It is his nature to do so. It takes no effort nor thought on his part.

Evil is as innocent as a child, and perniciously selfish. An evil person does not consider others, only themselves. They view others only as tools to their end. Their actions are evil continually, flowing from them like a stream. They do not try to be destructive. It is their nature to destroy.

Most people fall in the middle and we cannot see where or

what we are. As an eye cannot see itself, men cannot see their own nature. However, true awakening from God allows us to see ourselves as we really are and Gnosis brings about change as the inside and outside are made the same.

Luke 6:43-45 For no good tree bears bad fruit, nor again does a bad tree bear good fruit; for each tree is known by its own fruit. For figs are not gathered from thorns, nor are grapes picked from a bramble bush. The good man out of the good treasure of his heart produces good, and the evil man out of his evil treasure produces evil; for out of the abundance of the heart his mouth speaks.

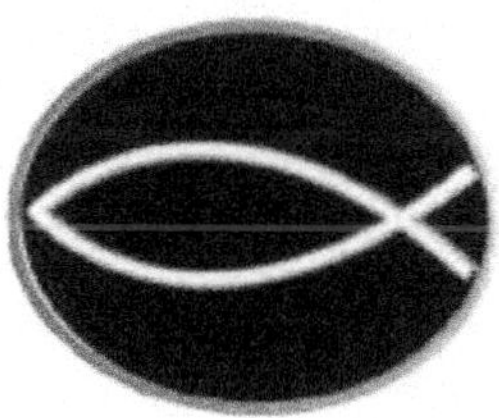

46. Jesus said: From Adam until John the Baptist there is none born of women who surpasses John the Baptist, for his eyes were not destroyed / broken (his eyes should not be downcast or lowered). Yet I have said that whoever among you becomes like a child will know / understand the Kingdom, and he will be more exalted (greater) than John.

Jesus expresses appreciation for few people. James, Thomas and John are mentioned with plaudits in the Gospel of Thomas.

Remembering that the Kingdom is another expression of Gnosis, this saying is similar to others, such as the saying exhorting the apostles to become childlike, strip of their clothes and dance on them.

R. McL. Wilson writes: "The Synoptic parallels here are Matthew xi. 11 and Luke vii. 28, but the words here rendered 'so that his eyes will not be broken' have so far baffled the commentators. Grant and Freedman plausibly suggest that the opening words are modelled on the following verse in

Matthew (xi. 12), in which case Thomas has re-written the saying. One possible line of interpretation may be to link this saying with logion 22 and with the Synoptic sayings about children and the Kingdom. The enigmatic words about eyes may, perhaps, have some connection with Matthew vi. 22 f., the passage about the 'single eye'; eyes that are broken (or divided?) are no longer 'single.' If this be so, the saying would be a mosaic of Synoptic elements, but here we have clear signs of redaction, possibly of textual corruption, and almost certainly of confusion on the part of the translator. It must be remembered that our present Coptic text is probably a translation of a translation, and that in both versions it has been subjected to the vagaries of the scribe; moreover, the sayings have passed through a process of oral tradition, whether or not they are derived from our Gospels, and were originally uttered neither in Greek nor in Coptic, but in Aramaic. When we add the probability of redaction at the hands of one or more editors, who had ends of their own in view, the difficulties in the path of the investigator are manifest." (Studies in the Gospel of Thomas, p. 62)

The comment regarding John's eyes not being broken may be much less complicated than scholars are making it. When we come into this world we no longer see things as they truly are. We have to be awakened. Yet, there are several verses that indicate small children still see the truth. An old man should ask a child of seven days about the kingdom... The saying here could simply mean John's eyes were not broken or blinded by his birth and journey here. He still sees the kingdom as if her were there. So shall we when we become as children again, not attached or involved, but carefree, playful, loving.

Matthew 6:22-23 New International Version (NIV)
22 "The eye is the lamp of the body. If your eyes are healthy,[a] your whole body will be full of light. 23 But if your eyes are unhealthy,[b] your whole body will be full of darkness. If then the light within you is darkness, how great is that darkness!
Footnotes:
Matthew 6:22 The Greek for healthy here implies generous.
Matthew 6:23 The Greek for unhealthy here implies stingy.

Matthew 11:11 Truly I tell you, among those born of women no one has arisen greater than John the Baptist; yet the least in the kingdom of heaven is greater than he.

Luke 7:28 I tell you, among those born of women none is greater than John; yet he who is least in the kingdom of God is greater than he.

Matthew 18:2-4 He called a child, whom he put among them, and said, Truly I tell you, unless you change and become like children, you will never enter the kingdom of heaven. Whoever becomes humble like this child is the greatest in the kingdom of heaven.

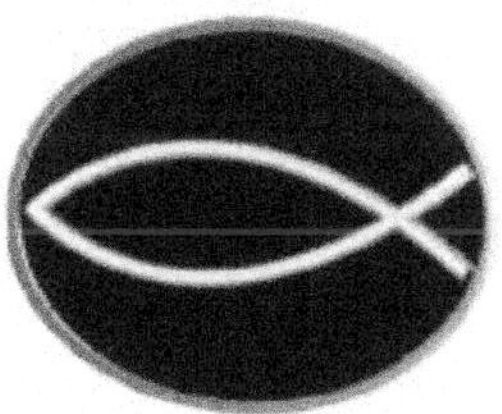

47. Jesus said: It is impossible for a man to mount two horses or to draw two bows, and a servant cannot serve two masters, otherwise he will honor the one and disrespect the other. No man drinks vintage wine and immediately desires to drink new wine, and they do not put new wine into old wineskins or they would burst, and they do not put vintage wine into new wineskins or it would spoil (sour). They do not sew an old patch on a new garment because that would cause a split.

This verse reminds us once more that there must be single-mindedness, solidarity and unity inside and outside. Leave old ways. Embrace the new ways. Let go of the old master of the world and cleave to the new spiritual master.

A new garment will shrink when washed, but an old one will not. Luke 5:36-37 says we should not place a new patch on an old garment. As the patch shrinks and the garment remains the same the patch will tear away from the garment, leaving a bigger hole.

Old wine containers made of skin are hard and do not stretch. If you put new wine in them the wine is still "working" and producing gasses. If the bottle is sealed it will burst. Also, the bacteria of old bottles that have been used and have set up bad bacteria will contaminate the new wine and cause it to sour.

The sequences of old and new wine and patches are reversed from the Gospels. Thomas is pointing out the folly of trying to keep the old life when you are reborn. It will end in damage to your spirit.

There is a Zen saying: If you sit, sit; if you stand, stand; do not wobble. There must be a full commitment to the spiritual life in order to reach complete enlightenment. The secular world and the spiritual world do not mix well.

When Peter walked on the water he began to sink when he took his spiritual eyes off Jesus and began to fear. We must stay single-minded. This is wholeness and unity of being. It is not stubbornness.

Matthew 6:24 No one can serve two masters; for a slave will either hate the one and love the other, or be devoted to the one and despise the other. You cannot serve God and wealth.

Matthew 9:16-17 No one sews a piece of cloth, not yet shrunk, on an old cloak, for the patch pulls away from the cloak, and a worse tear is made. Neither is new wine put into old wineskins; otherwise, the skins burst, and the wine is spilled, and the skins are destroyed; but new wine is put into fresh wineskins, and so both are preserved.

Mark 2:21-22 No one sews a piece of unshrunk cloth on an old garment; if he does, the patch tears away from it, the new from the old, and a worse tear is made. And no one puts new wine into old wineskins; if he does, the wine will burst the skins, and the wine is lost, and so are the skins; but new wine is for fresh skins.

Luke 5:36-39 He told them a parable also: No one tears a piece from a new garment and puts it upon an old garment; if he does, he will tear the new, and the piece from the new will not match the old. And no one puts new wine into old wineskins; if he does, the new wine will burst the skins and it will be spilled, and the skins will be destroyed. But new wine must be put into fresh wineskins. And no one after drinking old wine desires new; for he says, "The old is good."

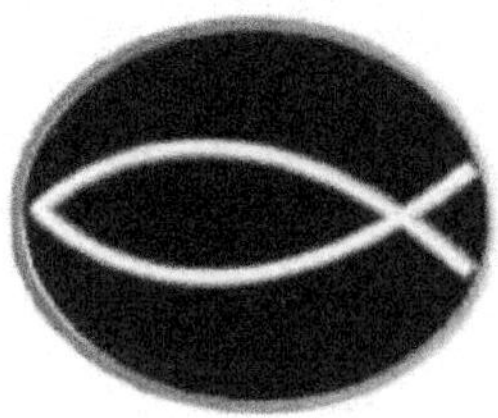

48. Jesus said: If two make peace with each other in this one house, they will say to the mountain: Be moved! and it will be moved.

This saying is similar to saying 106, Jesus says: "When you make the two one, you will become sons of Man and if you say: 'Mountain, move!', it will move." It is assumed that "making peace" is the same as being one, at least in agreement. Therefore, within this house, which is the body, reside the spirit and the soul. The soul is made up of mind and emotion. If spirit, mind, and heart are made one, there is power beyond imagination. This act is full individuation.

In the Gnostic world, where one seeks to return to an undifferentiated form of male-female, mind-spirit, the act of achieving this brings the realization of how the cosmos works and thus it brings great power. Like Faust as he deals with the devil, we may realize, "Alas, there are two souls at war within my breast". To be at peace, at one, undivided and unencumbered emotionally and spiritually, we have great potential.

In "The Process of Individuation", Scott Jeffrey writes: "Consider how the values and worldviews of masculine and feminine principles can vary. The masculine seeks autonomy. The feminine seeks communion or relationship.

Can you imagine what it would be like to integrate both masculine and feminine principles within your mind, not favoring either perspective over the other?

It's not easy, but this is part of the goal of the individuation process.

Jung found that opposites create tension in the psyche. If we don't learn to address these tensions, denying the opposites instead, we repress or push the pressure out of our consciousness.

But repressing doesn't eliminate the opposites or the tension itself. It only makes them more destructive in our psyche by strengthening our shadows.

Repressing tension makes us one-sided, and it leads us to

project our unconscious fantasies on to reality.

When we deny these internal tensions, we enforce our delusions and self-deception.

Besides the tension between masculine and feminine principles, here are two other common internal tensions:
A key pair of opposites in Jung's work are instincts and psyche. The instincts are our biological roots, our body. The psyche, in Jung's conception, is the totality of mental processes that include both conscious and unconscious forces.

Any time we try to favor psyche over instincts—mind over body, spirit over nature—or vice versa, we cut ourselves off (dissociate) from a part of what we are."

Matthew 18:19 Again, truly I tell you, if two of you agree on earth about anything you ask, it will be done for you by my Father in heaven.

Mark 11:23-24 Truly I tell you, if you say to this mountain, Be taken up and thrown into the sea, and if you do not doubt in your heart, but believe that what you say will come to pass, it will be done for you. So

I tell you, whatever you ask for in prayer, believe that you have received it, and it will be yours.

Matthew 17:20 He said to them, Because of your little faith. For truly, I say to you, if you have faith as a grain of mustard seed, you will say to this mountain, Move from here to there, and it will move; and nothing will be impossible to you.

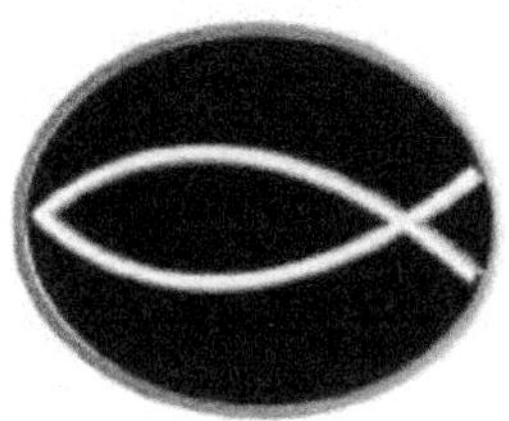

49. Jesus said: Blessed is the solitary (single/unified) and chosen (superior), for all of you will find the Kingdom. Because have come (issued forth) from it, you will return to it once again.

Here, we again find the idea of completeness. The word, "solitary" is unity. Blessed are the complete or unified. You are selected because you will find the kingdom (or find your way back to the kingdom) because you will remember where you came from and find your way home. This is the knowledge or gnosis we seek.

John 16:28: "I have come out from the Father and I have come into the world. I am again leaving the world and return to the Father." But, Jesus also said he was preparing the way for us and preparing a place for us. We are supposed to follow him. Out of the kingdom he came and he returned, and so shall we.

Matthew 5:1-3 And seeing the multitudes, he went up into a mountain: and when he was set, his disciples came unto him: And he opened his mouth, and taught them, saying, Blessed are the poor in spirit: for theirs is the kingdom of heaven.

John 20:28-30 And Thomas answered and said unto him, My LORD and my God. Jesus saith unto him, Thomas, because thou hast seen me, thou hast believed: blessed are they that have not seen, and yet have believed. And many other signs truly did Jesus in the presence of his disciples, which are not written in this book:

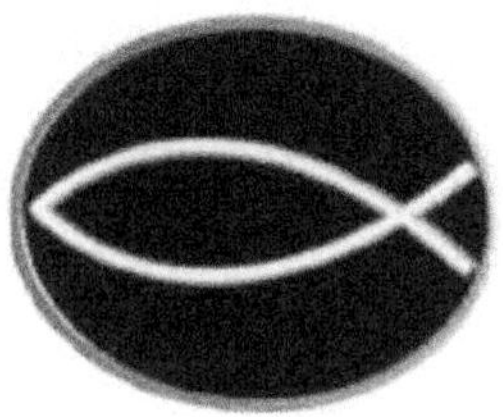

50. Jesus said: If they say to you all: From where do you come? Say to them: We have come from the Light, the place where the Light came into existence of its own accord and he stood and appeared in their image. If they say to you: (Is it you?) Who are you?, say: We are his Sons and we are the chosen / the elect of the Living Father. If they ask you: What is the sign of your Father in you? Say to them: It is movement with rest (peace in the midst of motion and chaos).

Stillness and peace comes from a state of non-attachment. Only here can the ego be at rest and we become an observer instead of a participant caught up in the moment.

"The Master acts without doing anything
And teaches without talking.
He allows things to come and go naturally.
He does not hold on.
He has but doesn't possess, works but takes no credit,
He has no expectations.

It is done and then forgotten, therefore, it lasts forever."
Lao Tsu , Tao Te Ching verse 2. - The Tao of Thomas by Joseph Lumpkin

Collect money, jewels, and possessions
And you cannot protect them.
Gather wealth and position
And your heart will be their captive.
Do your work, then let it go.
This is the only path to inner peace.
Lao Tsu , Tao Te Ching verse 9 - The Tao of Thomas by Joseph Lumpkin

The man who apprehends the spark of life and light, in his realization of what he truly is, will show forth light and life, for God is in him and he in God and God is all of this and more.

Robert M. Grant and David Noel Freedman write: "This saying continues the thought of Saying 50. The disciples are the light of the world (Matthew 7:14) because Jesus is the light of the world (John 8:12). They are from above, from the place where the light shines in the darkness (John 1:5). They are sons of the light (?), and the elect. If men ask for a sign, as they asked Jesus (Mark 8:11-12; Matthew 16:1-4; Luke 11:16, 29-30), no startling miracle can be shown them, but only 'a movement and a rest.'

The 'rest' must be the rest characteristic of the kingdom (Sayings 1 [Greek], 52, 90); the 'movement' is ultimately that of the unmoved mover, according to the Naassenes (Hippolytus, Ref., 5, 7, 25)." (The Secret Sayings of Jesus, pp. 160-161)

Movement is the action of obtaining the realm of fullness. Once there we have rest. Our spirits came from the place of light, and there we return.

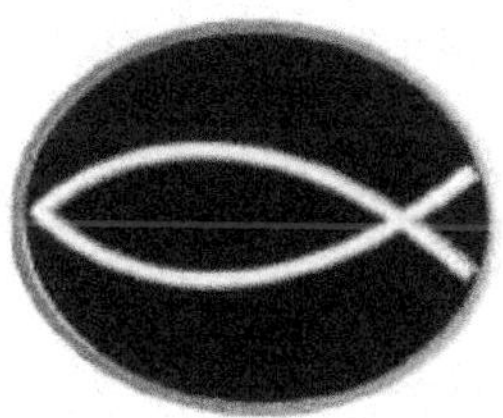

51. His Disciples said to him: When will the rest of the dead occur, and when will the New World come? He said to them: That which you look for has already come, but you do not recognize it.

DORESSE

[51]. His disciples said to him: "On what day shall rest come to those who are dead, and on what day shall the new world come?" He said to them: "This <rest> that you wait for has (already) come, and you have not recognized it."

The Treatise on the Resurrection, (From the Nag Hammadi Library, Translated by Malcolm L. Peel)

"Those who are living shall die. How do they live in an illusion? The rich have become poor, and the kings have been overthrown. Everything is prone to change. The world is an illusion! - lest, indeed, I rail at things to excess! But the resurrection does not have this aforesaid character, for it is the truth which stands firm. It is the revelation of what is, and the transformation of things, and a transition into newness. For imperishability descends upon the perishable; the light flows down upon the darkness, swallowing it up; and the Pleroma fills up the deficiency. These are the symbols and the images of the resurrection. He it is who makes the good. Therefore, do not think in part, O Rheginos, nor live in conformity with this flesh for the sake of unanimity, but flee from the divisions and the fetters, and already you have the resurrection. For if he who will die knows about himself that he will die - even if he spends many years in this life, he is brought to this - why not consider yourself as risen and (already) brought to this? If you have the resurrection but continue as if you are to die - and yet that one knows that he has died - why, then, do I ignore your lack of exercise? It is fitting for each one to practice in a number of ways, and he shall be released from this Element that he may not fall into error but shall himself receive again what at first was."

Funk and Hoover write: "The question posed in v. 1 employs the characteristic Thomean term 'rest': this term is a synonym for salvation in Thomas (see 50:3; 60:6; 90; in addition, the Greek fragment of Thomas 2 adds the additional verse: 'and having reigned, one will rest.') The term 'rest' with a similar meaning is not unknown in other texts, both Christian (Matt 11:28-29; Rev 14:13) and Judean (Sir 51:26-27), but it carried special significance among gnostic Christians and Platonists. To achieve 'rest' meant to find one's place again in unity with the highest God. (In developed gnostic systems, at the beginning was the incomprehensible, invisible, eternal, and ungenerated Forefather, Depth; Depth gave rise to a female counterpart, Silence. Together they produced the next pair of Aeons, which eventuate in fourteen such pairs, each pair with lesser power and memory of its origin than the previous pair. At the lowest level is Wisdom and the creator God. Salvation consists in reascending the ladder of divine emanations and rejoining the godhead.)" (The Five Gospels, p. 502)

NIV 1 Corinthians 4:8 Already you have all you want! Already you have become rich! You have begun to reign—and that without us! How I wish that you really had begun to reign so that we also might reign with you!

Luke 17:20 And when he was demanded of the Pharisees, when the kingdom of God should come, he answered them and said, The kingdom of God cometh not with observation: 21 Neither shall they say, Lo here! or, lo there! for, behold, the kingdom of God is within you. 22 And he said unto the disciples, The days will come, when ye shall desire to see one of the days of the Son of man, and ye shall not see it. [23] And they shall say to you, See here; or, see there: go not after them, nor follow them.[24] For as the lightning, that lighteneth out of the one part under heaven, shineth unto the other part under heaven; so shall also the Son of man be in his day.[25] But first must he suffer many things, and be rejected of this generation.

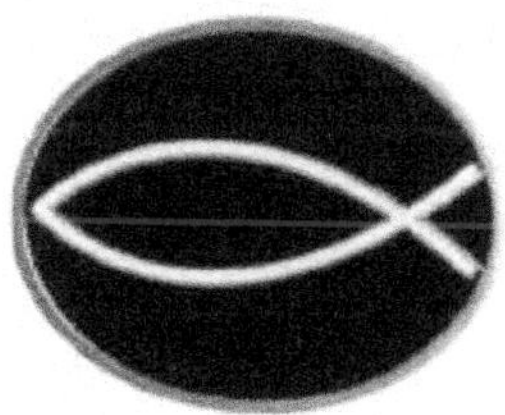

52. His Disciples said to him: Twenty-four prophets preached in Israel, and they all spoke of you (in you / by you). He said to them: You have abandoned (ignored) the Living-One who is in your presence (in front of your eyes) and you have spoken only of those who are dead.

The 24 referred to are the 24 books of the Hebrew bible. Christ is the fulfillment of all of these. The books are not living, although it is said they contain the living word. Jesus IS the living word, the Logos, and he is there with them. Some had rather read about truth than experience it because that may cause them to change and upset their viewpoints and their life.

The Jews relied on the written words of 24 books written by dead men rather than the living word.

Numerically, 24 reduces to 6 (2+4=6) and six is the highest number humanly attainable. It represents man's imperfection and man's enmity with God. It is not 7, which is represents spiritual perfection. Jesus is the 25th word and represents the Seven.

Marvin Meyer writes: "Augustine, Against the Adversary of the Law and the Prophets 2.4.14, provides a close parallel to this saying: 'You have rejected the living one who is before you, and you speak idly of the dead.' Also noteworthy is Acts of Thomas 170: 'Since you do not believe in the living, how do you wish to believe in the dead? But do not fear. Jesus the Christ, through his great goodness, treats you humanely.' Compare also John 5:37-40; 8:52-53." (The Gospel of Thomas: The Hidden Sayings of Jesus, p. 90)

> *John 5: 33 "You have sent to John and he has testified to the truth. 34 Not that I accept human testimony; but I mention it that you may be saved. 35 John was a lamp that burned and gave light, and you chose for a time to enjoy his light. 36 "I have testimony weightier than that of John. For the works that the Father has given me to finish – the very works that I am doing – testify that the Father has sent me. 37 And the Father who sent me has himself testified concerning me. You have never heard his voice*

nor seen his form, 38 nor does his word dwell in you, for you do not believe the one he sent. 39 You study[c] the Scriptures diligently because you think that in them you have eternal life. These are the very Scriptures that testify about me, 40 yet you refuse to come to me to have life.

John 8:52-53 New International Version (NIV)

52 At this they exclaimed, "Now we know that you are demon-possessed! Abraham died and so did the prophets, yet you say that whoever obeys your word will never taste death. 53 Are you greater than our father Abraham? He died, and so did the prophets. Who do you think you are?"

John 13:31 Therefore, when he was gone out, Jesus said, Now is the Son of man glorified, and God is glorified in him.[32] If God be glorified in him, God shall also glorify him in himself, and shall straightway glorify him.[33] Little children, yet a little while I am with you. Ye shall seek me: and as I said unto the Jews, Whither I go, ye cannot come; so now I say to you.[34] A new commandment I give unto you, That ye love one another; as I have loved you, that ye also love one another.[35] By this shall all men know that ye are my disciples, if ye have love one to another.[36] Simon Peter said unto him, Lord, whither goest thou? Jesus answered him, Whither I go, thou canst not follow me now; but thou shalt follow me afterwards.

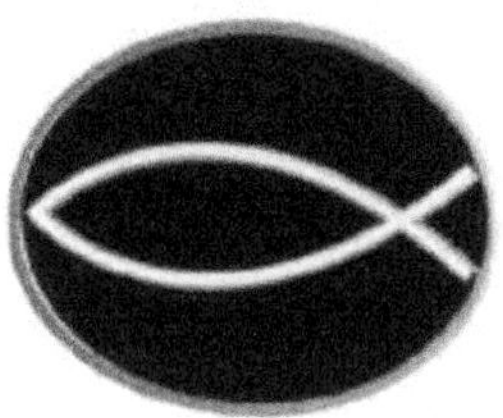

53. His Disciples said to him: Is circumcision beneficial or not? He said to them: If it were beneficial, their father would beget them already circumcised from their mother. However, the true spiritual circumcision has become entirely beneficial.

Over and again in Gnostic literature the theme of inner and outer occurs wherein the outer of the physical world is deemed worthless to the spirit. This is one of the issues that brought contention between Gnostics and the other movements claiming orthodoxy. In Gnosticism fasting, prayer, almsgiving, and dietary regulations are all rejected as useless outer displays, which do not touch the spirit. Yet, when the spirit is changed, outward signs will be apparent.

According to a Jewish tradition, a governor of Judea once commented to Rabbi Akiba, 'If he (that is, God) takes such pleasure in circumcision, why then does not a child come circumcised from his mother's womb?'" (Marvin Meyer, The Gospel of Thomas: The Hidden Sayings of Jesus, pp. 90-91)

If outward circumcision were useful, we would be born circumcised. The outward circumcision is useless, but the circumcision of the heart is of great use. Cut away that which is useless and it reveals the truth. You might ask, If heart circumcision were useful why were we not born that way? We were. Little children do not need this. They already understand. Thus, we must cut away all those things that have incased our hearts and return to our primal, beginning, our childlike state. We must circumcise the heart because it has become grown over and it has been covered up.

Acts 15:5-17 But there rose up certain of the sect of the Pharisees which believed, saying, That it was needful to circumcise them, and to command them to keep the law of Moses. And the apostles and elders came together for to consider of this matter. And when there had been much disputing, Peter rose up, and said unto them, Men and brethren, ye know how that a good while ago God made choice among us, that the Gentiles by my mouth should hear the word of the gospel, and believe. And God, which knoweth the hearts, bare them witness, giving them the Holy Ghost, even as he did unto us; And put no difference between us and them, purifying their hearts by faith. Now therefore why tempt ye God, to put a yoke upon the neck of the disciples, which neither our fathers nor we were able to bear? But we believe that through the grace of the LORD Jesus Christ we shall be saved, even as they. Then all the multitude kept silence, and gave audience to Barnabas and Paul, declaring what miracles and wonders God had wrought among the Gentiles by them. And after they had held their peace, James answered, saying, Men and brethren, hearken unto me: Simeon hath declared how God at the first did visit the Gentiles, to take out of them a people for his name. And to this agree the words of the prophets; as it is written, After this I will return, and will build again the tabernacle of David, which is fallen down; and I will build again the ruins thereof, and I will set it up: That the residue of men might seek after the Lord, and all the Gentiles, upon whom my name is called, saith the Lord, who doeth all these things.

Jeremiah 4:3-5 For thus saith the LORD to the men of Judah and Jerusalem, Break up your fallow ground, and sow not among thorns. Circumcise yourselves to the LORD, and take away the foreskins of your heart, ye men of Judah and inhabitants of Jerusalem: lest my fury come forth like fire, and burn that none can quench it, because of the evil of your doings. Declare ye in Judah, and publish in Jerusalem; and say, Blow ye the trumpet in the land: cry, gather together, and say, Assemble yourselves, and let us go into the defenced cities.

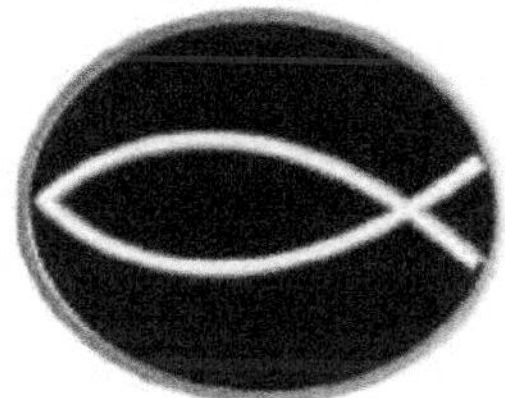

54. Jesus said: Blessed be the poor, for yours is the Kingdom of the Heaven.

The poor have less of the material world for attachments. Maybe the poor have already learned that this world offers little to stay for.

Often we fall into the trap of thinking that God has blessed those who are wealthy. Wealth, as we see from the parable of the rich young ruler, can be a curse.

If the sun shines on the just and unjust, and the rain falls on the just and unjust, how can we not see that the fate of wealth can come to the just as well as the unjust?

Many of us would have more peace if we were not so stressed about collecting more possessions. He who knows that enough is enough will have enough.

R. McL. Wilson writes: "On logion 54: 'Blessed are the poor, for yours is the kingdom of heaven,' Grant and Freedman say that it combines Luke vi. 20 with Matthew v. 3, but it may, perhaps, be doubted if Matthew comes into question at all. The only difference between Luke and Thomas lies in the use of the phrase 'kingdom of heaven,' and Thomas, as already noted, habitually avoids the name of God. It is at least possible that Thomas here preserves the original form, which Luke has altered by substituting 'God' and Matthew interpreted by adding 'in spirit' after 'the poor.' There are, however, other possibilities: deliberate alteration of Luke by Thomas, or the transmission of the saying from Luke to Thomas through a Jewish-Christian milieu in which the change was made." (Studies in the Gospel of Thomas, pp. 55-56)

Matthew 6:20 Then he looked up at his disciples and said: Blessed are you who are poor, for yours is the kingdom of God.

Luke 6:20 And he lifted up his eyes on his disciples, and said: Blessed are you poor, for yours is the kingdom of God.

Matthew 5:3 Blessed are the poor in spirit, for theirs is the kingdom of heaven.

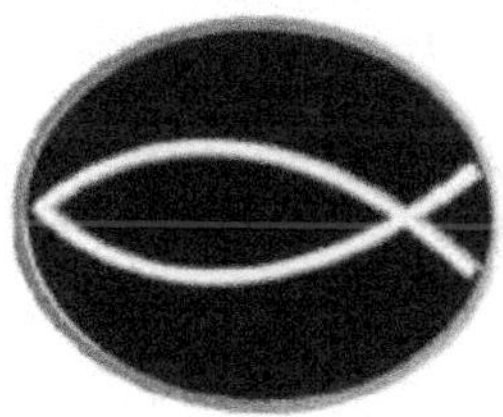

55. Jesus said: Those who do not hate his father and his mother will not be able to become my Disciple. And those who do not hate his brothers and his sisters and does not take up his own cross in my way will not become worthy of me.

"I have left father and mother and brother and sister. I have come a stranger for the sake of your name. I have taken up my cross, and I have followed you. I have left the things of the body for the sake of the things of the spirit. I have disregarded the glory of the world for the sake of your glory that does not pass away." (Manichaean Psalm Book 175:25-30)

In "The Secret Sayings of Jesus", pp. 163-164, Robert M. Grant and David Noel Freedman write: "This saying is a combination of Luke 14:26-27 (hating father and mother, brothers and sisters, carrying cross, becoming disciple) with Matthew 10:37-38 (being worthy of me). From Luke, Thomas omits mention of wife and children, perhaps because the Gnostic will have neither; he adds to carrying the cross 'as I do' (or 'like me,'

Doresse, page 177), perhaps because as in John 19:17, Jesus bears his own cross (Simon of Cyrene carries it in the synoptic gospels)."

This saying should not be taken literally. There is no room for hate in the way we interpret it. Mother, father, and brother are those in this world following the outward way, attached to the world, including family, and ignoring or numbed to the truth, being that all things placed here in the physical world, including family, are a distraction to the journey. As a matter of fact, drama within families can serve as the greatest distraction and impede us in our journey. Dysfunctional families tend to bind tightly together to protect the dysfunctional ways they behave. No one wants to disturb their way of life, at least not until they see a higher truth. We have seen in other sayings that our true families are those souls we walk with in the solidarity of the truth.

Luke 14:26-27 If any one comes to me and does not hate his own father and mother and wife and children and brothers and sisters, yes, and even his own life, he cannot be my disciple. Whoever does not bear his own cross and come after me, cannot be my disciple.

John 17:11-21 And now I am no more in the world, but these are in the world, and I come to thee. Holy Father, keep through thine own name those whom thou hast given me, that they may be one, as we are. While I was with them in the world, I kept them in thy name: those that thou gavest me I have kept, and none of them is lost, but the son of perdition; that the scripture might be fulfilled. And now come I to thee; and these things I speak in the world, that they might have my joy fulfilled in themselves. I have given them thy word; and the world hath hated them, because they are not of the world, even as I am not of the world. I pray not that thou shouldest take them out of the world, but that thou shouldest keep them from the evil. They are not of the world, even as I am not of the world. Sanctify them through thy truth: thy word is truth. As thou hast sent me into the world, even so have I also sent them into the world. And for their sakes I sanctify myself, that they also might be sanctified through the truth. Neither pray I for these alone, but for them also which shall believe on me through their word; That they all may be one; as thou, Father, art in me, and I in thee, that they also may be one in us: that the world may believe that thou hast sent me.

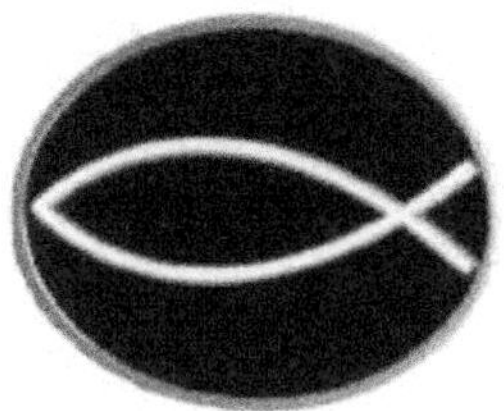

56. Jesus said: Whoever has come to understand the world (system) has found a corpse, and whoever has found a corpse, is superior to the world (of him the world is not worthy).

When you see the world system for what it is, a sham, place of the spiritually dead, and a trap, you will know its lack of worth and you will know you are superior to the world. You are the eternal children of the Father. This idea of the world being a corrupt, dying, or rotten place is a repeating theme of Gnosticism and was so important to them that the idea is repeated almost word for word, and certainly idea for idea, in verse 80. The main difference between the two is one verse uses the word "body" and the other uses "corpse".

To see the world for what it is, a corpse, is a good thing. It means the seeker has seen through the illusion.

F. F. Bruce had another insight into the interpretation when he wrote: The Naassenes, according to Hippolytus, spoke of the spiritual body as a 'corpse'. [The reason for this strange use of 'corpse' was that the spiritual essence is 'buried' in the body as a corpse is buried in a tomb (Hippolytus, Refutation v.8.22).] But the analogy of Saying 111 ('as for him who finds himself, the world is not worthy of him') suggests that here 'corpse' means 'body' as used in the sense of 'self'. If so, we may have a cryptic parallel to the canonical saying about gaining the world and losing one's own self, or vice versa (Luke 9.24f.; Matthew 16.25f.), which follows a saying about denying self and taking up the cross (cf. Saying 55)." (Jesus and Christian Origins Outside the New Testament, p. 135)

Luke 9:24 And he said to them all, If any man will come after me, let him deny himself, and take up his cross daily, and follow me.

Hebrews 11:37-40 They were stoned, they were sawn asunder, were tempted, were slain with the sword: they wandered about in sheepskins and goatskins; being destitute, afflicted, tormented; (Of whom the world was not worthy:) they wandered in deserts, and in mountains, and in dens and caves of the earth. And these all, having obtained a good report through faith, received not the promise: God having provided some better thing for us, that they without us should not be made perfect.

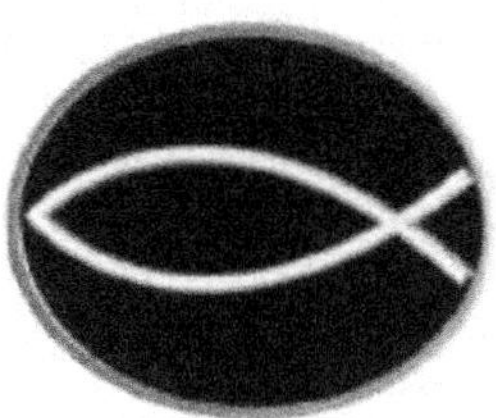

57. Jesus said: The Kingdom of the Father is like a person who has good (kind of) seed. His enemy came by night and sowed (scattered) weed (thorn) seeds among the good seed. The man did not permit them to pull up the weeds, he said to them: perhaps you will intend to pull up the weed and you pull up the wheat along with it. But, on the day of harvest the weeds will be very visible and then they will pull them and burn them.

This verse draws us back to the Gnostic belief that the physical realm was put in place by a lower god, an insane angel, who viewed himself as god, and who seeks to entrap men into a continuing worship of him and his creation. In time the differences between his captives and the free enlightened ones will be very clear.

The verse is an apocalyptic reference suggesting the Gnostic view of duality in the world between those who have gnosis or salvation and those who do not, and the eternal separation between the two groups.

Every major religion is somewhat exclusive in their view of "others". The mainline Christians believe people are saved or they are doomed to hell. After judgement, in eternity the twain shall never meet. There is separation based on which is wheat and which is weed or thorn. This is a judgement of sorts. In this verse, we see the weeds are removed and burned, alluding to a state where one ceases to exist. It is not "hell" in that it is not eternal punishment, but instead it is a quick, effortless return to nothingness. In the Gnostic mind, there is a spiritual chasm and void between those who understand the nature of existence and those who do not.

Matthew 13:24-30 He put before them another parable: The kingdom of heaven may be compared to someone who sowed good seed in his field; but while everybody was asleep, an enemy came and sowed weeds among the wheat, and then went away. So when the plants came up and bore grain, then the weeds appeared as well. And the slaves of the householder came and said to him, Master, did you not sow good seed in your field? Where, then, did these weeds come from? He answered, An enemy has done this. The slaves said to him, Then do you want us to go and gather them? But he replied, No; for in gathering the weeds you would uproot the wheat along with them. Let both of them grow together until the harvest; and at harvest time I will tell the reapers, Collect the weeds first and bind them in bundles to be burned, but gather the wheat into my barn.

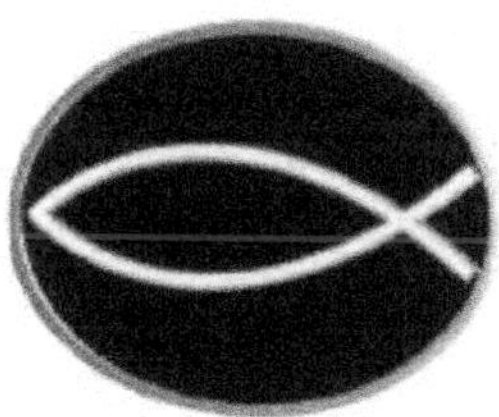

58. Jesus said: Blessed is the person who has suffered, for he has found life. (Blessed is he who has suffered (labored) to find life and has found life).

The major scholars seeking to interpret this saying diverge in small ways, causing major differences.

BLATZ
(58) Jesus said: Blessed is the man who has suffered; he has found life.

LAYTON
(58) Jesus said, "Blessed is the person who has labored and found life."

The search for truth is a labor. Being truthful and authentic with oneself is suffering. The seeker will find truth, but only in God's time, since it is the Father who must reveal himself to us.

In the Gnostic mind, there is no need to suffer or labor to find Gnosis. The knowledge is there, waiting to be seen. Yet, it does take "work" to fight ones way through the traps of the world and societies, to mentally disengage from the rat race, and then to keep the truth in the forefront of the mind. It takes focus and work to fight against the distractions of the world so as not to lose sight of the truth. If you exert this will and energy, you will find life and rest.

Funk and Hoover write: "In form, this aphorism mimics the beatitudes found in Matthew (5:3-12) and Luke (6:20-22). But in content it recalls the 'labors' of Hercules. In early Christian times, Cynics and Stoics, two dominant schools of philosophy during the Greco-Roman period, 300 B.C.E. - 300 C.E., looked to Hercules as a kind of heroic founder. This sort of borrowing from popular culture was common in the early Christian movement as the followers of Jesus added to the legacy of their teacher. Also, the promise of life echoes the prologue to Thomas and related motifs elsewhere in this gospel (101:3; 114:1; further, 18:3; 19:4; 85:2; 111:2)." (The Five Gospels, p. 506)

Matthew 11:28 Come to me, all you that are weary and are carrying heavy burdens, and I will give you rest.

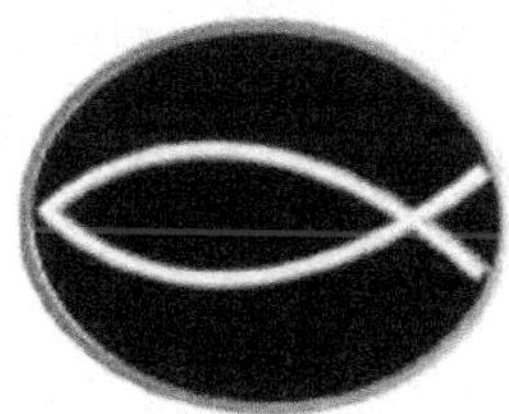

59. Jesus said: Look to the Living-One while you all are alive, otherwise, you might die and then seek to see him and will be unable to find him.

There are many pearls hidden in the saying. It seems to connect directly to saying 52.

52. His Disciples said to him: Twenty-four prophets preached in Israel, and they all spoke of (in or by) you. He said to them: You have abandoned (ignored) the Living-One who is in your presence (in front of your eyes) and you have spoken only of those who are dead.

The Living-One refers to Jesus after the resurrection. Reach for God while you are still awake from the initial jolt of the enlightened truth because you may fall back to sleep if you wait too long. Unused epiphanies tend to fade away.

In this saying, we are told there will be individuality, will, and choice after death. We are told that we will remember the lessons of gnosis, or regret the rejection of the truth as well as the giver of truth and life, Jesus. However, this concept redefines the story of the wheat and tares, where the weeds are quickly burned up. Both may be true, if Thomas is saying between the uprooting and destruction there is a time of realization and regret of our errors and ways.

Gerd Ludemann writes: "The key word 'living' links the present logion with the previous one ('found life'). Jesus is speaking of himself as the living one (cf. Prologue; 52.2) and emphasizing the either-or between (spiritual) life and (spiritual) death." (Jesus After 2000 Years, p. 619)

John 7:34 You will search for me, but you will not find me; and where I am, you cannot come.

John 13:33 Little children, I am with you only a little longer. You will look for me; and as I said to the Jews so now I say to you, Where I am going, you cannot come.

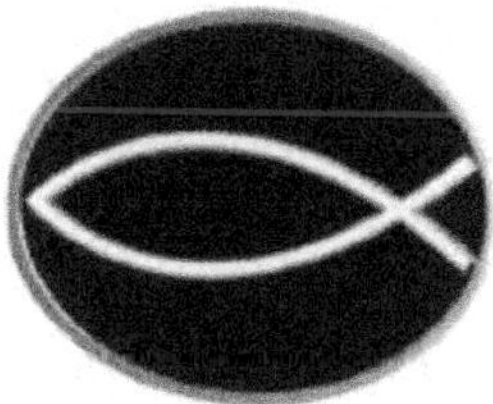

60. On Jesus' way to Judea, they (Jesus and the apostles) saw a Samaritan carrying a lamb. Jesus said to them: Why does he take the lamb with him? They said to him: So that he may kill it and eat it. He said to them: While it is alive he will not eat it, but only after he kills it and it becomes a corpse. They said: How could he do otherwise? He said to them: Look for a place of rest for yourselves, otherwise, you might become carcasses (corpses) and be devoured.

The codex is damaged here and the verse is unclear. It is reconstructed as a best-guess, based on content and context available.

The place of rest always refers to our realization of the truth and place or state of enlightenment. Seeing the truth makes us alive. While we are alive the world can no longer keep us or destroy us. We must seek the Gnosis and rest that comes with it before we are turned into the world and are trapped.

"The Lord said truly: You shall be as lambs in the midst of wolves! Peter answered: But what if the wolves tear open the lambs? And Jesus said to Peter: After their death, the lambs have nothing further to fear from the wolves. You also, do not need to fear those who kill you because then they cannot make you suffer any further. But fear him who after your death has power to cast your soul and your body into Gehenna, that place of fire! Know then . . . that the promise of Christ is great . . . as also the Repose of the Kingdom . . .!" II Epistle of Clement

Gehenna is a valley in Jerusalem where some of the kings of Judah sacrificed their children by fire. It was in the valley of Hinnom, near Jerusalem, where sacrifices were made to pagan god, Moloch. II Kings 23:10. Thereafter, it was deemed to be cursed (Jer. 7:31, 19:2-6). In rabbinic literature Gehenna is a destination of the wicked.

Since the manuscript here is damaged, its reconstruction is unclear. We assume Jesus is the lamb. He is going to be taken and killed. He is inviting his disciples to eat of him, take his teachings, while he is still alive. They do not understand. While you find the truth standing before you, alive, eat of it. When it dies, and is presented in book, history, stories, and myths, it cannot sustain you as well spiritually. Jesus then warns his followers to find rest "salvation" soon, before they also become carcasses and are devoured when they are dead. This is indeed what has happened.

We read the words, but it is difficult to make them alive. We hear teaching, but it is difficult to know how history and transmission has altered it. The Gnostics valued direct transmission and an awakening of the person that proved the validity of the knowledge.

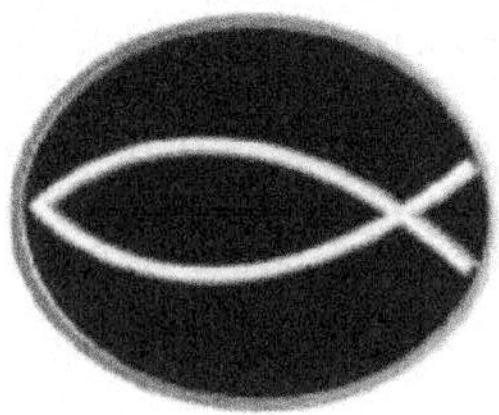

61. Jesus said: Two will recline on a bed and one will die and the other will live. Salome said: Who are you, man (whose son are you)? It is as if you are a stranger sent by someone (as if from one). You reclined (laid) upon my couch (bed) and you ate from my table. Jesus said to her: I-Am he who has come forth from and was created by the one who is equal (that which is whole and undivided). I have been given those thing that belong to my Father. Salome said: I'm your Disciple. Jesus said to her: Because of that, I say that whenever someone is one fully integrated (undivided) he will be filled with light, yet whenever he is divided he will be filled with darkness.

The Coptic translation "as if you were from one" or from someone special. This harkens back to the protest heard from the Pharisee that Jesus called himself the son of God, thus making himself equal to God.

In those days, they reclined on a couch or bed near the table to eat. There were certain positions at the table reserved for those who were invited. Jesus reclined to eat. His actions beg a challenge, as if he is baiting her to speak. Then he pours this simply, yet complex truth out like food before her. You must be whole or you will be in darkness and filled with darkness.

Funk and Hoover write of 61:1, "Live or die": "Most of the Fellows were of the opinion that the version in Thomas was older than the Q version because it is simpler. However, in its Thomean form it was probably a piece of common wisdom: death strikes when we least expect it and rather arbitrarily. Two on a couch probably refers to a dinner party or symposium - a place one is least likely to anticipate death. This context is confirmed by the remark of Salome in v. 2: 'Who are you, mister? You have climbed onto my couch and eaten from my table as if you are from someone.' Jesus is here represented as an intruder at a dinner party." (The Five Gospels, p. 507)

This idea of integration, wholeness, and undividedness so intrigued C.G. Jung that many of his psychological theories sprang from it. We stop here, at saying 61, to point out the great and wonderful power of being fully integrated. When actions, will, mind, and spiritual beliefs line up, we are no longer at war within ourselves. When inner conflict no longer exists, there is rest and peace, clarity of thought, and a deep, abiding understanding of ourselves and others.

Moreover, having been in deep conflict at one time, and now being at rest, we can see the struggles of others and have a depth of compassion not felt before. Judgement can vanish and replacing it is sympathy.

The process of integration and unity takes time and effort, as we continually apply the absolute truth to our intentions, our thoughts and our actions. The gnosis of what this world system is, the traps it sets, the greed, conflicts, wars, and malice it generates through the illusions of control and worldly success will become clear. We will see how useless and empty it all is, and the realization, knowledge or gnosis will allow us to separate our minds and spirits from the trap and see the love and potential in ourselves and others.

2 Timothy 4:4-6 New Living Translation (NLT)
4 They will reject the truth and chase after myths.
5 But you should keep a clear mind in every situation. Don't be afraid of suffering for the Lord. Work at telling others the Good News, and fully carry out the ministry God has given you.
6 As for me, my life has already been poured out as an offering to God. The time of my death is near.

Eph. 4: 21 Surely you heard of him and were taught in him in accordance with the truth that is in Jesus.

22 You were taught, with regard to your former way of life, to put off your old self, which is being corrupted by its deceitful desires;
23 to be made new in the attitude of your minds;
24 and to put on the new self, created to be like God in true righteousness and holiness.
25 Therefore each of you must put off falsehood and speak truthfully to his neighbor, for we are all members of one body.

Luke 17:34 I tell you, on that night there will be two in one bed; one will be taken and the other left.

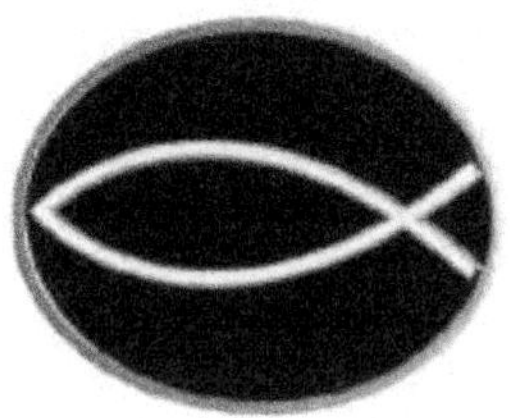

62. Jesus said: I tell my mysteries to those who are worthy of my mysteries. Do not let your right hand know what your left hand is doing.

The right hand is the symbol of rightness, power, and good. The word for "left" is where we get the words, "sinister" and "gauche". I have told you things because you have become righteous (sacred). Do not give what is sacred to those who are not. Do not give these teaching to those who are not ready for them.

The word "hand" is not in the Coptic version. Left and right are metaphors for inner and outer, soul and world, bride and groom, male and female, sacred and mundane.

Mark 4:11 And he said to them, To you has been given the secret of the kingdom of God, but for those outside, everything comes in parables.

Matthew 6:3 But when you give alms, do not let your left hand know what your right hand is doing.

Luke 8:10 He said, To you it has been given to know the secrets of the kingdom of God; but for others they are in parables, so that seeing they may not see, and hearing they may not understand.

Matthew 13:10-11 Then the disciples came and said to him, Why do you speak to them in parables? And he answered them, To you it has been given to know the secrets of the kingdom of heaven, but to them it has not been given.

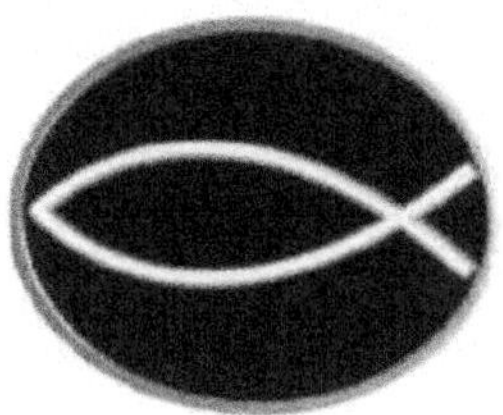

63. Jesus said: There was a wealthy person who had much money, and he said: I will use my money so that I may sow and reap and replant, to fill my storehouses with grain so that I lack nothing (so that need will not touch me). This was his intention (is what he thought in his heart) but that same night he died. Whoever has ears, let him hear!

A rich man from the city has plans to invest his money, but he should have taken care of the more important thing first. Death is inevitable and many times it is unexpected. Take care of your spirit because it will endure. The body is always a heartbeat away from death.

Funk and Hoover write: "As a single, unelaborated tale the Thomas version retains more of the characteristics of orally transmitted tradition and is probably an earlier form of the parable than Luke's. Thomas has nevertheless shifted the social location of the parable. His rich man is no longer a farmer. He is an investor who seeks such a high return that he will lack nothing. But on very day he has such thoughts he dies and thus loses everything. Thomas' version seems to turn on its incongruity between his thoughts and his end, whereas Luke's version focuses on the farmer's folly." (The Five Gospels, p. 508)

Luke 12:21 Then he told them a parable: The land of a rich man produced abundantly. And he thought to himself, What should I do, for I have no place to store my crops? Then he said, I will do this: I will pull down my barns and build larger ones, and there I will store all my grain and my goods. And I will say to my soul, Soul, you have ample goods laid up for many years; relax, eat, drink, be merry. But God said to him, You fool! This very night your life is being demanded of you. And the things you have prepared, whose will they be? So it is with those who store up treasures for themselves but are not rich toward God.

King James Bible - Matt 16:26 For what is a man profited, if he shall gain the whole world, and lose his own soul? or what shall a man give in exchange for his soul?

Christian Standard Bible- Matt 16:26 For what will it benefit someone if he gains the whole world yet loses his life? Or what will anyone give in exchange for his life?

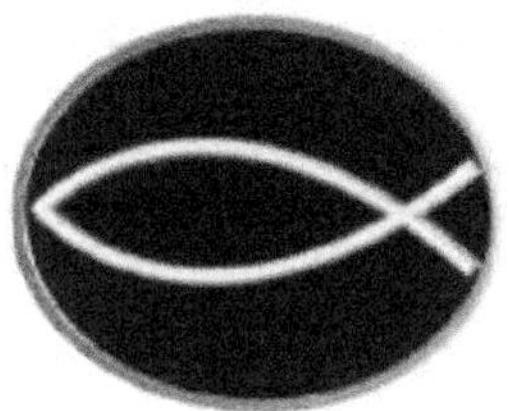

64. Jesus said: A person had houseguests, and when he had prepared the banquet in their honor he sent his servant to invite the guests. He went to the first, he said to him: My master invites you. He replied: I have to do business with some merchants. They are coming to see me this evening. I will go to place my orders with them. I ask to be excused from the banquet. He went to another, he said to him: My master has invited you. He replied to him: I have just bought a house and they require me for a day. I will have no spare time. He came to another, he said to him: My master invites you. He replied to him: My friend is getting married and I must arrange a banquet for him. I will not be able to come. I ask to be excused from the banquet. He went to another, he said to him: My master invites you. He replied to him: I have bought a farm. I go to receive the rent. I will not be able to come. I ask to be excused. The servant returned, he said to his master: Those whom you have invited to the banquet have excused themselves. The master said to his servant: Go out to the roads, bring those whom you find so that they may feast.

And he said: Businessmen and merchants will not enter the places of my Father.

Jesus is the Bridegroom. It is customary to come to the reception and receive a gift, but few came and took the gift that was offered. Those who are too busy will be overlooked in place of those who are less rooted in the world and thus have more time for spiritual matters.

The tradesmen and merchants, the investors and real estate moguls in the parable cover the spectrum of wealth at the time. The parable is an indictment against the wealthy, who wish to complete the next deal for the sake of acquiring more wealth to feed their pride and ego instead of coming to a free banquet and there receive a gift that has little value in the world system.

Marvin Meyer writes: "The Palestinian Talmud recounts a similar story about the rich tax-collector Bar Ma'jan, who arranged a feast for the city officials; when they did not come, he invited the poor instead." (The Gospel of Thomas: The Hidden Sayings of Jesus, p. 94)

Luke 14:16-24 Then Jesus said to him:, Someone gave a great dinner and invited many. At the time for the dinner he sent his slave to say to those who had been invited, Come; for everything is ready now. But they all alike began to make excuses. The first said to him, I have bought a piece of land, and I must go out and see it; please accept my regrets. Another said, I have bought five yoke of oxen, and I am going to try them out; please accept my regrets. Another said, I have just been married, and therefore I cannot come. So the slave returned and reported this to his master. Then the owner of the house became angry and said to his slave, Go out at once into the streets and lanes of the town and bring in the poor, the crippled, the blind, and the lame. And the slave said, Sir, what you ordered has been done, and there is still room. Then the master said to the slave, Go out into the roads and lanes, and compel people to come in, so that my house may be filled. For I tell you, none of those who were invited will taste my dinner.

Matthew 19:23 Then Jesus said to his disciples, Truly I tell you, it will be hard for a rich person to enter the kingdom of heaven.

Matthew 22:1-14 And Jesus answered and spake unto them again by parables, and said, The kingdom of heaven is like unto a certain king, which made a marriage for his son, and sent his servants to call those who were invited to the marriage feast; but they would not come. Again he sent other servants, saying, Tell those who are invited, Behold, I have made ready my dinner, my oxen and my fat calves are killed, and everything is ready; come to the marriage feast. But they made light of it and went off, one to his farm, another to his business, while the rest seized his servants, treated them shamefully, and killed them. The king was angry, and he sent his troops and destroyed those murderers and burned their city. Then he said to his servants, The wedding is ready, but those invited were not worthy. Go therefore to the thoroughfares, and invite to the marriage feast as many as you find. And those servants went out into the streets and gathered all whom they found, both bad and good; so the wedding hall was filled with guests. But when the king came in to look at the guests, he saw there a man who had no wedding garment; and he said to him, Friend, how did you get in here without a wedding garment? And he was speechless. Then the king said to the attendants, Bind him hand and foot, and cast him into the outer darkness; there men will weep and gnash their teeth. For many are called, but few are chosen.

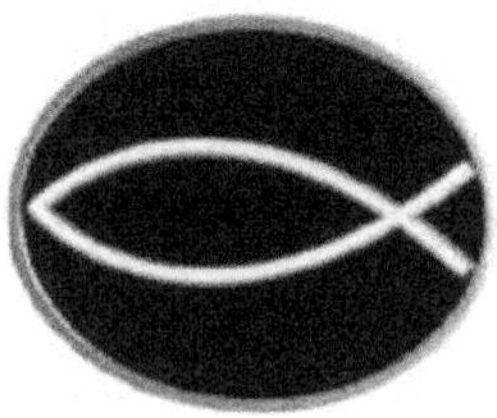

65. He said: A kind person who owned a vineyard leased it to tenants so that they would work it and he would receive the fruit from them. He sent his servant so that the tenants (cultivators / farmers) would give to him the fruit of the vineyard. They seized his servant and beat him nearly to death. The servant went, he told his master what had happened. His master said: Perhaps they did not recognize him. So, he sent another servant. The tenants (cultivators) beat him also. Then the owner sent his son. He said: Perhaps they will respect my son. Since the tenants knew that he was the heir to the vineyard, they seized him and killed him. Whoever has ears, let him hear!

Judaism accepts the fact that there have been multiple messiahs. Kind David was considered one, but when God's servant was sent to take the people the truth and introduce them to the true God they crucified him because they did not want to give up the fruits of the world.

Likewise, those who see the world differently should expect to be rejected in some form. The Gnostics assumed that if almost everyone was deluded and asleep the few who had clarity and were awake would think and act so differently that they would be stopped, ceased, or assaulted. How much more resistant would be inflicted on the one who was sent to awaken those who sleep?

John S. Kloppenborg, Marvin W. Meyer, Stephen J. Patterson, and Michael G. Steinhauser state: "When one compares this version of the Parable of the Tenants to those which occur in Mark, Matthew, and Luke, one notices immediately its distinguishing characteristic: this version is a true parabolic story, not an allegory. Form critics have long held that allegorization of the parables was a relatively late development in the history of their interpretation. In fact, even without access to the Coptic Gospel of Thomas, the great parables scholar C. H. Dodd had offered a conjectural reconstruction of the Parable of the Tenants as it would have been read before the synoptic tradition had allegorized it. His reconstruction matched Saying 65 almost to the word." (Q-Thomas Reader, p. 102)

What does the above opinion mean? According to Dodd, this verse in Thomas agrees very closely to that of the Q document and is therefore older in form than the corresponding verses in the Gospels.

Matthew 21:33-39 Listen to another parable. There was a landowner who planted a vineyard, put a fence around it, dug a wine press in it, and built a watchtower. Then he leased it to tenants and went to another country. When the harvest time had come, he sent his slaves to the tenants to collect his produce. But the tenants seized his slaves and beat one, killed another, and stoned another. Again he sent other slaves, more than the first; and they treated them in the same way. Finally he sent his son to them, saying, They will respect my son. But when the tenants saw the son, they said to themselves, This is the heir; come, let us kill him and get his inheritance. So they seized him, threw him out of the vineyard, and killed him.

Mark 12:1-9 And he began to speak to them in parables. A man planted a vineyard, and set a hedge around it, and dug a pit for the wine press, and built a tower, and let it out to tenants, and went into another country. When the time came, he sent a servant to the tenants, to get from them some of the fruit of the vineyard. And they took him and beat him, and sent him away empty-handed. Again he sent to them another servant, and they wounded him in the head, and treated him shamefully. And he sent another, and him they killed; and so with many others, some they beat and some they killed. He had still one other, a beloved son; finally he sent him to them, saying, They will respect my son. But those tenants said to one another, This is the heir; come, let us kill him, and the inheritance will be ours. And they took him and killed him, and cast him out of the vineyard. What will the owner of the vineyard do? He will come and destroy the tenants, and give the vineyard to others.

Luke 20:9-16 And he began to tell the people this parable: A man planted a vineyard, and let it out to tenants, and went into another country for a long while. When the time came, he sent a servant to the tenants, that they should give him some of the fruit of the vineyard; but the tenants beat him, and sent him away empty-handed. And he sent another servant; him also they beat and treated shamefully, and sent him away empty-handed. And he sent yet a third; this one they wounded and cast out. 13 Then the owner of the vineyard said, What shall I do? I will send my beloved son; it may be they will respect him. 14 But when the tenants saw him, they said to themselves, This is the heir; let us kill him, that the inheritance may be ours. 15 And they cast him out of the vineyard and killed him. What then will the owner of the vineyard do to them? 16 He will come and destroy those tenants, and give the vineyard to others. When they heard this, they said, God forbid!

Isaiah 5 New International Version (NIV)
The Song of the Vineyard

5 I will sing for the one I love
a song about his vineyard:
My loved one had a vineyard
on a fertile hillside.
2 He dug it up and cleared it of stones
and planted it with the choicest vines.
He built a watchtower in it
and cut out a winepress as well.
Then he looked for a crop of good grapes,
but it yielded only bad fruit.

3 "Now you dwellers in Jerusalem and people of Judah,
judge between me and my vineyard.
4 What more could have been done for my vineyard
than I have done for it?
When I looked for good grapes,
why did it yield only bad?
5 Now I will tell you
what I am going to do to my vineyard:
I will take away its hedge,
and it will be destroyed;
I will break down its wall,
and it will be trampled.
6 I will make it a wasteland,
neither pruned nor cultivated,

and briers and thorns will grow there.
I will command the clouds
not to rain on it."

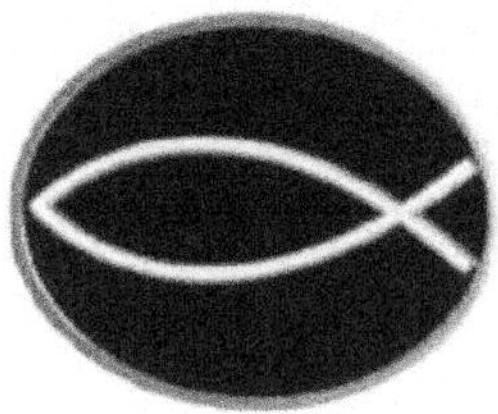

66. Jesus said: Show me the stone which the builders have rejected. It is that one that is the cornerstone (keystone).

Another rendering is: Jesus says: "Would that you could tell me about the stone which the builders have rejected. That is it, the cornerstone."

There are two ways to approach this verse, based on the rendering of the word for cornerstone. F.F. Bruce believes this to be the word for pediment, which is defined as the triangular upper part of the front of a building in classical style, typically surmounting a portico of columns. This would mean the stone should have been elevated above the others. Jesus, who should have been elevated and made visible the everyone was rejected.

If the standard definition of "cornerstone" is used, it would mean that Jesus and his teachings would have formed the solid and correct foundation.

The truth is contrary to what is considered normal or good. It is therefore discarded by most. This means, in the Gnostic mind, that the world system is not built on the truth and is therefore a lie with no foundation. It will fall in time. Likewise, the real truth was rejected by the builders of this world, which is the true cornerstone.

F. F. Bruce writes: "In all three Synoptic Gospels the parable of the vineyard is followed by the quotation of Psalm 118.22: 'The stone which the builders rejected has become the head of the corner' (i.e. top of the pediment). The point is that Christ, rejected by the leaders of Israel, is exalted by God (cf. Acts 4.11). Here no reference is made to its being an Old Testament quotation. Hippolytus tells us that the Naassenes spoke of the archetypal heavenly Man (whom they called Adamas) as 'the chief corner stone'. [Refutation v.7.35.]" (Jesus and Christian Origins Outside the New Testament, p. 139)

Thomas goes to great lengths to avoid mentioning or quoting the Old Testament or Torah directly. To the Gnostic mind, the seemingly vengeful, jealous, angry God of the Old Testament could not be the same kind, gracious, loving God of the New Testament. To avoid religiously induced cognitive dissonance, they separated the personalities into two Gods, believing the Old Testament God was the insane creator of this world, Yaldabaoth, and the New Testament God was the Divine

Father, who sent Jesus to awaken us to this truth.

Matthew 21:42 Jesus said to them, Have you never read in the scriptures: The very stone which the builders rejected has become the head of the corner; this was the Lord's doing, and it is marvelous in our eyes?

Mark 12:10-11 Have you not read this scripture: The very stone which the builders rejected has become the head of the corner; this was the Lord's doing, and it is marvelous in our eyes?

Luke 20:17 But he looked at them and said, What then does this text mean: The stone that the builders rejected has become the cornerstone?

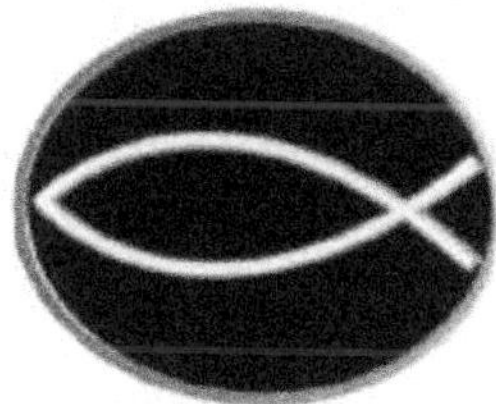

67. Jesus said: He who knows The All but does not know himself has missed everything (fallen completely short).

The exact meaning of this verse is complicated and difficult to translate. Several vantage points will be explored.

Jesus said, "If anyone becomes acquainted with All and falls short of all, that person falls short completely."

Jesus says: "He who knows the All, but has failed to know himself, has failed completely to find that Place."

R. McL. Wilson writes: "Logion 67 Grant and Freedman, using a different translation, found incomprehensible, and they suggest that it may have been garbled in the transmission. The clue, however, had already been provided by Dr. Till, who after observing 'For him who wants to be saved it is necessary above all to recognize the vanity of the material world,' and quoting sayings to that effect, continues 'It is by no means sufficient to know the worthlessness of the material world. The indispensable perfection of knowledge is knowing oneself. For even "he who knows all the universe but does not know himself has missed everything".'" (Studies in the Gospel of Thomas, p. 28)

To know, or be aware, of all parts of our body, mind, and spirit, and to have all thoughts, feelings, and actions acting in one accord is both powerful and peaceful.

As Joseph Campbell writes in The Portable Jung:
"Individuation' is Jung's term for the process of achieving such command of all four functions (Sensation, Feeling (emotion), Thinking, and Intuition) that, even while bound to the cross of this limiting earth, one might open one's eyes at the center, to see, think, feel and intuit transcendence, and to act out of such knowledge."

Self-knowledge is a very important tenant in the Gospel of Thomas. If we do not know ourselves and examine ourselves how can we know that we lack something?

There is a theme in Gnosticism of a "homesickness." As my grandfather, Rev. W.R. Lumpkin, has been quoted, "I am homesick for a place I have never been." Yet, maybe we have been there and do not fully remember. The place still calls to us in our deeper spirit.

Jeremiah 17:5- 10 Thus saith the LORD; Cursed be the man that trusteth in man, and maketh flesh his arm, and whose heart departeth from the LORD. For he shall be like the heath in the desert, and shall not see when good cometh; but shall inhabit the parched places in the wilderness, in a salt land and not inhabited. Blessed is the man that trusteth in the LORD, and whose hope the LORD is. For he shall be as a tree planted by the waters, and that spreadeth out her roots by the river, and shall not see when heat cometh, but her leaf shall be green; and shall not be careful in the year of drought, neither shall cease from yielding fruit. The heart is deceitful above all things, and desperately wicked: who can know it? I the LORD search the heart, I try the reins, even to give every man according to his ways, and according to the fruit of his doings.

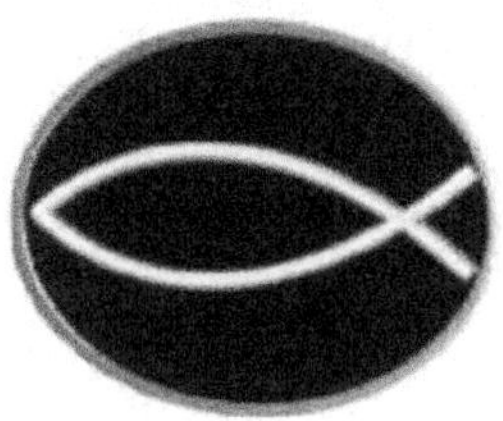

68. Jesus said: Blessed are you when you are hated and persecuted, but they themselves will find no position (place) (reason) where (why) you have been persecuted.

The meaning is unclear, so here we present three more interpretations.

Jesus said: Blessed are you when you are hated and persecuted, but they find no reason for why they pursue you.

DORESSE 68. Jesus says: "Blessed are you when you are hated and persecuted; but they will not find a position in that place to which they shall pursue you!"

LAYTON (68) Jesus said, "Blessed are you whenever they hate you and persecute you. And wherever they have persecuted you, they will find no place."

The world, its maker, and those trapped by the system its

illusions are in enmity with the real God and those seeking him. They would rather destroy the seeker than to free him.

Their hate is instinctual and not founded in reason or logic. It you ask them why they hate you, they would not be able to find a reason. It is only a reaction to the truth that opposes their reality. It is their ego fighting against being exposed to the transience of its existence.

When one's reality is threatened, or when one's worth is questioned, as it would be if the lack of value of possessions and stations in this life were to be revealed, the ego will react strongly and negatively. But do not fear. You live in a state, and will transcend to a place where the attackers cannot pursue or find you.

Matthew 5:11 Blessed are you when people revile you and persecute you and utter all kinds of evil against you falsely on my account.

Luke 6:22 Blessed are you when men hate you, and when they exclude you and revile you, and cast out your name as evil, on account of the Son of man!

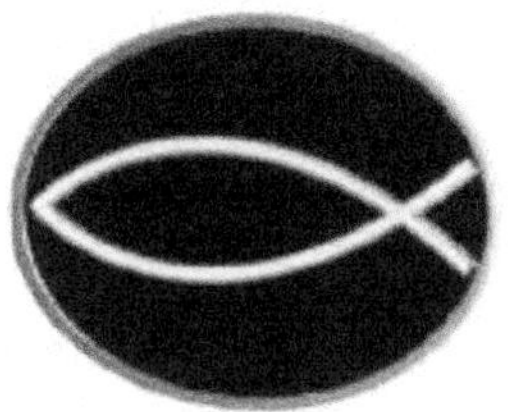

69. Jesus said: Blessed are those who have been persecuted in their heart. These are they who have come to know the Father in truth. Jesus said: Blessed are the hungry, for the stomach of him who desires to be filled will be filled.

Rumi said: "I am waiting for the guest. It is the longing that does the work." It is the hunger for the truth and for the father that guides us and draws Him. When your own heart is persecuting you, how can you escape? This is the state of most of mankind. We are haunted by what we need to be, should be, and could be. We know there is more to us than this existence. There is more to us than this shell. There is more to life than the one we are living. These people hunger for more. It is interesting that in certain Asian cultures, the stomach and not the heart, is the seat of emotion. Thomas states, you will be filled.

Robert M. Grant and David Noel Freedman write: "Like Saying 68, this one is based on gospel Beatitudes. From the blessing on those who are persecuted (Matthew 5:10), Thomas turns to add materials taken from Matthew 5:8: 'Blessed are the pure in heart, for they shall see God'; for him the vision of God is equivalent to knowing 'the Father in truth' (knowing and worshiping the Father in truth, John 4:22-23). Then he goes back to Matthew 5:6 (hungering for righteousness, being filled), though with the parallel verse in Luke (6:21) he omits 'for righteousness.'" (The Secret Sayings of Jesus, p. 174)

Matthew 5:8 Blessed are the pure in heart, for they will see God.

Luke 6:21 Blessed are you who are hungry now, for you will be filled.

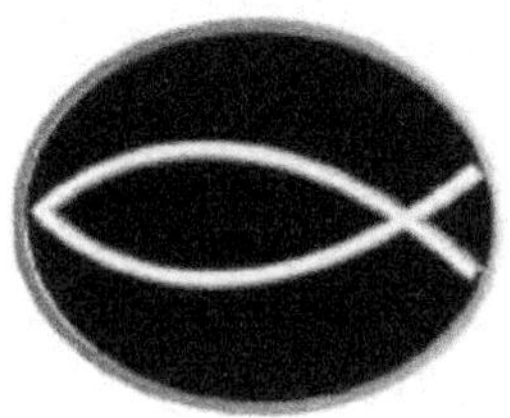

70. Jesus said: If you bring forth what is within you, it will save you. If you do not have it within you to bring forth, that which you lack will destroy you.

Out of all mysteries written within the Gospel of Thomas, this verse is the most profound. It is perhaps the simplest, yet the most difficult to fulfill. If the person has within the soul what is needed to be whole, integrated, and complete, and if these things are brought forth it will save that person.

But, what exactly does is mean to be saved? What is salvation? The Greek word for salvation is "sótéria". According to Strong's Concordance, it means deliverance, health, preservation, safety, and "salvation" in the spiritual sense. Deliverance from the molestation of enemies, preservation of physical life. In an ethical sense, that which concludes to the soul's safety or salvation. Of Messianic salvation.

To be saved is to be made safe, healthy and whole. It is to preserve life, to be delivered from harm, and to be spiritually saved.

If the truth of God is within us it will save us. If the spirit and soul, the various parts of the psyche, the inside and outside, and the male and female parts can be made one again they will be saved (made whole). If the person does not have these things inside them they will be lost in spiritual blindness, not because God does not love them, but because in such a state of chaos and disconnection within themselves, they could not find the truth.

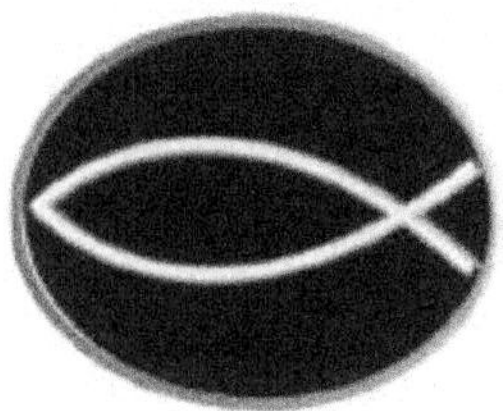

71. Jesus said: I will destroy this house (building), and no one will be able to build it (again).

The metaphor here is unclear. Is Jesus speaking of his body? The body was considered a vessel or house entrapping the soul. To destroy it was to free the soul. It is upon this idea that the Gospel of Judas hangs.

Is Jesus speaking of the temple in Jerusalem? It was totally destroyed in 70 A.D. and could not be restored.

It Jesus speaking of the world itself? The destruction of the world would be considered a good thing, as it would bring to an end captivity in this realm and cause all the souls to be released from their "buildings" or bodies, to return to the Pleroma or heaven in which the divine All resides.

Funk and Hoover write: "The Fellows conceded that Jesus

could have predicted the destruction of the temple and its replacement by another 'not made with hands.' And they agreed that some such saying must have circulated as an independent remark during the oral period, since it appears in three independent sources. Yet they were hesitant to identify its original form. The saying in Thomas, unfortunately, is fragmentary." (The Five Gospels, p. 513)

Mark 14:58 We heard him say, I will destroy this temple that is made with hands, and in three days I will build another, not made with hands.

John 2: 18 The Jews then responded to him, "What sign can you show us to prove your authority to do all this?" 19 Jesus answered them, "Destroy this temple, and I will raise it again in three days." 20 They replied, "It has taken forty-six years to build this temple, and you are going to raise it in three days?" 21 But the temple he had spoken of was his body. 22 After he was raised from the dead, his disciples recalled what he had said. Then they believed the scripture and the words that Jesus had spoken.

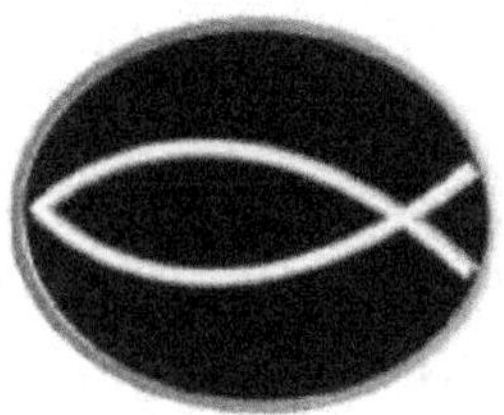

72. A person said to him: Tell my brothers to divide the possessions of my father with me. He said to him: Oh man, who made me a divider (sharer / arbitrator)? He turned to his Disciples, he said to them: I'm not a divider (sharer / arbitrator), am I?

This verse seems to be a pun or double entendre. Jesus is sharing an inside joke with his friends. In the Gnostic view, Jesus has spent his entire ministry preaching a central message of unity within the person. Personal wholeness and unity, and unity with the Divine All were the main points of his teaching. Now he takes this event to have a bit of fun with those who have heard the message every day for years. The other point of the double entendre was a message to the Jews at the time. There was a growing uneasiness about Jesus, his message, and the movement, which was gaining momentum. Jesus is asking people to decide if they think he was trying to divide the Jewish religion and the families within it. Jesus was preaching unity within the person, knowing the message would be receive by some and rejected by other, thus being a division among men.

Jesus does not care for the laws of man but instead is working to teach the laws of God. These trivial material matters do not matter. He communicates this almost as a joke. He has already said he has come to divide and set ablaze. He seems to be mocking the man for caring about such minor issues and causing division when Jesus is about to divide the world. Oddly and ironically, Jesus will divide the world between those who are internally and spiritually divided, and those who are whole.

'Abd al Jabbar in the Book on the Signs of Muhammed's Prophecy states: "A man said to him, 'Master, my brother (wishes) to share (with me) my father's blessing.' (Jesus) said to him, 'Who set me over you (in order to determine your) share?'" (from Shlomo Pines, The Jewish Christians of the Early Centuries of Christianity According to a New Source, p. 13)

Luke 12:13-15 Someone in the crowd said to him, Teacher, tell my brother to divide the family inheritance with me. But he said to him, Friend, who set me to be a judge or arbitrator over you? And he said to them, Take care! Be on your guard against all kinds of greed; for one's life does not consist in the abundance of possessions.

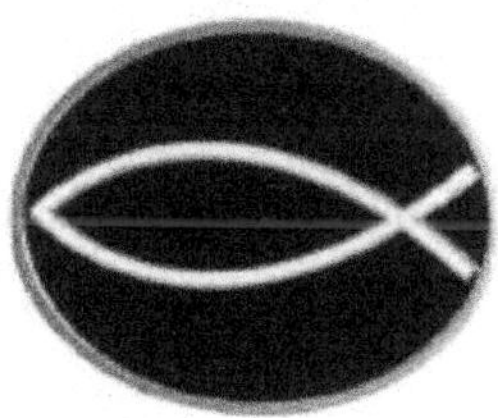

73. Jesus said: The harvest is indeed plentiful, but the workers are few. Ask the Lord to send workers for the harvest.

Although time is running out and the fire of Gnosis has been set, even with eternal life at stake, there are few willing to come forward, leave their old ways, and work for the kingdom.

This saying seems to be closer to the Q document than the Gospels. Q does not mention "the lord of the harvest", but instead simply says "the lord". See Matthew 9:37 below.

Matthew 9:37-38 Then he said to his disciples, The harvest is plentiful, but the laborers are few; therefore ask the Lord of the harvest to send out laborers into his harvest.

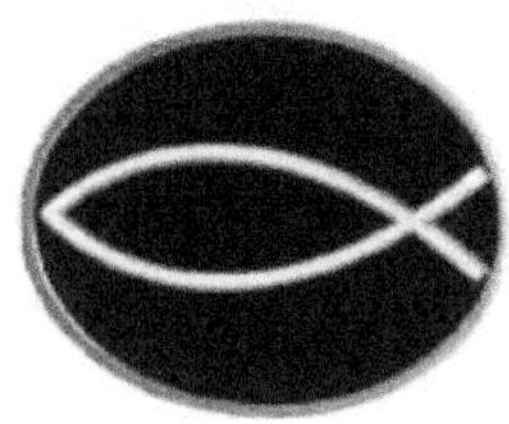

74. He said: Lord, there are many around the well, yet there is on one in the well (no one goes into it).

Plato: "The wand-bearers are many, but the initiates are few" (Phaedo 69c).

The Gnostic group, of the Ophites (serpent worshippers) wrote in "Heavenly Dialogue": 'Why are there many around the well and no one in the well?'

There is no water (truth) around the well, and nothing of value left on the outside for the thirsty. But if one goes down the metaphorical well and digs he will find running (living) water. Many talked about what Jesus was saying. Few dug in to apply it. You cannot be only a hearer of the word. You must study, understand, apply it, do it, and practice it.

James 1:22-25 New King James Version (NKJV)

22 But be doers of the word, and not hearers only, deceiving yourselves. 23 For if anyone is a hearer of the word and not a doer, he

is like a man observing his natural face in a mirror; 24 for he observes
himself, goes away, and immediately forgets what kind of man he was.
25 But he who looks into the perfect law of liberty and continues in it,
and is not a forgetful hearer but a doer of the work, this one will be
blessed in what he does.

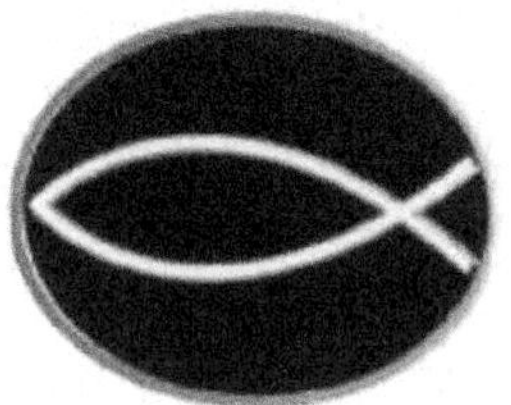

75. Jesus said: There are many standing at the door, but only those who are solitary (a single one, alone) are the ones who will enter into the Bridal Chamber.

The many who stood before the door are probably the foolish virgins of Matthew 25:1-13. The foolish had no oil for their lamps, and therefore no light, a symbol of gnosis. Only the wise virgins enter.

Only those who are solitary, one, or unified could enter. This takes us back to the idea of the undifferentiated whole and the individuated person.

The Bridal Chamber is referred to in the Gospel of Philip as a sacrament. In the chamber the male and female are united. The person is made whole as spirit and soul come together. The splitting apart and cleaving of wholeness is symbolized in the story of Adam and Eve, according to the Gnostics. When Eve came out of Adam it symbolized the separation or division within the person and within their mind and emotion. Inner unity was cut away from their spirit, splitting that once intergraded part first imparted by the divine. Keeping with the theory of wholeness and Jung's individuation, these parts must once again be merged to form a complete person, capable of accessing their true divine nature.

The Valentinian Gnostics observed a sacred ceremony called, the bridal chamber or wedding suite. In this initiation or ceremony only free men and virgins could enter. Within the ritual, the light or gnosis was received. According to the Gospel of Philip, if any one becomes a son of the bridal chamber, he will receive the light; but if he does not receive it there, he will not receive it at any other time or place.

Matthew 25:1-8 Then shall the kingdom of heaven be likened unto ten virgins, which took their lamps, and went forth to meet the bridegroom. And five of them were wise, and five were foolish. They that were foolish took their lamps, and took no oil with them: But the wise took oil in their vessels with their lamps. While the bridegroom tarried, they all slumbered and slept. And at midnight there was a cry made, Behold, the bridegroom cometh; go ye out to meet him. Then all those virgins arose, and trimmed their lamps. And the foolish said unto the wise, Give us of your oil; for our lamps are gone out.

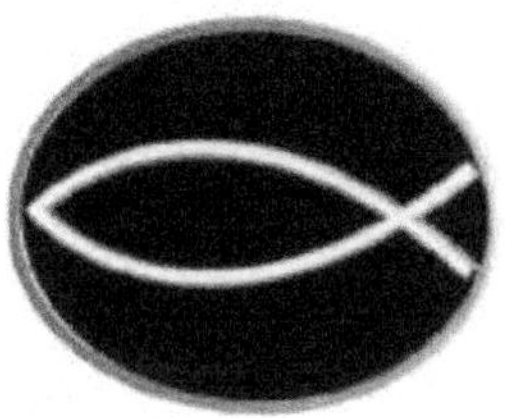

76. Jesus said: The Kingdom of the Father is like a merchant with a stock of goods who learned of a particular pearl. The merchant was shrewd because he sold his stock of goods and bought that one, single pearl for himself. You also, seek after his face (his treasure) , which does not fail, but is ceaseless, where no moth can come near to devour it nor worm to destroy it.

There was a scribal alteration in which the word "face" was corrected to be treasure. It is difficult to know if this was changed or corrected. We do not know if "treasure" or "face" was original to the saying.

In ancient days, the pearl was one of the most precious of "stones". The creation of a pearl only comes through pain, for the pearl is the tears of the oyster.

This verse is similar to Matt. 6.19, Luke 12.33 and Q, and calls on the reader to give up what they own and seek the peril of truth. Thomas shines a negative light on merchants and implores the reader to give up worldly goods to seek the treasure or face of God.

Matthew 13:45-46 Again, the kingdom of heaven is like a merchant in search of fine pearls; on finding one pearl of great value, he went and sold all that he had and bought it.

Matthew 6:19-20 Do not store up for yourselves treasures on earth, where moth and rust consume and where thieves break in and steal; but store up for yourselves treasures in heaven, where neither moth nor rust consumes and where thieves do not break in and steal.

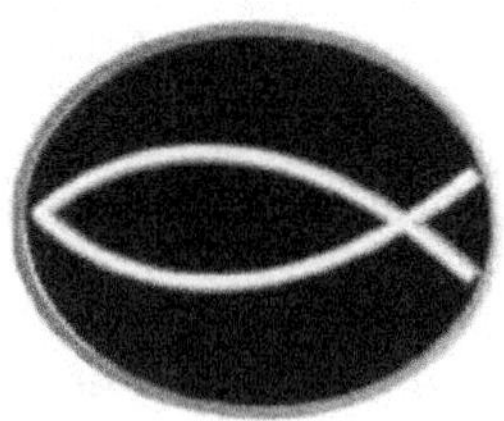

77. Jesus said: I-Am the Light who is over (above them) all things, I-Am the All. From me The All came forth and to me all has returned (The All came from me and the All has come to me). Split wood, there am I. Lift up the stone and there you will find me there.

Acts of Peter, Chapter 39: You are The All, and The All is within you, and (therefore) you exist! And there is nothing else that exists, except you alone!'

Colossians 3: 11: 'Christ is all and in all.'"

Note:
Many scholars believe the order of verses 30 and 77 were misplaced and these two verses should be connected as one verse.

30. Jesus said: Where there are three gods, they are gods (Where there are three gods they are without God). Where there is only one, I say that I am with him. Lift the stone and

there you will find me, Split the wood and there am I.

ATTRIDGE - Oxyrhynchus (Greek)

30 "Where there are [three], they are without God, and where there is but [a single one] I say that I am with [him]. Lift up the stone, and you will find me there. Split the piece of wood, and I am there."

God is everywhere and in every mundane object and task of life he can be found if you look for him.

A famous Zen Koan reads: Before enlightenment, carrying water, chopping wood. After enlightenment, carrying water, chopping wood.

Layman Pang, a Zen Buddhist (740–808) wrote:
My daily activities are not unusual,
I'm just naturally in harmony with them.
Grasping nothing, discarding nothing.
In every place there's no hindrance, no conflict.
How miraculous and wondrous
Drawing water and chopping wood.

Before we experience the truth, the world turns, and after we experience the truth the world turns in the same way. We go about working, sleeping, and eating as before, but how we perceive the world and our place in it is quite different. How many thousands of times have we carried out some menial task, lost in the mindlessness of repetition and boredom? Now the world is new and we find God everywhere.

John 8:12 Again Jesus spoke to them, saying, I am the light of the world. Whoever follows me will never walk in darkness but will have the light of life.

John 1:3 All things came into being through him, and without him not one thing came into being.

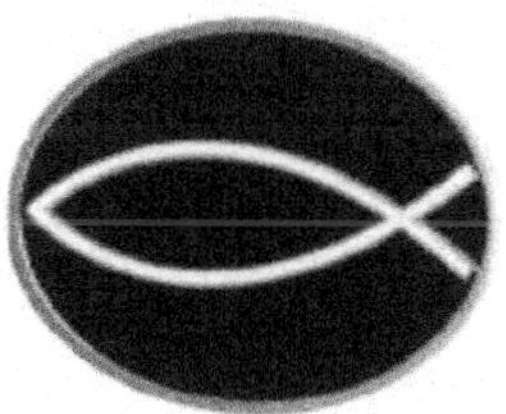

78. Jesus said: Why did you come out into the country (rural /wilderness)? Was it to see a reed shaken by the wind? And to see a person dressed in fine (soft – plush) garments like your rulers and your dignitaries? They are clothed in plush garments, and they are not able to recognize (understand / know) the truth.

Contrary to what we were taught, clothes do not make the man. Wisdom and knowledge make the man. As we proceed through the Gospel of Thomas we hear calls for asceticism repeated. Do not fall into the trap of wanting, acquiring, storing and worrying over the possessions of this world. Fine clothes and high positions will not get you to truth, unity, individuation, or peace. Do not become attached and do not depend on the things of value here. In a blink of an eye everything here can change or disappear, but the truth remains.

Matthew 11:7-9 As they went away, Jesus began to speak to the crowds about John: What did you go out into the wilderness to look at? A reed shaken by the wind? What then did you go out to see? Someone dressed in soft robes? Look, those who wear soft robes are in royal palaces. What then did you go out to see? A prophet? Yes, I tell you, and more than a prophet.

Another place where the words for "rulers and dignitaries" occurs in Revelation 6, where it the terms are translated "kings and great men".

Rev 6:13 And the stars of heaven fell unto the earth, even as a fig tree casteth her untimely figs, when she is shaken of a mighty wind. 14 And the heaven departed as a scroll when it is rolled together; and every mountain and island were moved out of their places. 15 And the kings of the earth, and the great men, and the rich men, and the chief captains, and the mighty men, and every bondman, and every free man, hid themselves in the dens and in the rocks of the mountains;

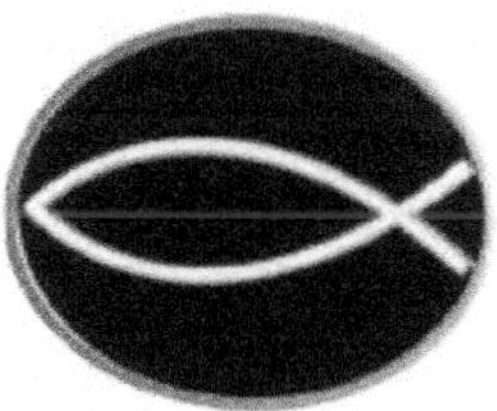

79. A woman from the crowd (multitude) said to him: Blessed is the womb which bore you, and the breasts which nursed you! He said to her: Blessed are those who have heard the word (utterance / meaning) of the Father and have truly kept it. For there will be days when you will say: Blessed be the womb which has not conceived and the breasts which have not nursed.

A cynic may interpret this as meaning Motherhood is a blessed thing but the state of motherhood binds both mother and child together to the material world, making escape all the more difficult. However, it is more likely this refers to the trials to come in which Jesus is saying it is better not to bring a child into the world in conditions to come.

F. F. Bruce writes: "Two quite independent sayings are conflated here. Jesus's reply to the woman who says how wonderful it must be to be his mother indicates that to do the will of God is more wonderful still (Luke 11.27 f.), but this is merged with his words to the weeping woman on the Via

Dolorosa (Luke 23.29). The two sayings are linked by the common theme of bearing and suckling children, but the historical perspective of the second (the impending siege and capture of Jerusalem in A.D. 70) is here replaced by a suggestion that motherhood is incompatible with 'hearing the Father's word and keeping it in truth'. As regularly (except in Saying 100), 'God' in the canonical text is here replaced by 'the Father'." (Jesus and Christian Origins Outside the New Testament, p. 143)

How many times have we heard a young couple say, "We would really like kids, but we do not know if it is right to bring a child into this world in the state it is in."? People have bemoaned the state of mankind since mankind began. Yet, even within the midst of war there have been people who could find peace, happiness, and truth.

Luke 11:27-28 While he was saying this, a woman in the crowd raised her voice and said to him, Blessed is the womb that bore you and the breasts that nursed you! But he said, Blessed rather are those who hear the word of God and obey it!

Luke 23:29 For the days are surely coming when they will say, Blessed are the barren, and the wombs that never bore, and the breasts that never nursed.

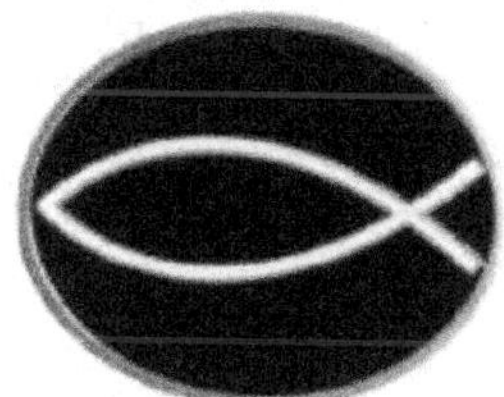

80. Jesus said: Whoever has come to understand (recognize) the world (world system) has found the body, and whoever has found the body, of him the world (world system) is not worthy.

This saying is nearly identical with saying 56, which likens the world to a 'corpse' (Greek ptoma) rather than the body (Greek to soma).

If you understand the world is dead spiritually you are already above the world.

Helmut Koester writes: "Understanding the world - a thing that is really dead - leads inevitably to a proper understanding of the body and corporeal existence. Becoming superior to the world involves deprecation of the flesh in favor of the spirit." (Ancient Christian Gospels, p. 126)

Hebrews 11:37-40 They were stoned, they were sawn asunder, were tempted, were slain with the sword: they wandered about in sheepskins and goatskins; being destitute, afflicted, tormented; (Of whom the world was not worthy:) they wandered in deserts, and in mountains, and in dens and caves of the earth. And these all, having obtained a good report through faith, received not the promise: God having provided some better thing for us, that they without us should not be made perfect.

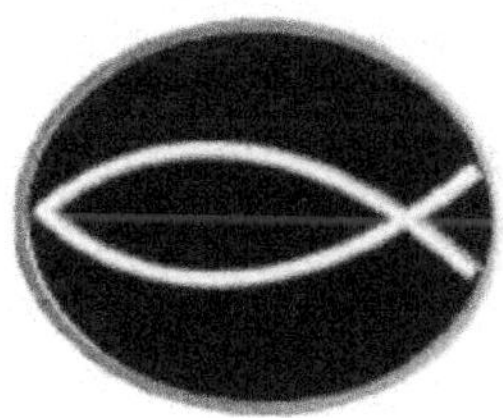

81. Jesus said: Whoever has become rich should reign (become king), and let whoever has power renounce it (refrain from its use).

This paradoxical saying refers to the richness of the spiritual life as opposed to the power wielded in the material life.

Though some scholars have trouble discerning the meaning of this verse, it may be much more straightforward than they think. In the mind of Thomas, becoming rich is obtaining Gnosis and he who comes to this knowledge will renounce his perceived place in the world and in doing so he will spiritually reign.

This saying is about putting things in their proper place with proper perspective. When we become spiritually rich we see the worthless and transitory nature of this world. Our social position, wealth, and power are seen as the illusions they are. We can easily renounce them, knowing what true wealth is.

Revelation 1:5 and from Jesus Christ, who is the faithful witness, the firstborn from the dead, and the ruler of the kings of the earth. To him who loves us and has freed us from our sins by his blood, 6 and has made us to be a kingdom and priests to serve his God and Father – to him be glory and power for ever and ever! Amen.

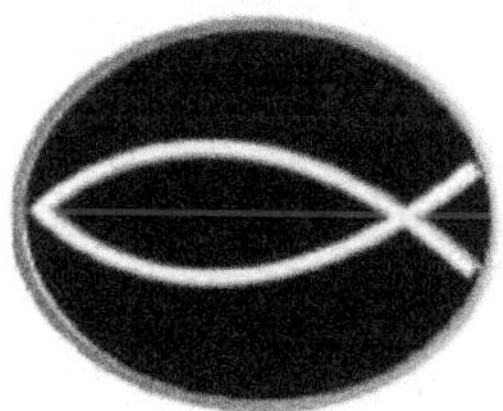

82. Jesus said: Whoever is close to me is close to the fire, and whoever is far from me is far from the Kingdom.

The fire is the gnosis that Jesus came to cast on the earth. It is referred to in sayings 9 and 16. Gnosis leads to the kingdom. The journey is not an easy one. Standing close to the fire is uncomfortable. Fire changes you, purifies you, burns out the dross in you, and leaves you in an altered state and form, one capable of entering the kingdom.

F. F. Bruce writes: "The fire is a symbol of the 'kingdom of the Father' (cf. Sayings 10, 16). We may recall that, according to Justin Martyr and others, a fire was kindled on Jordan when Jesus was baptized. [Justin Martyr, Dialogue with Trypho 88.3: 'When Jesus went down into the water a fire was kindled in the Jordan.' Cf. the 'light' which shone on the same occasion according to the Gospel of the Ebionites (p. 107)." (Jesus and Christian Origins Outside the New Testament, p. 144)

John 14:6-9 Jesus saith unto him, I am the way, the truth, and the life: no man cometh unto the Father, but by me. If ye had known me, ye should have known my Father also: and from henceforth ye know him, and have seen him. Philip saith unto him, Lord, show us the Father, and it sufficeth us. Jesus saith unto him, Have I been so long time with you, and yet hast thou not known me, Philip? he that hath seen me hath seen the Father;

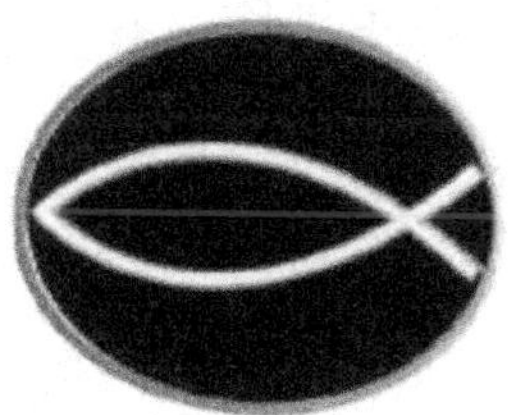

83. Jesus said: Images are visible to man but the light which is within them is hidden. The light of the father will be revealed, but he (his image) is hidden in the light.

Sophia hid the light of God when she created the Demiurge. It was just a spark from the light that she captured. She tricked the Demiurge into breathing the light into Adam in order to impart a spirit into the form called man. Yet, when one looks into the pure light only the light can be seen. The source is hidden behind the light.

We are given the truth in the forms of signs, symbols, allegories, metaphors, and the words of prophets. Truth is never presented in its full form, which is The Father. No one has seen the Father. The images of truth are seen and some are understood...by some, but, just as one can look at the sun and see only its light, but never its surface, so it is with the image of God that is hidden in his light.

Funk and Hoover write: "This saying makes use of the

language of the Platonic schools, which were active at the time the Christian movement began. According to Plato, God or the Demiurge brought the world into being, but crafted it according to an eternal archetype or 'image' (sometimes called a 'form'). The sensory world was contrasted in Platonism with the world of 'images' or 'forms,' which were eternal and fixed. Platonism influenced Philo, a Jewish philosopher of considerable stature living in Alexandria, Egypt, at the time of Jesus. A little later, Clement of Alexandria, and Origen, another Egyptian Christian philosopher-theologian, began to integrate Platonism and Christian thought. This saying in Thomas thus reflects early Christian attempts to formulate its theology in Greek philosophical terms, something entirely alien to Jesus, but quite common in many parts of Christendom." (The Five Gospels, p. 518)

"In the beginning the church was a fellowship of men and women centering on the living Christ. Then the church moved to Greece, where it became a philosophy. Then it moved to Rome, where it became an institution. Next it moved to Europe where it became a culture, and, finally, it moved to America where it became an enterprise." Dick Halverson

Matthew 4:16 the people living in darkness have seen a great light; on those living in the land of the shadow of death a light has dawned."

1 John 1: 5 This is the message we have heard from him and declare to you: God is light; in him there is no darkness at all. 6 If we claim to have fellowship with him and yet walk in the darkness, we lie and do not live out the truth. 7 But if we walk in the light, as he is in the light, we have fellowship with one another, and the blood of Jesus, his Son, purifies us from all sin.

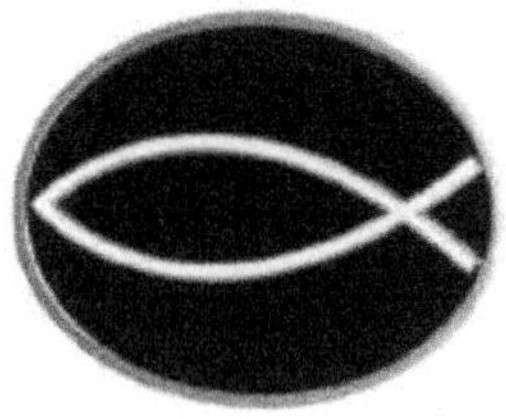

84. Jesus said: When you all see your reflections, you rejoice. Yet when you perceive your images which have come into being before you, which are immortal (do not die) nor can be seen (do not show themselves / are invisible), how will you bear the greatness of it?

Remembering that in Gnostic belief, all things are duality and are made in pairs. The earthly creature is just a likeness of our heavenly image. If we are happy to see a reflection of this likeness, think how we will react when we see the heavenly and real counterpart from which this flesh was "coined". In the Valentinian sect of the early 2nd century AD, the special rite, called the bridal chamber, celebrated the reunion of the lost spirit (which was trapped within the mortal body) with its heavenly counterpart. Christ and Sophia await the spiritual man at the entrance of the Pleroma. They help him to enter the bridal chamber for final reunion. In the fullness of time, every spiritual being will receive Gnosis and will be united with its higher Self or the angelic Twin, which is the heavenly or spiritual component to the earth-bound divine spark trapped within each person. The unity of these two parts brings us unity or wholeness and qualifies us to enter the Pleroma. Keep this metaphor of unity of higher-self and lower-self in mind when Thomas quotes Jesus when He urges us to make the inside like the outside or the high like the low. We are being called to make our earthly image like our heavenly image in one sense, and to unify them in another sense.

When we see Christ we will see that we are like him. We have been changed to be like him. Christ is the light of the world. Gnosis is fire and fire is light and we shall be alight.

1 John 3:2 Aramaic Bible in Plain English
Beloved, now we are the children of God, and it has not been revealed until now what we are going to be, but we know that when he has been revealed, we shall be in his likeness, and we shall see him just as what he is.
1 John 3:2 Holman Christian Standard Bible
2 Dear friends, we are God's children now, and what we will be has not yet been revealed. We know that when He appears, we will be like Him, because we will see Him as He is.

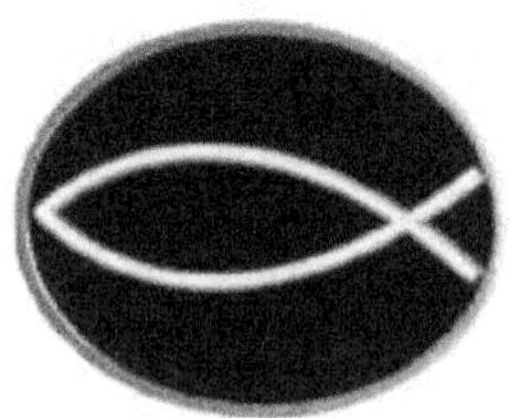

85. Jesus said: Adam came into existence out of a great power and a great wealth, and yet he was not worthy of (any of) you. For if he had been worthy, he would not have tasted death.

It has been suggested that verses 83, 84, and 85 should be read as a single statement. It would look something like this:
Jesus said: Images are visible to man but the light which is within them is hidden. The light of the father will be revealed, but his image is hidden in the light. When you all see your reflections, you rejoice. Yet when you perceive your images which have come into being before you, which are immortal and invisible to you now, how will you bear the greatness of it? Adam came into existence out of a great power and a great wealth, and yet he was not worthy of (any of) you. For if he had been worthy, he would not have tasted death.

Robert M. Grant and David Noel Freedman write: "Doresse (pages 192-93) treats his equivalent of Sayings 83 and 84 together, but it would be better to treat 83, 84, and 85 as a unit. We begin with Saying 85. We know that Adam originated from a great power and great wealth because he was a copy of the 'image' and 'likeness' of god; he was both male and female (Genesis 1:26-27). He was not worthy of Gnostic believers, however, for he sinned - by increasing and multiplying, by being divided into male and female when Eve was taken from his rib. (Eve mus trutrn to Adam, as in Saying 112 [114].) Apparently (Saying 84), men in general can see the 'likeness,' which they still retain. Not all can see the 'images,' for to see the image is to see Christ, which means to see the kingdom and, indeed, the inner man. This true image neither dies nor is openly manifest. At this time the image cannot be seen openly or perfectly; it is fully seen only after death (1 Corinthians 13:12, quoted by Doresse). Saying 83 explains why the image cannot be fully seen now. The image contains light (see Saying 51), but this light is overshadowed by the image of the light of the Father (cf., 2 Corinthians 4:4, 6). Later, however, 'If he is manifest we shall be like him, for we shall see him as he is' (1 John 3:2). If this is what these sayings mean, Thomas has expressed it rather obscurely, using image terminology perhaps like that of the Naassenes (Hippolytus, Ref., 5, 8, 10)." (The Secret Sayings of Jesus, p. 181-182)

Yaldabaoth stole great power from his mother, Sophia and created man, very imperfectly and without a spirit. Sophia took pity and gave man a spirit. Yet Adam never received full

Gnosis because he did not know Jesus or His wisdom. Adam could not find his way back to the unity, nor the full knowledge of God. He saw only the earthly division and not the heavenly wholeness.

In Jung's idea of wholeness the metaphor within this saying speaks volumes. We are created whole, as Adam was created whole. Yet, through decisions that caused cognitive dissonance, outward trauma that fractured the soul, or through the violence of simply existing, we split, cracked, and splintered. Realizing this fact is the beginning of the search for Gnosis. When we find it we will make ourselves whole again.

International Standard Version 1 Corinthians 13: 12
Now we see only an indistinct image in a mirror, but then we will be face to face. Now what I know is incomplete, but then I will know fully, even as I have been fully known.

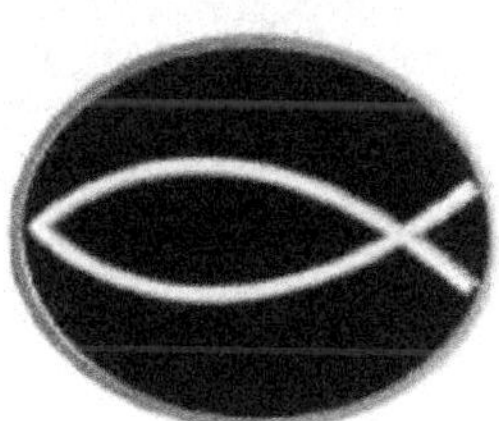

86. Jesus said: The foxes have their dens and the birds have their nests, yet the Son of Man has no place to lay his head and rest (repose).

The Greek text, "ho huios tou anthropou" may not be a title at all but probably refers to mankind. Human Beings have no place to lay their heads or rest. The ultimate goal is to find rest, which comes from Gnosis, and Jesus was sent to deliver this. In the Gnostic sense, it makes no sense that Jesus has no place to rest.

Jesus has assumed the highest level of material life, that of a pilgrim. He had renounced the material world and has given up even his bedroll.

Matthew 8:20 And Jesus said to him, Foxes have holes, and birds of the air have nests; but the Son of Man has nowhere to lay his head.

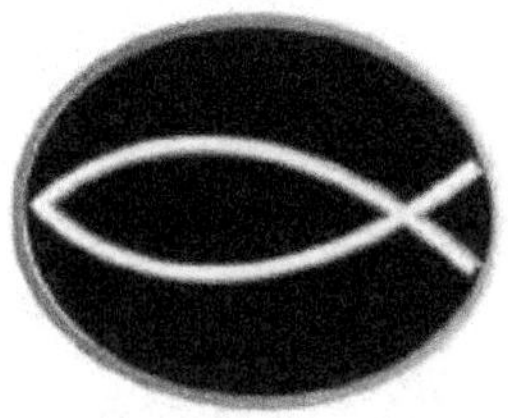

87. Jesus said: Wretched is the body which depends upon another body, and wretched is the soul which depends on these two (upon their being together).

Our bodies come into existence through birth, which requires another body. That of our mothers. In this way, our body depends on another body to even exist. After death, our body depends on the body of our children to bury it. The spirit should not depend on these two. The spirit is free from the mortal body. It does not matter where the body dies. The spirit has flown.

Jean Doresse writes: "No doubt this is to be explained by *Luke* IX, 57-60 and *Matt.* VIII, 21-2: 'Let the dead bury the dead.' In this case, 'the body which depends on a body' is a living person who, through care for earthly obligations, wishes to bury his dead person. 'The soul which depends on these two' is the soul of such a person, a living body depending on a dead body." (*The Secret Books of the Egyptian Gnostics*, p. 377)

To break all earthly ties, we should leave the dead. This includes the physically dead and the spiritually dead.

KJV Matt 8:21 And another of his disciples said unto him, Lord, suffer me first to go and bury my father. 22 But Jesus said unto him, Follow me; and let the dead bury their dead.
23 And when he was entered into a ship, his disciples followed him.

NIV Luke 9: 59 He said to another man, "Follow me."
But he replied, "Lord, first let me go and bury my father."
60 Jesus said to him, "Let the dead bury their own dead, but you go and proclaim the kingdom of God."

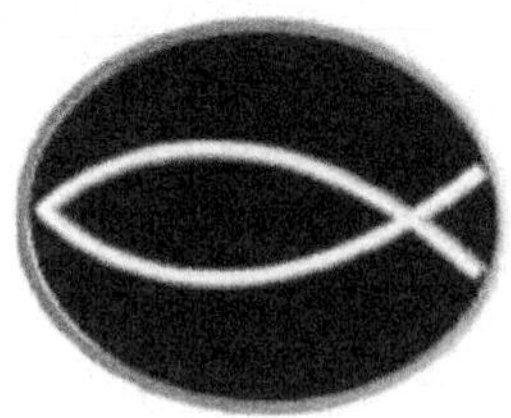

88. Jesus said: The messengers (angels) and the prophets will come to you all, and what they will give you are the things you already possess. And you will give them what you have, and say among yourselves: When will they come to take (receive) what belongs to them?

The angels will come to give you the kingdom. This is at your death. But you already possess the kingdom. You will give the angels the life you have when they come. We wonder when that time may be.

The old prophets and messengers are trying to preach to you about things you know more about than they do. You will ask yourself when they will come to understand they do not have the complete truth and when will they seek it? Preachers speak about things they have only read but do not know. It is necessary to experience it to know it.

NIV Luke 10" 21 At that time Jesus, full of joy through the Holy Spirit, said, "I praise you, Father, Lord of heaven and earth, because you have hidden these things from the wise and learned, and revealed them to little children. Yes, Father, for this is what you were pleased to do. 22 "All things have been committed to me by my Father. No one knows who the Son is except the Father, and no one knows who the Father is except the Son and those to whom the Son chooses to reveal him." 23 Then he turned to his disciples and said privately, "Blessed are the eyes that see what you see. 24 For I tell you that many prophets and kings wanted to see what you see but did not see it, and to hear what you hear but did not hear it."

Luke 12:20 New International Version (NIV)
16 And he told them this parable: "The ground of a certain rich man yielded an abundant harvest. 17 He thought to himself, 'What shall I do? I have no place to store my crops.' 18 "Then he said, 'This is what I'll do. I will tear down my barns and build bigger ones, and there I will store my surplus grain. 19 And I'll say to myself, "You have plenty of grain laid up for many years. Take life easy; eat, drink and be merry."' 20 "But God said to him, 'You fool! This very night your life will be demanded from you. Then who will get what you have prepared for yourself?'

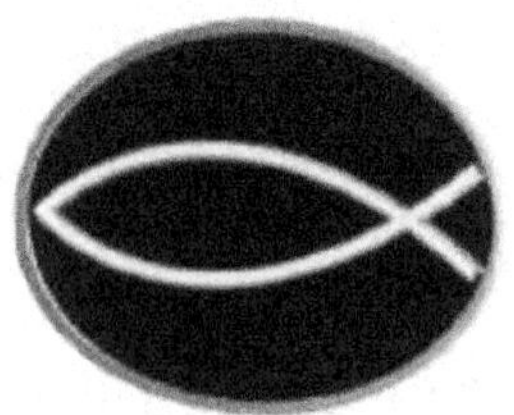

89. Jesus said: Why do you all wash the outside of your cup? Do you not understand (mind / think) that He who created the inside is also He who created the outside?

Marvin Meyer writes: "Note also the Babylonian Talmud, Berakoth 51a, with its provisions for rinsing the inside and washing the outside of a cup."

This saying has its parallel in Luke 11:29-40. Early manuscripts have the comments regarding the inside and outside reversed. The entire saying is an indictment against ritual practices without spiritual understanding. Rote memorization, mumbled liturgies, or actions without thought cannot move the spirit or reveal the truth. The Gospel of Thomas cries out for us to be present in the moment, fully realizing what you are, where you are, and what you are doing. We may look good on the outside and still our minds and hearts may be filled with greed, envy, and hate. We should be concerned about this cleansing more than the outside appearance.

The Jews were very concerned about keeping the laws. By the time of Jesus there were over 600 laws to be kept, yet if you are so concerned about the law you have no time left for the spirit. This is why Jesus broke everything down to two laws. Love others and love God. Then he said, if you hate doing something, do not do it because your hate will betray you.

Luke 11:39-40 Then the Lord said to him, Now you Pharisees clean the outside of the cup and of the dish, but inside you are full of greed and wickedness. You fools! Did not the one who made the outside make the inside also?

Matthew 23:23 "Woe to you, teachers of the law and Pharisees, you hypocrites! You give a tenth of your spices – mint, dill and cumin. But you have neglected the more important matters of the law – justice, mercy and faithfulness. You should have practiced the latter, without neglecting the former. 24 You blind guides! You strain out a gnat but swallow a camel. 25 "Woe to you, teachers of the law and Pharisees, you hypocrites! You clean the outside of the cup and dish, but inside they are full of greed and self-indulgence. 26 Blind Pharisee! First clean the inside of the cup and dish, and then the outside also will be clean. 27 "Woe to you, teachers of the law and Pharisees, you hypocrites! You are like whitewashed tombs, which look beautiful on the outside but on the inside are full of the bones of the dead and everything unclean. 28 In the same way, on the outside you appear to people as righteous but on the inside you are full of hypocrisy and wickedness.

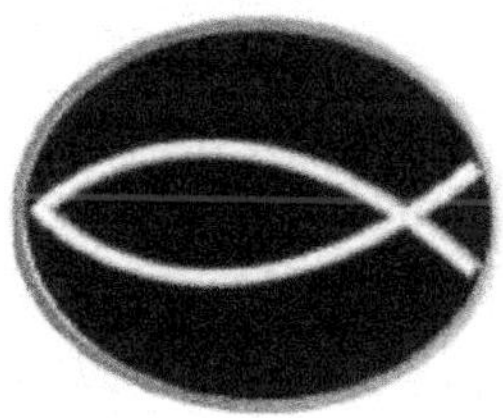

90. Jesus said: Come unto me, for my yoke is comfortable (easy to use) (natural) and my lordship (authority) is gentle (sweet / mild) – and you will find rest for yourselves.

Jesus was at peace and rest, even in the midst of chaos and persecution. Come under the mastership of Jesus and do as he instructs and all will be well with you. The implication of this verse differs from the Gospel version. In the Gospels, we are told Jesus will give us rest. Thomas says if you do as Jesus has instructed, you will find rest for yourself.

A yoke is a wooden crosspiece that is fastened over the necks of two animals and attached to the plow or cart that they are to pull. Jesus promises us a yoke that is easy, comfortable, or natural feeling.

Except for "lordship" instead of "burden" (Matt. 11:30) the shorter version of Thomas could be more original than Matthew's version.

Matthew 11:28-30 Come to me, all you that are weary and are carrying heavy burdens, and I will give you rest. Take my yoke upon you, and learn from me; for I am gentle and humble in heart, and you will find rest for your souls. For my yoke is easy, and my burden is light.

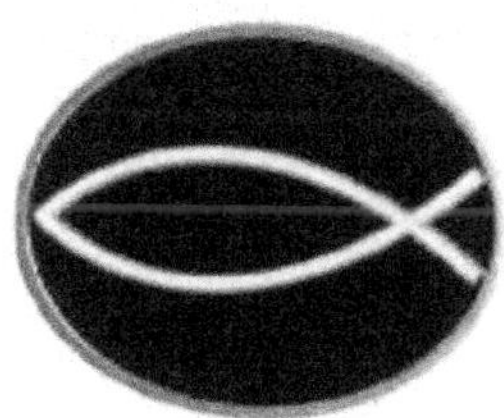

91. They said to him: Tell us who you are, so that we may believe in you. He said to them: You examine (know / can discern) the face of the sky and of the earth, yet you do not recognize the living one who is here with you, and you do not know how to test (inquire of) him at this moment (you do not know how to take advantage of this opportunity).

There is no obvious gender due to fragmentation of the Greek version and the Coptic version is neuter, so the word "him" could be rendered "the person" or "the living one".

We have lived with, are acquainted with and know the signs of the physical world. We can tell if it is going to rain or not. We know what kind of plants and animals are growing in a place, but we are not familiar with the spiritual world. We are so blind to the spiritual world we do not even recognize the messiah is walking among us.

John 9:36 He answered, And who is he, sir? Tell me, so that I may believe in him.

Luke 12:54-56 He also said to the crowds, When you see a cloud rising in the west, you immediately say, It is going to rain; and so it happens. And when you see the south wind blowing, you say, There will be scorching heat; and it happens. You hypocrites! You know how to interpret the appearance of earth and sky, but why do you not know how to interpret the present time?

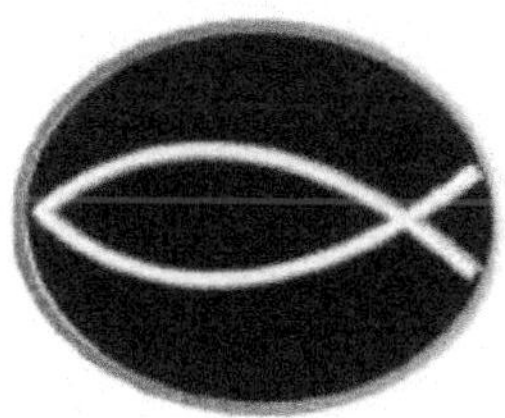

92. Jesus said: Seek and you will find. But in the past I did not answer the questions you asked. Now I wish to tell them to you, but you do not ask about (no longer seek) them.

God reveals himself in his own time. It is up to us to stay open and keep searching. In this verse, Jesus tells his followers he did not tell them certain things because it was not the proper time. Now, his time is short and he wishes to reveal more but they have stopped asking the deeper questions. As he is ready to tell them what they asked long ago, they are walking away. He asks, "Where are you going?"

Gerd Ludemann writes: "This verse calls on the reader not to give up the search, even though signs of neglect are becoming evident (v. 2b). Gnostic existence is grounded in a 'religion of searching'." (Jesus After 2000 Years, p. 635)

Berean Study Bible John 16 :1 I have told you these things so that you will not fall away. 2 They will put you out of the synagogues. In fact, a time is coming when anyone who kills you will think he is offering a service to God. 3 They will do these things because they have not known the Father or Me. 4 But I have told you these things so that when their hour comes, you will remember that I told you about them. I did not tell you these things from the beginning, because I was with you. 5 Now, however, I am going to Him who sent Me; yet none of you asks Me, 'Where are You going?'

Matthew 7:7 Ask, and it will be given you; search, and you will find; knock, and the door will be opened for you.

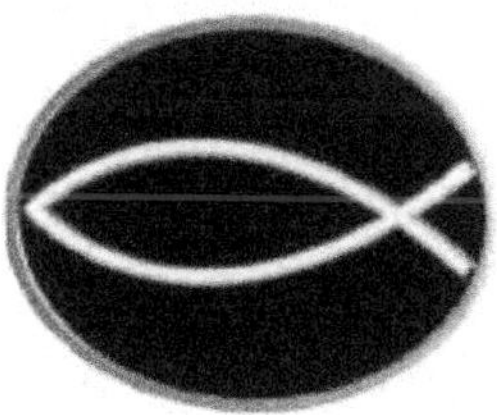

93. Jesus said: Do not give what is sacred to the dogs, because they may carry it to (lest they throw it on) the dung heap. Do not cast the pearls to the swine, lest they cause it to become dung (mud).

The last line of this verse is corrupted and fragmented. It cannot be read and so what the pigs do to the pearl is assumed.

Unless the person is seeking, and has come to a point of asking the correct question, you are wasting your time when you try to teach or convince them of the truth. They will ignore the truth, throw it away, or twist it to use against you.

This passage has been said by various scholars to refer to intercourse, Eucharist, Baptism, or knowledge. Whatever a sect believes to be sacred can apply this verse to it. This is a "Gnostic" gospel, after all, so we will assume he is referring to the secret and holy knowledge. The Gnosis.

Robert M. Grant and David Noel Freedman write: "The disciples are to seek and to find; but they are not to make public what they have found. The holy is not to be given to dogs; pearls are not to be cast to swine (outsiders are dogs and swine, as the Basilidians taught: Epiphanius, Pan., 24, 5, 2). Gnostics and Christians alike were fond of this mysterious saying (Matthew 7:6). Both Gnostics (Basilidians; Elchasaites in Hippolytus, Ref., 9, 17, 1) and Christians (Clement of Alexandria, Strom., 1, 55, 3; 2, 7, 4; Origen, Homily on Joshua, 21, 2; Tertullian, De praescriptione, 26 and 41) applied it to secret doctrines, while in the second-century Didache (9, 5) it is referred to the Eucharist, in Tertullian (De baptismo, 18, 1) to baptism. The Naassenes took it to refer to sexual intercourse (Hippolytus, Ref., 5, 8, 33), but Thomas probably does not have this interpretation in mind, at least not here." (The Secret Sayings of Jesus, p. 186)

Matthew 7:6 Do not give what is holy to dogs; and do not throw your pearls before swine, or they will trample them under foot and turn and maul you.

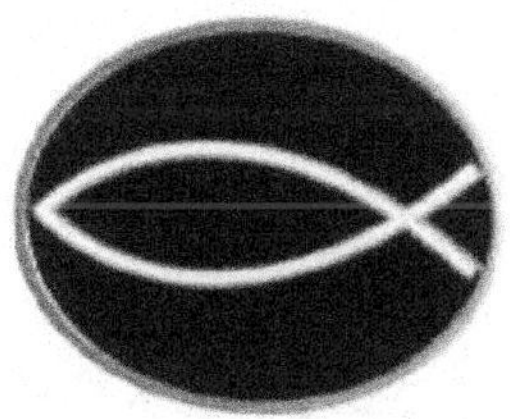

94. Jesus said: Whoever seeks will find. And whoever knocks, it will be opened to him.

When this passage appears in the Bible, some authors are quick to point out that the verb tense indicates a continuing action. That is, continue to knock and continue to seek, Do not stop knocking and seeking. A casual attempt will not get you where you need to go.

J. D. Crossan writes: "There is a lacuna in this text because the left bottom center of the manuscript page is missing. But the restoration is probably as certain as such things can be. The restored '[he who knocks]' presumes the Coptic [pettohm e]hun (literally, 'knocks inward,' and this is still residually visible in the final tip of the -h- and the complete -un. And 'will be let in' is, literally, 'they will open to him,' which is normal circumlocution for Coptic's absent passive voice.

Matthew 7:8 For everyone who asks receives, and everyone who searches finds, and for everyone who knocks, the door will be opened.

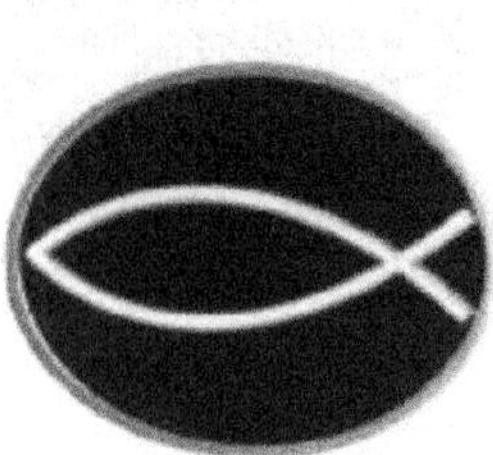

95. Jesus said: If any of you have money, do not lend at interest, but rather give it to those from whom you will not be repaid.

Do not give with the though to what you will get back. Give freely, out of compassion, not greed or expectation.

Funk and Hoover write: "Thomas records a saying that is parallel to Matt 5:42b: 'Don't turn away the one who triest to borrow from you.' Thomas' version may well be the earlier version since it is absolute: lend to those from whom you can't expect to get your capital back." (The Five Gospels, p. 522)

Comparing Thomas to Matthew and Luke, Koester finds that the Thomas form is more original: "The ending of Luke 6:34 ('Even sinners lend to sinners . . .') is a secondary addition in analogy to the ending of the preceding saying Luke 6:33 ('Even sinners do that'). Matt 5:42 reads, 'Give to the one who asks you, and do not refuse one who wants to borrow from you.' This may have preserved the wording of the original saying better than Luke 6:34, and Thomas's version can be best explained as a development of this form." (Ancient Christian Gospels, p. 90)

Matthew 5: 40 And if anyone wants to sue you and take your shirt, hand over your coat as well. 41 If anyone forces you to go one mile, go with them two miles. 42 Give to the one who asks you, and do not turn away from the one who wants to borrow from you.

Luke 6:34-35 If you lend to those from whom you hope to receive, what credit is that to you? Even sinners lend to sinners, to receive as much again. But love your enemies, do good, and lend, expecting nothing in return. Your reward will be great, and you will be children of the Most High; for he is kind to the ungrateful and the wicked.

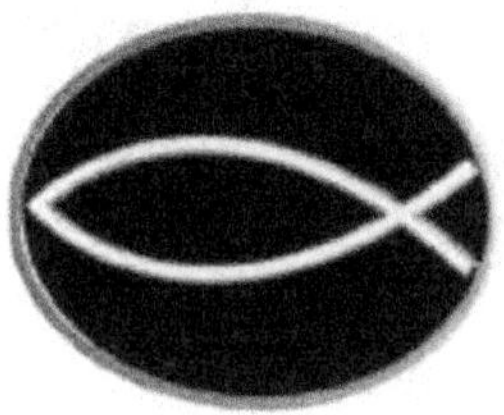

96. Jesus said: The Kingdom of the Father is like a woman who has taken a little yeast and hidden it in dough (three measures of flour). She produced large loaves with it. Whoever has ears, let him hear!

In the Gospel version of Luke, the Kingdom is like the yeast. In Thomas, the kingdom is like the woman, not the bread or yeast. The dough is the world. The yeast is Gnosis. It is the woman that impregnates the dough, with the yeast. She is the person who has Gnosis. She is the Lord and the Gnostic who has the knowledge. The reader is to emulate her. Gnostics are few and the Gnosis is hidden, but it will gestate, grow, spread, and burst forth. The truth is like cream. It eventually rises to the surface and make itself known.

Joachim Jeremias writes: "Again we are shown a tiny morsel of leaven (cf. 1 Cor. 5.6; Gal. 5.9), absurdly small in comparison with the great mass of more than a bushel of meal. The housewife mixes it, covers it with a cloth, and leaves the mass to stand overnight, and when she returns to it in the morning the whole mass of dough is leavened." (The Parables of Jesus, p. 148)

Gnosis will be hidden in the world, scattered among the seekers, but when it breaks forth it will have spread and will be a notable force. This parable is like that of the tiny mustard seed growing into a large tree.

New International Version (NIV)Luke 13 :20 Again he asked, "What shall I compare the kingdom of God to? 21 It is like yeast that a woman took and mixed into about sixty pounds[a] of flour until it worked all through the dough.

Matthew 13:33 He told them another parable: The kingdom of heaven is like yeast that a woman took and mixed in with three measures of flour until all of it was leavened.

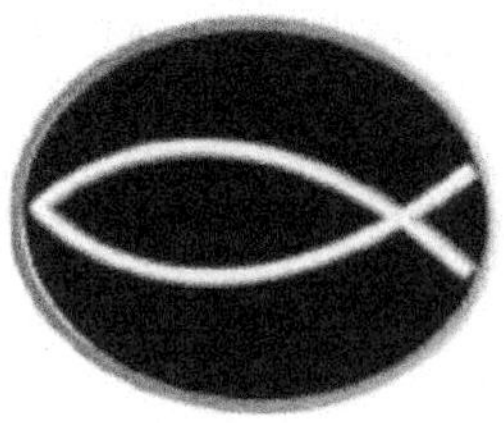

97. Jesus said: The Kingdom of the Father is like a woman who was carrying a jar full of grain (meal or flour). While she was walking on a road far from home, the handle of the jar broke and the grain (meal or flour) poured out behind her onto the road. She did not know it. She had not noticed the problem. When she arrived at her house she set the jar down and found it empty.

Many times men stumble over the truth and then, after picking themselves up, they walk away as if nothing has happened. One of the dangers of epiphanies is that they are powerful at the time but if you do not nurture them they will fade away little by little and be lost.

This is an odd parable, which is not contained in the Gospels. It is considered inauthentic by most. It is possibly a later addition by the Gnostic community. There is no hole in the container in this parable, instead the handle broke on the jar (probably a clay pot). We assume it tilted and jostled. Pouring out the meal or grain as she went. In this interpretation, it becomes a warning against letting the Gnosis fade away and losing it little by little until you are fully back in the world. One has to wonder what, if anything, the handle itself represents. Our handle on the truth? Is the handle our control of our minds, which contains the knowledge? If we do not keep our focus we can be pulled back into the mundane, carnal word and be left with nothing.

Let us not live our lives by accident or on auto-pilot, mindlessly. At the end, we will find our lives empty. We will have produced and accomplished nothing of consequence. Be aware of your actions and your thoughts. Be in the present.

Since we are unsure if the word in the parable should mean meal or seed, the Parable could take on an entirely different meaning. A possible meaning is an unnoticed spreading of seed as we go through life. This meaning would give hope to the Gnostics about growing their numbers in the Kingdom. As we move through our day, our actions and words drop along our path as seeds. If they land in the fertile heart of those around us the Kingdom may receive another soul. This is a far less likely application of the parable, since Jesus warns us in various ways in other parables about personal cost and loss of the Kingdom.

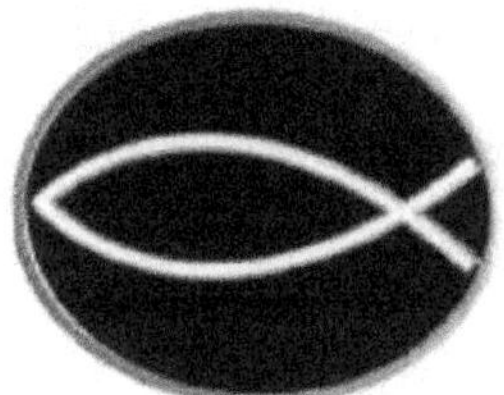

98. Jesus said: The Kingdom of the Father is like someone who wished to assassinate a prominent person. While still in his own house he (the assassin) drew his sword and thrust it into the wall in order to test whether his hand would be strong enough. Then he went and killed the prominent person.

There are several messages here. Before beginning this journey we should count the cost and then test your strength and tenacity before you begin. Half measures leave you worse off than before. Be prepared to lay down your life and count the person you are today dead. The strong man you are slaying is you. Your ego, your ignorance, and your splintered self; the you that you know will not endure. You will be reborn.

Gerd Ludemann writes: "The parable appears only at this point in the early Christian Jesus tradition. It has a high degree of offensiveness, since as in Luke 16.1-7; Matt. 13.44; Matt. 24.43-44/Luke 12.39 Jesus uses an immoral hero to make a statement about the kingdom of God. Cf. in addition the original version of the saying about 'men of violence' in Matt. 11.12/Luke 16.16 (= Q) as a further example of Jesus being deliberately offensive in what he says. . . . The parable is authentic. Because of its offensiveness it probably fell victim to moral censorship at an early stage and therefore does not appear in any other text." (Jesus After 2000 Years, p. 637)

Because of the offensive nature of the verse and moral censorship of the exact quote there are no parallel Bible verses. The following verses may capture the general meaning, framed in the light of orthodox Christianity.

Romans 6:4-7 NASB

4 Therefore we have been buried with Him through baptism into
death, so that as Christ was raised from the dead through the glory of
the Father, so we too might walk in newness of life. 5 For if we have
become united with Him in the likeness of His death, certainly we
shall also be in the likeness of His resurrection, 6 knowing this, that
our old self was crucified with Him, in order that our body of sin
might be done away with, so that we would no longer be slaves to sin;
7 for he who has died is freed from sin.

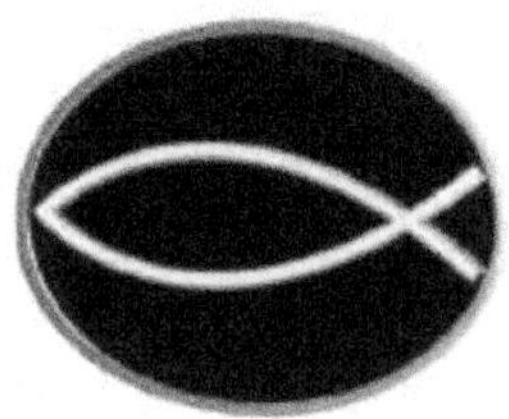

99. His Disciples said to him: Your brethren and your mother are standing outside. He said to them: It is those who are here and who do my Father's desires that are my brothers (siblings) and my Mother. It is they who will enter the Kingdom of my Father.

The operative phrase here is "the kingdom of MY FATHER". Those who are connected to the Father and part of his family are siblings. None other can make that claim. The heavenly family trumps the corporeal familial connections. Seldom are members of the same family born under the same roof. Family is gathered along the way.

In keeping with this line of thinking, some have speculated Jesus was making a point that some in his birth family as well as the Jews in general were not his true family, but pointing to the Gentiles gathered to hear him, he stated they were his family now because they heard and accepted his teaching. The Gentiles were not plotting to kill him.

Small words and short statements can make great theological differences. The Ebionites were a group of early Christians that denied the virgin birth of Jesus, and instead believed he was a spirit who only appeared to have a body. They seized upon this first to prove their point. When Jesus seemed to deny Mary and her children were his mother and brothers, the Ebionites took this literally and declared Jesus was claiming he had no earthly relatives, only spiritual ones. If it more likely Jesus was simply drawing a bright line between who is and who is not "family".

Matthew 12:46-50 While he was still speaking to the crowds, his mother and his brothers were standing outside, wanting to speak to him. Someone told him, Look, your mother and your brothers are standing outside, wanting to speak to you. But to the one who had told him this, Jesus replied, Who is my mother, and who are my brothers? And pointing to his disciples, he said, Here are my mother and my brothers! For whoever does the will of my Father in heaven is my brother and sister and mother.

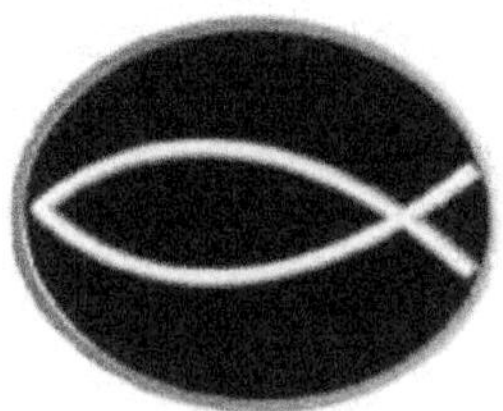

100. They showed Jesus a gold coin, and said to him: The agents of Caesar extort taxes from us. He said to them: Give the things of Caesar to Caesar, give the things of God to God, and give to me what is mine.

Here, we must remember the Gnostic stance on the God of the Old Testament. He was an inferior and insane deity who created a cruel and corrupt world. Because of his arrogance and cruelty, he attempts to keep us here, trapped by being blind to the truth there is a higher, divine source above him. He also attempts to keep us from personal integration and individuation, wherein me may discover our spiritual power and its source. The "source", father, or divine all sent Jesus to us to reveal this knowledge. Thus, in this saying the order of power and importance goes, Caeser, God, Jesus. The God of this world is inferior to Jesus, who was sent by the Divine Father.

R. McL. Wilson writes: "Grant and Freedman rightly note that Thomas does not speak of the kingdom *of God*, and that indeed 'God' is mentioned only once (logion 100), and there evidently as subordinate to Jesus. Their inference that Thomas may be reserving the name 'God' for use as that of an inferior power is also probably correct, and serves to confirm the Gnostic character of the book; as already noted, the God of the Old Testament is in the Gnostic systems degraded to the status of creator and ruler of this present evil world." (*Studies in the Gospel of Thomas*, p. 27)

It is the Demiurge that created this world. He fights to keep all souls enslaved to him in worship and obedience. Caesar and the Demiurge are both tyrants. Give them what is owed them but Jesus demands those that are his. These are the ones who have heard the word, receive Gnosis through the word, and are now free of the Demiurge's illusion.

Mark 12:14-17 Is it lawful to pay taxes to the emperor, or not? Should we pay them, or should we not? But knowing their hypocrisy, he said to them, Why are you putting me to the test? Bring me a denarius and let me see it. And they brought one. Then he said to them, Whose head is this, and whose title? They answered, The emperor's. Jesus said to them, Give to the emperor the things that are the emperor's, and to God the things that are God's. And they were utterly amazed at him.

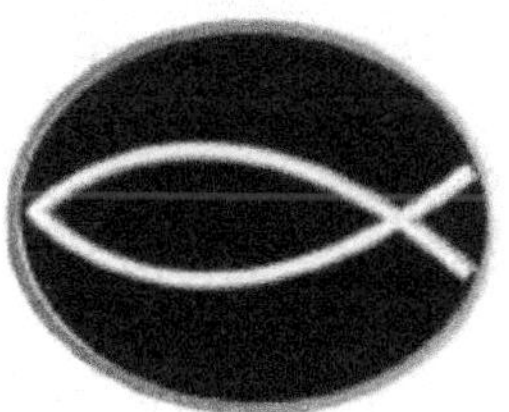

101. Jesus said: Whoever does not hate his father and his mother, in my way (as I do), will not be able to become my Disciple. And whoever does not love his father and his mother, as I do, will not be able to become my disciple. For my mother (bore me), yet my true Mother gave me the life.

The text is broken and fragmentary at the word "for my mother..." We assume "bore me" are the missing words but cannot be sure. In any case, it is obvious from the use of paradoxical couplets used in Thomas that the missing words must match this form. The earthly parents are rejected and the spiritual parents are embraced. Gnosticism, in keeping with the idea of balance of energies and power, accepts the idea of the Holy Spirit being a feminine force.

According to the Old Testament book of Genesis in the Hebrew text, there was a balance of male and female forces within God from the beginning. God was neither male nor female and both male and female, God showed the male energy of forming and shaping, as well as the female energy of nurturing and brooding. Although one may have a difficult time in distinguishing God the Spirit from the Spirit of God, the word for "spirit" is "ruach" and is a female word. However, this is the Old Testament God and thus in Gnostic eyes it is the Demiurge we speak of. His image and structure may be entirely different from that of the Divine Father.

Genesis 1 Amplified Bible

1) In the beginning God (prepared, formed, fashioned, and) created the heavens and the earth. 2) The earth was without form and an empty waste, and darkness was upon the face of the very great deep. The Spirit of God was moving (hovering, brooding) over the face of the waters.

The Holy Spirit is the designated representation of the feminine principle. This idea is supported by the Hebrew word for "spirit". Jerome, the author of the Latin Vulgate knew this when he rendered the passage into Latin. He is quoted as saying: "In the Gospel of the Hebrews that the Nazarenes read it says, 'Just now my mother, the Holy Spirit, took me.' Now, no one should be offended by this, because "spirit" in Hebrew is feminine, while in our language [Latin] it is masculine, and in Greek it is neuter. In divinity, however, there is no gender."

In Jerome's Commentary on Isaiah 11, an ex-planation contains a pointed observation. There was a tradition among a sect of Early Christians which believed that the Holy Spirit was our Lord's spiritual mother. Jerome comments that the Hebrew word for "spirit" (ruach or ruak) is feminine, meaning, that for the 1st Century Christians in the Aramaic world, the Holy Spirit was a feminine figure. This was likely because in the beginning, the converts to this new cult of Judaism, called Christianity, were mostly Jews. The gender was lost in the translation from the Hebrew into the Greek, rendering it neuter, and then it was changed to a masculine gender when it was translated from the Greek into the Latin.

The Bible in Genesis describes a male/female God with male creating and female brooding.

Although the balance of male and female energies were presented in Genesis from the outset, primitive man was not ready to accept or understand the spiritual truth of balance. Instead, mankind had to evolve spiritually over thousands of years until they were ready to resume the search for the Sacred Feminine. This time, it was within their one true God. Monotheism does not easily reveal the dualism of male and female forces.

Even today, the churches continue to struggle with the fact that

God is at once male and female. God is neither. God is both. God is all.

In Thomas, verse 101, we again see the divergent views of earthly family ties and heavenly family ties. In this case, the mother is the Holy Spirit, which in Hebrew is a feminine word and entity that gives spiritual life. In the Gnostic myth, it was Barbelo that was created as the Divine All shined forth. She was the feminine balance point.

Matthew 10:37 Whoever loves father or mother more than me is not worthy of me; and whoever loves son or daughter more than me is not worthy of me.

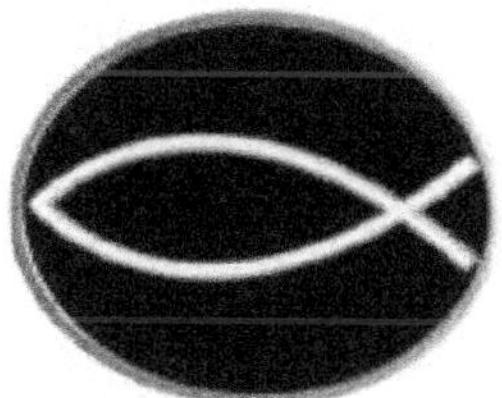

102. Jesus said: Curse these Pharisees. They are like a dog sleeping in the feed trough of cattle. For neither does he eat, nor does he allow the cattle to eat.

The learned teachers had all the information at hand to understand the kingdom, but they held to tradition and law and forced others to do the same, refusing to let them come to the knowledge of the truth and refusing to teach the people those things that could lead them to the kingdom.

J. D. Crossan writes: "The 'dog in the manger' is apparently a Greek proverb going back to 'very ancient times'. It is included among the Greek proverbs attributed to Aesop: 'a dog lying in the manger who does not eat himself but hinders the donkey from doing so'. It is also among the Latin fables as follows: 'A dog without conscience lay in the manger full of hay. When the cattle came to eat of the hay he would not let them, but showed his teeth in an ugly mood. The oxen protested: "It is not right for you to begrudge us the satisfaction of indulging our natural appetite when you yourself have no such appetite. It is not your nature to eat hay, and yet you prevent us from eating it". Lucian of Samosata (c. A.D. 125-180) gives the following version in 'Timon, or The Misanthrope': 'Not that they were able to enjoy you themselves, but that they were shutting out everyone else from a share in the enjoyment, like the dog in the manger that neither ate the barley herself nor permitted the hungry horse to eat it'. Again, in 'The Ignorant Book-Collector,' he says: 'But you never lent a book to anyone; you act like the dog in the manger, who neither eats the grain herself nor lets the horse eat it, who can' (In Fragments, pp. 34-35)

Matthew 2:13 But woe unto you, scribes and Pharisees, hypocrites! because you shut the kingdom of heaven against men; for you neither enter yourselves, nor allow those who would enter to go in.

Mark 7:13 King James Version (KJV) 13 Making the word of God of none effect through your tradition, which ye have delivered: and many such like things do ye.

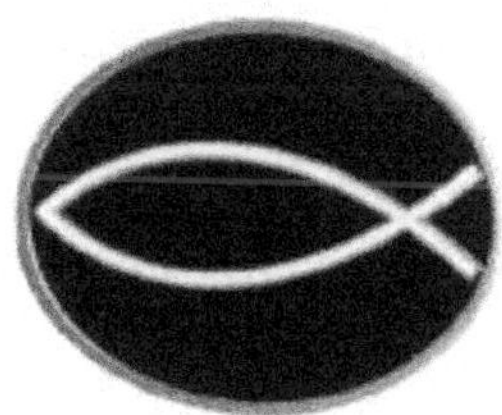

103. Jesus said: Blessed (happy) is the person who knows at what place of the house the bandits (robbers) may break in, so that he can rise and collect his things (forces) and prepare himself before they enter.

Layton

(103) Jesus said, "Blessed is the man who recognizes [which] district the brigands are going to enter, so as to arise, gather (the forces of) his domain, and arm himself before they enter."

This parable or saying looks like #21, but instead of addressing the time of an attack, this one addresses the place.

21.c - **Therefore, I say, if the owner of the house knows that the thief is coming, he will be alert before he arrives and will not allow him to break in (dig through the walls into) the royal house (the master's home) to carry away his belongings. You, must be on guard and beware of the world (system).**

Still, watch, keep vigilant, and be prepared. The approach in 103 parallels the Q version. This version literally reads, "Fortunate (blessed) is the man who knows in what part the robbers are coming." There is a rip in the text at the word we assume to be "domain". The word seems to fit well with the meaning and structure but it is a best guess.

Between 21 and 103 we are warned that we should be aware of the time and place of the attacks on us. It is as if we are being told that if we keep alert we can thwart the robbers' attack, but if we do not know when to stop him, once he gets to the house we must be aware of where he may attack. That is to say - know your weaknesses and guard them.

Keep your distance from the world. People will try to rob you of your Gnosis by trying to convince you that you are wrong. They will drag you back into the world and spoil your peace and rest.

Matthew 24:43 But understand this: if the owner of the house had known in what part of the night the thief was coming, he would have stayed awake and would not have let his house be broken into.

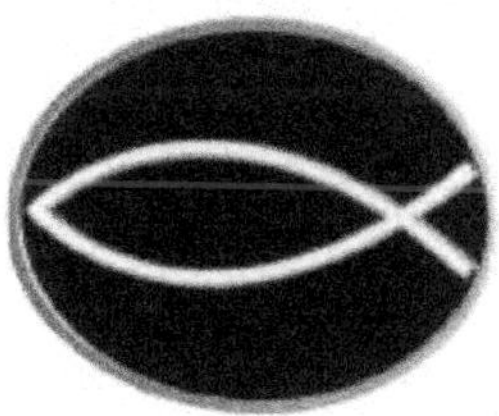

104. They said to him: Come, let us pray and let us fast today. Jesus said: What sin have I committed? How have I been overcome (undone) (been at fault)? When the Bridegroom comes forth from the bridal chamber, then let them fast and let them pray.

Jesus is telling them that these external trapping of religion make no difference and they do not reflect the state of the person. A person who has committed no sin has no need of prayer and fasting.

Jesus goes on to tell them that when the bridegroom exits the chamber they can fast, but in the Gnostic world the initiate spiritually lives in the metaphorical bridal chamber forever. This differs from Mark 2:19, in which we are told the day will come that the bridegroom is "taken" from them and on that day of grief and sadness, referring to his death, Jesus said they will indeed fast and pray.

This saying, as well as 6, 14, and 27 address the fruitlessness of ritual exterior practices in a spiritual search. Yet, in Mark the acts are not depicted as ritualistic but instead are a result of immediate, real, and compelling feelings.

This goes back to Jung's theory of individuation where one's emotions, thoughts, and actions should align and integrate. To be "authentic" and in the moment is our eternal challenge.

Mark 2:18-22 New International Version (NIV)
18 Now John's disciples and the Pharisees were fasting. Some people came and asked Jesus, "How is it that John's disciples and the disciples of the Pharisees are fasting, but yours are not?" 19 Jesus answered, "How can the guests of the bridegroom fast while he is with them? They cannot, so long as they have him with them. 20 But the time will come when the bridegroom will be taken from them, and on that day they will fast.

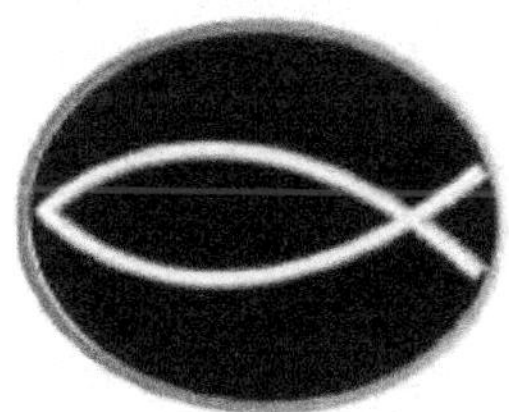

105. Jesus said: Whoever acknowledges (comes to know) father and mother, will be called the son of a whore.

The established religious leaders often called Jesus a bastard, referring to the fact that there were claims he was not Joseph's child. Indeed, strictly speaking, on the mundane physical level, this is true. God, not Joseph, whom Mary is married to under Jewish law, is the father. Jesus knows his heavenly father and mother and knows from where he came.

In Against Celsus 1.28; 32 Origen cites the tradition that Jesus was the illegitimate child of Mary, who 'bore a child from a certain soldier named Panthera.' It is known from a gravestone that a Sidonian archer named Tiberius Julius Abdes Pantera was in fact stationed in Palestine around the time of the birth of Jesus.

Another way of interpreting this verse may allude to the aesthetic demands of some Gnostic. These were celibate and decried any sexual relationship. In the Book of Thomas, Nag

Hammadi index NHC II,7, 144,8-10 declares, "Damn you who love intercourse and filthy association with womankind."

This approach to the texts leave us to wonder if Jesus feels so negatively toward women and sex if this verse is not hinting that Jesus was not born of a woman, and as some Gnostics claimed, he was only a spirit walking among us. This view must reject since it flies in the face of his association with women, his relationship with Mary of Magdala, and the Gnostic writings of Mary, Philip, and others.

The most likely meaning is the simplest - If you come to know your real mother and father (The Divine All and the Holy Spirit) you will see that you do not belong to your earthly parents. In relation to them you will feel orphaned, widowed, alone, a misfit, and a bastard.

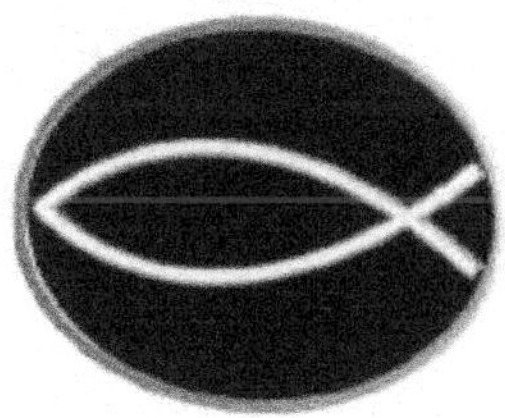

106. Jesus said: When you make the two one, you will become Sons of Man (children of Adam), and when you say to the mountain: Move! It will move.

Once again, we have the theme of unity. The inner and outer, the male and female, and the higher and lower parts of a person must be brought into unity so that when one sets oneself to a task there is not a single part of the person arguing against the envisioned goal. It is not faith that moves the mountain. It is the unity of the person. Nowhere in this saying is faith mentioned.

It should be abundantly clear by now that the Gospel of Thomas is in fact a book of mystical unity. This is its theme and purpose. The theme is visited and repeated over and over in the gospel. Verses 47, 48, 49, and 106 speak loudly about unity of mind, spirit, and action. Achieving this unity frees up vast amounts of energy, as we no longer have to partition, control, or restrain various parts of our mind or heart. We no longer have to fight the guilt or shame of the past, or the fear and anxiety of the future. We are at peace, at rest, in the present, and we are whole.

Mark 11:23 Truly I tell you, if you say to this mountain, Be taken up and thrown into the sea, and if you do not doubt in your heart, but believe that what you say will come to pass, it will be done for you.

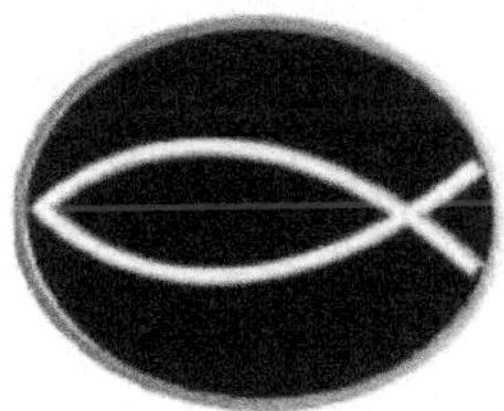

107. Jesus said: The Kingdom is like a shepherd who has a hundred sheep. The largest one of them went astray. He left the ninety-nine and sought for the one until he found it. Having searched until he was weary, he said to that sheep: I desire you more than the ninety-nine.

In this parable, we do not know if the shepherd is Jesus and the hundredth sheep is the Gnostic believer, or the shepherd is the Gnostic believer and the sheep is the knowledge. Keeping with the Gospel account we will assume the shepherd is Jesus and this is simply a Gnostic interpretation of the parable. Various versions of this story circulated at the time, and even in this collection there are similar stories. In this version, the shepherd leaves the other sheep to look for the biggest and most valuable sheep. This is not unlike the biggest fish in saying 8 and the best pearl of saying 76. The largest or best object represents the most full and deepest gnosis, or the Gnostic with the most complete gnosis. This attribute of the Gnostic version runs counter to the synoptic gospels, since they explain the father does not wish for even the smallest to perish.

Matt 18:14 So it is not the will of my father who is in heaven that one of these little ones should perish.

The number ninety-nine is found in several stories and always stands for a completion. In this case, it is a complete set. All there is. Nine represents the entire collection, set, members, or allotment. It also represents the end of a period of time.

Matthew 18:12-13 What do you think? If a shepherd has a hundred sheep, and one of them has gone astray, does he not leave the ninety-nine on the mountains and go in search of the one that went astray? And if he finds it, truly I tell you, he rejoices over it more than over the ninety-nine that never went astray.

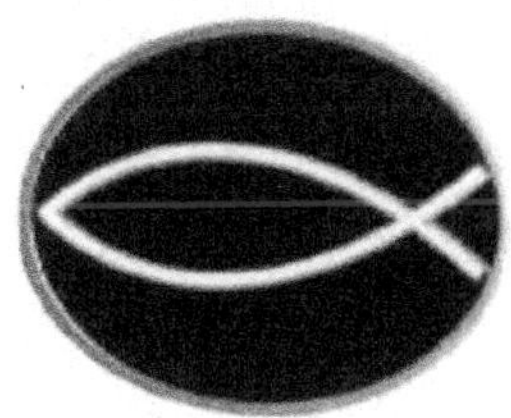

108. Jesus said: Whoever drinks from my mouth will become like me. I will become him, and the secrets will be revealed to him.

The mouth of the master feeds the soul. The mouth is the gateway to the soul thus the words of his mouth is a soul-to-soul communication. The Odes of Solomon 30:1, 5, says that living water flows from the lips of the Lord. Knowledge is imparted from the mouth and so it follows that for the Gnostics salvation comes from the mouth as the transmission of gnosis. In many mystery religions, there are rituals where the priest breathes into the mouth of the initiate as a symbol of the passing of the mystery from one to the other. Jesus breathed on his disciples and said, "Receive ye the Holy Ghost (Spirit). Ghost, breath, wind, and spirit are the same Greek word. So it was for the initiation of the Knights Templar whose master breathed on them as part of the initiation. Jesus is the breath and spirit of God. He is the water of life, the living water, the well, the ever-flowing river. Drink deeply.

Let us not forget the environment this saying was written in. Jesus lived in a desert region. The average rainfall in Jerusalem in the months of June, July, and August is 0 inches, while May and September may yield about one-tenth of an inch. Beginning in October and cycling into April of the next year, there is rainfall ranging from .5 inches per month to 5 inches per month. Water is precious. Water is life. Water can be priceless.

Spiritually, water is cleansing and purifying. It is used in christening, sprinkling, and baptism. It can represent the spirit, and in baptism, the grave giving way to the resurrection and new birth of the believer.

John 4:14 New International Version (NIV)
14 but whoever drinks the water I give them will never thirst. Indeed, the water I give them will become in them a spring of water welling up to eternal life."

Revelation 22:17 New International Version (NIV)
17 The Spirit and the bride say, "Come!" And let the one who hears say, "Come!" Let the one who is thirsty come; and let the one who wishes take the free gift of the water of life.

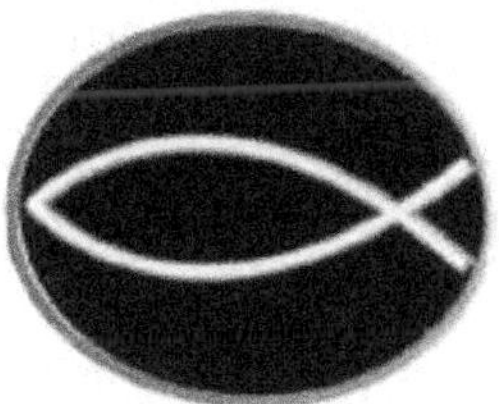

109. Jesus said: The Kingdom is like a person who had a treasure hidden in his field and knew nothing of it. After he died, he bequeathed it to his son. The son accepted the field knowing nothing of the treasure. He sold it. Then the person who bought it came and plowed it. He found the treasure. He began to lend money at interest to whomever he wished.

There is truth hidden everywhere and in everything. Split wood and it is there. Look under a stone and it is there. It is priceless, yet we give it away. We pass it by and we sell our treasure because we are too slothful to dig. The point is almost lost in this saying that the field was obviously not used by the son. It lay fallow. If the son had plowed the field he would have found the treasure. We must dig for truth, not because it is inherently buried, but because as we experience this world, its influences cover the truth in us, or force us to cover and ignore the truth we already know.

The Jews had this treasure in front of them but they did not use it. They rejected it and it was passed to the Gentiles. The Gentiles listened, asked questions, and dug for the truth - and found it.

The statement about lending at interest is troubling, since it is forbidden in saying 92. We must therefore look at this saying as a spiritual lending, or sharing of the gnosis, which always comes back many fold.

Joachim Jeremias quotes a parallel in Midrash on Canticles 4.12: "(The quotation from Canticle 4.12) is like a man who inherited a place full of rubbish. The inheritor was lazy and sold it for a ridiculously small sum. The purchaser dug therein industriously and found in it a treasure. He built therewith a great palace and passed through the bazaar with a train of slaves whom he had bought with the treasure. When the seller saw it he could have choked himself (with vexation).

Robert M. Grant and David Noel Freedman write: "It might mean that the kingdom which the Jews, or people in general, could have known was given to others [cf. Mt 8:11-12, Lk 13:29] . . . The 'lending at interest' at the end of the story would then be spiritual, for taking interest is rejected in Saying 92. On the other hand, it might mean that unless you look for the treasure within your own field it will pass to others who will profit from it. The second interpretation seems more probable." (The Secret Sayings of Jesus, p. 194)

Matthew 13:44 The kingdom of heaven is like treasure hidden in a field, which someone found and hid; then in his joy he goes and sells all that he has and buys that field.

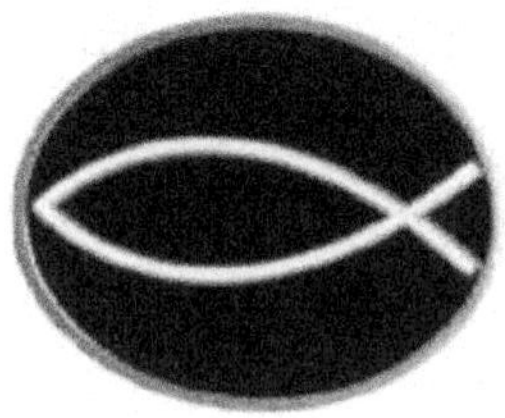

110. Jesus said: Whoever has found the world (system) and becomes wealthy (enriched by it), let him renounce the world (system).

As is stated in saying 27, we should not depend on the world or society to define us or give us our worth. Our values or self-image should not come from the world. Jung observed that those who relied on the materal world for their identity became anxious and fearful because of the uncontrollable and transient nature of life. Renounce this identity, walk away, untangle, and be free.

This saying is the same challenge to us as the one given to the rich young ruler. It is actually a question veiled in a challenge. Who do you love? What do you love? The world sets us in competition and holds those who gather the most money and possessions higher and more worthy than those who have gathered less. Yet, while we are chasing wealth we are forced to leave the spiritual aspects behind. It is not a matter of our conscious decision but a matter of time, focus, and energy, which in this life are limited resources. So, the question becomes, how will you use your resources and your allotted time on earth? Even more importantly, after you are fully invested in the meaningless race for acquisition and consumption, when the truth is revealed to you, will you give up your prizes and possessions to walk a more meager but spiritual path?

Mark 10:17-24 17 As Jesus started on his way, a man ran up to him and fell on his knees before him. "Good teacher," he asked, "what must I do to inherit eternal life?"

18 "Why do you call me good?" Jesus answered. "No one is good – except God alone. 19 You know the commandments: 'You shall not murder, you shall not commit adultery, you shall not steal, you shall not give false testimony, you shall not defraud, honor your father and mother.'" 20 "Teacher," he declared, "all these I have kept since I was a boy." 21 Jesus looked at him and loved him. "One thing you lack," he said. "Go, sell everything you have and give to the poor, and you will have treasure in heaven. Then come, follow me." 22 At this the man's face fell. He went away sad, because he had great wealth. 23 Jesus looked around and said to his disciples, "How hard it is for the rich to enter the kingdom of God!" 24 The disciples were amazed at his words. But Jesus said again, "Children, how hard it is[e] to enter the kingdom of God! 25 It is easier for a camel to go through the eye of a needle than for someone who is rich to enter the kingdom of God."

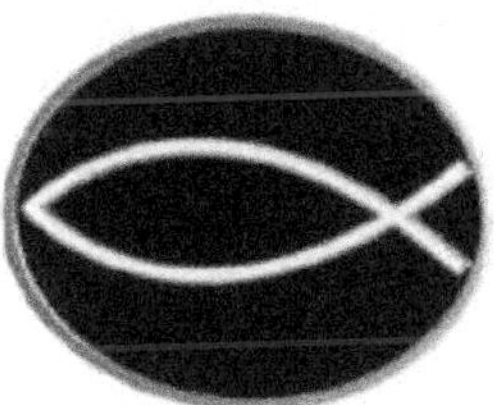

111. Jesus said: Heaven and earth will roll up (collapse and disappear) before you, but he who lives within the Living-One will neither see nor fear death. For, Jesus said: Whoever finds himself, of him the world is not worthy.

Another way of reading the verse may be:

Heaven and earth will open before you and the living (people) will come forth out of the Living One and he will not see death or fear death for, Jesus said: He who finds himself (keeps himself) of him the world is not worthy.

It is possible a later editor added the last part of this saying as an explanation, which was later made part of the saying by mistake. The line "He who finds himself, of him the world is not worthy…" is likely a later commentary that became part of the saying. Nonetheless, it is a good explanation of the text.

We must find our place in the living God and the way to do

that is to "find ourselves and keep ourselves" from the dividing power of the world, which pulls us in so many directions. In the present moment, with individual unity of all we are, we live within the living God. In doing this we will emerge from the Living One fully alive.

The imagery here is stunning. We come forth out of the living one. Not only do we realize this is how we are here now, but one day we will experience this. There is a saying: "Life is older than anything living." It means the force which brought about the human spirit is older than the first spirit. Life itself has existed long before anything or anyone was alive to witness it.

Funk and Hoover write: "In vv. 1-2, Jesus speaks as the redeemer sent from God to reveal the secrets of the universe. Such an understanding of Jesus' identity belongs to the early Jesus movement, not to Jesus himself." (The Five Gospels, p. 530)

Matthew 16:28 New International Version
"Truly I tell you, some who are standing here will not taste death before they see the Son of Man coming in his kingdom."

John 8:51 New International Version
Very truly I tell you, whoever obeys my word will never see death."

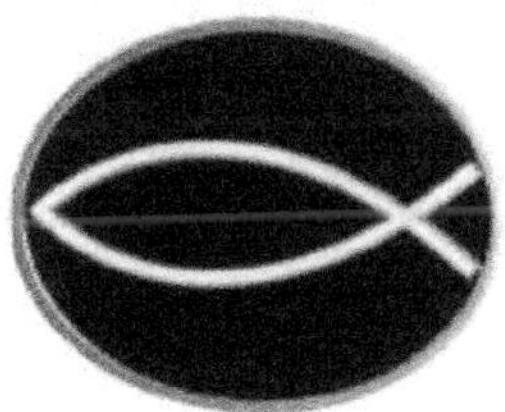

112. Jesus said: Damned is the flesh which depends upon the soul. Damned is the soul which depends upon the flesh.

In the ancient concept, soul and spirit are not the same. Soul is the mental - emotional makeup of a being. Spirit is the life force from God. Here we are told that if the mental - emotional state depends on what the flesh is going through we are lost. There is a state beyond faith. It is knowing (Gnosis) and this will not be swayed by circumstances of the flesh. If the flesh depends on the soul it will perish as the soul steps out of it into freedom from the world. If the soul depends on the flesh it will be lost in cravings and disunity.

Helmut Koester writes: "Flesh and spirit, body and soul, are two different components in a human being, joined in an unholy mix which spells doom for both" (Ancient Christian Gospels, p. 126).

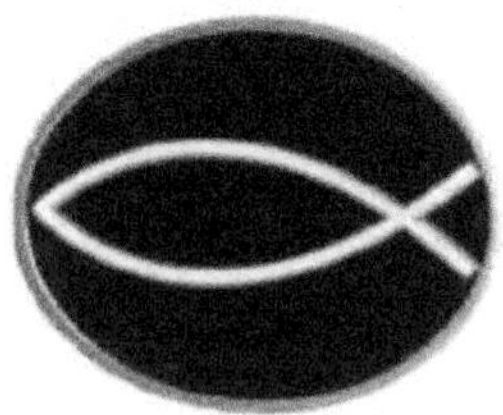

113. His Disciples said to him: When will the Kingdom come? Jesus said: It will not come by expectation (because you watch or wait for it). They will not say: Look over here! or: Look over there! But the Kingdom of the Father is spread upon the earth, and people do not realize it.

Do not look for an "advent". Do not look for a great sign that the kingdom has come. It is within you, gestating, growing as you learn the truth. It is in each of us. There is no apocalypse that will bring the Kingdom or be a sign of its coming, but we should hope that by the time an apocalypse comes we have found the kingdom. If all here is destroyed, the only safe place for the kingdom to reside is within the spirit.

In saying 2 we are told the Kingdom is within us. The Coptic version adds it is outside of us also. In saying 3 we are told not to believe those who say the kingdom is above or below you but it is inside you and outside you. It is everywhere if one were to see it. It is possible that saying 3 and 113 are different versions of the same saying. It develops a point also found in the Gospel of Mary, and other Gospel sources, such as Luke 17:20.

Gospel of Mary 8,11-22: "When the blessed one had said these things, he greeted them all, saying, 'Peace be with you. Acquire my peace for yourselves. Watch that no one misleads you, saying, "Look, here," or "Look, there," for the child of humankind is within you. Follow him. Those who seek him will find him. Go, then, and preach the gospel of the kingdom.'"

Luke 17:20 Once, on being asked by the Pharisees when the kingdom of God would come, Jesus replied, "The coming of the kingdom of God is not something that can be observed, 21 nor will people say, 'Here it is,' or 'There it is,' because the kingdom of God is in your midst."

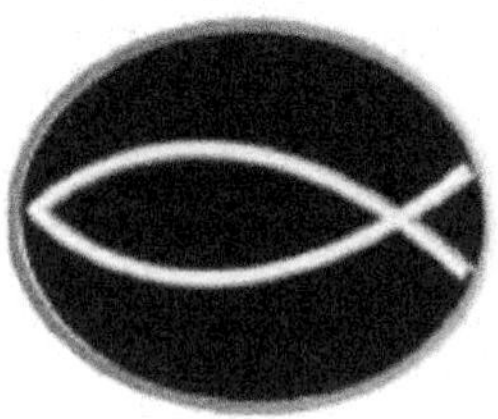

(Saying 114 was written later and was added to the original text.)

114. Simon Peter said to them: Send Mary away from us, for women are not worthy of life. Jesus said: See, I will draw her (lead her) so that I may make her male, in order that she herself will become a living spirit like you males. For every female who make themselves (becomes) male will enter the Kingdom of Heaven.

Even though we are told there is no gender in heaven, no marriage, no differences in spirit between male and female, all angels are male. This is a metaphor from the time indicating a high (male) and lower (female) state. It is a statement using social values. We are told to cast off our garments of this body and become spiritual beings. Separate ourselves from the world. Shake off this mortal coil. Become higher creatures. In saying 38 we all become bridegrooms. It is as if the default human condition is male, and so without the body we are all male.

“The 'house of God' is reserved 'for the spiritual ones alone; when they come there they cast off their garments [see Saying 38] and all become bridegrooms [Saying 75], having been made male by the virginal Spirit' (Hippolytus, Ref., 5, 8, 44). The high point of Thomas's eschatology is thus reached, at the end of his gospel, with the obliteration of sex." (The Secret Sayings of Jesus, p. 198)

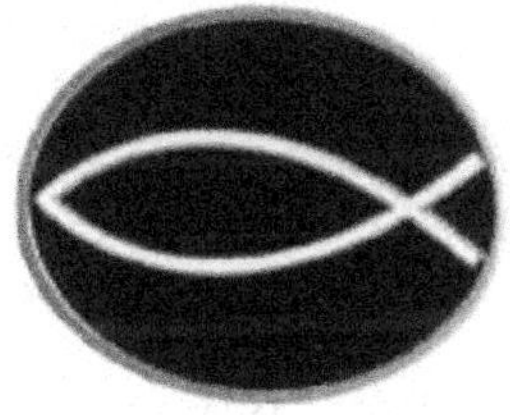

Summation

Having read the words of Thomas, what can we now say? Are these the words of Jesus? Is this a true catalog of the sayings, insights, and wisdom of the living Christ? Is Thomas simply conveying to us his memories of what he heard from Jesus when he walked the earth and taught the people? If these sayings are true they force us to reexamine modern, orthodox Christianity. Moreover, they force us to examine ourselves.

In the words of Jesus we find a plea, a command, to reach inside and reveal our true self. In discovering and knowing ourselves on the deepest level we will understand the Kingdom of Heaven, the Gnosis, is within us – it has always been. Upon realizing this truth we will know ourselves for what we are, the sons and daughters of the living God.

Jesus warns against organized religion. He steers us away from priests who steal the keys of the kingdom, keeping the truth from the people. Heaven is not above us, nor below us, nor in the hands of others, and not in any institution. The Kingdom is in you and around you and there heaven must be also. He adds that we cannot do this alone. We need God's grace to draw us and make us realize we want and need more. It is up to God to make us homesick for the Kingdom.

It is no wonder that the early church suppressed the Gospel of Thomas. As the church struggled to consolidate its authority and power, the enemy would have been individual, spiritual advancement, independent of ritual and rule. Yet, that is the essence of what the Protestant church calls salvation, if all other rituals and man-made rules were abandoned. It is the awakening caused by a personal encounter with truth itself - God, and when you are awake, fully awake, you can never fall asleep to the truth again. But the church has fallen asleep again and again, from reformation to reformation. Always, the body politic of the church struggles to suppress or even kill those rebels that have in some way awakened to the truth.

If you have ever felt as if there was more to existence than you could see, that there was another world just behind the curtain of your mind that was just out of reach which contained the full truth the words of Jesus will echo within you and lead you into light.

What is the essential wisdom within The Gospel of Thomas? Simply this; the search for self is the most difficult and troubling journey anyone could ever attempt, but it is also the only path with lasting spiritual results. If you can find what is real and honest within you, and if you have the courage to bring it forth, you will gain peace, strength and freedom forever. To deny your selfishness is to refuse to overcome it. To deny your blindness is to be held hostage by it. To ignore the longing in your heart for God is to die without knowing Him. Worst of all, to refuse to bring forth the true and holy part of you is to be destroyed by it as it sours and turns rancid within you, unborn and unseen. In this state we are neither true to God nor ourselves. We are lost and destined to suffer.

If we understand the Gospel we understand the clear and elegant truth. God is in us and outside of us, impossible to miss, undeniable to those who seek, and irresistible in His grace. He is the forgiving and loving father who awaits our return. A child knows the way and old men may realize they have lost the way, but the masses become so involved in the "world system" the way to God is forgotten or ignored.

"What must we do to be saved?" has been the same question posed for thousands of years. Jesus' answer in The Gospel of Thomas is shockingly simple. "Become passers by" and " bring forth what is within you". What does this mean? Become detached. Don't allow the world to posses you, but instead view it as though you are watching from a distance, and walking through a field. Become the observer. Separate yourself from feelings based in a world that is temporary and meaningless. Instead, focus on what is real within you. Find that part of you that is part of Him. Keep it, let it gestate, and give birth to it in your words, deeds, and thoughts. Reject all else.

How will you know it is done? What is the sign of your father in you? It is peace in the midst of motion. It is movement and rest. Whether the motion is external chaos or it is the emotions of anger or fear, there is peace and rest in your spirit. As Jesus commanded the storm, "peace, be still", He also commands us when he says, "Peace, peace I give to you. My peace I give to you, not as the world gives it, but as I alone can give it". But first, we must understand and obey.

Whoever finds the interpretation of these sayings will not taste death.

Let he who seeks not stop seeking until he finds, and when he finds he will be troubled, and when he has been troubled he will marvel and he will reign over all and in reigning, he will find rest.

If those who lead you say to you: Look, the Kingdom is in the

sky, then the birds of the sky would enter before you. If they say to you: It is in the sea, then the fish of the sea would enter ahead of you. But the Kingdom of God exists within you and it exists outside of you. Those who come to know themselves will find it, and when you come to know yourselves you will become known and you will realize that you are the children of the Living Father. Yet if you do not come to know yourselves then you will dwell in poverty and it will be you who are that poverty.

Recognize what is in front of your face, and what has been hidden from you will be revealed to you. For there is nothing hidden which will not be revealed, and nothing buried that will not be raised.

I will give to you what eye has not seen, what ear has not heard, what hand has not touched, and what has not occurred to the mind of man.

Unless you fast from the world (system), you will not find the Kingdom of God.

I stood in the midst of the world. In the flesh I appeared to them. I found them all drunk; I found none thirsty among them. My soul grieved for the sons of men, for they are blind

in their hearts and do not see that they came into the world empty and they are destined (determined) to leave the world empty. However, now they are drunk. When they have shaken off their wine, then they will repent (change their ways).

Many times have you yearned to hear these sayings which I speak to you, and you have no one else from whom to hear them. There will be days when you will seek me but you will not find me.

Become passers-by.

Blessed is the solitary and chosen, for you will find the Kingdom. You have come from it, and unto it you will return. If they said to you: From where do you come? Say to them: We have come from the Light, the place where the Light came into existence of its own accord and he stood and appeared in their image. If they say to you: Is it you? (Who are you?), say: We are his Sons and we are the chosen of the Living Father. If they ask you: What is the sign of your Father in you? Say to them: It is movement with rest.

Those who know everything but themselves, lack everything. (whoever knows the all and still feels a personal lacking, he

is completely deficient).

If you bring forth what is within you, it will save you. If you do not have it within you to bring forth, that which you lack will destroy you.

"I-Am" the Light who is over all things, "I-Am" the All. From me all came forth and to me all return (The All came from me and the All has come to me). Split wood, there am I. Lift up the stone and there you will find me.

Whoever is close to me is close to the fire, and whoever is far from me is far from the Kingdom.

Whoever drinks from my mouth will become like me. I will become him, and the secrets will be revealed to him.

Heaven and earth will roll up before you, but he who lives within the Living-One will neither see nor fear death. Whoever finds himself, of him the world is not worthy.

Bibliography

The Gospel of Thomas by Joseph Lumpkin, 2005 Fifth Estate Publishing

The Tao of Thomas by Joseph B. Lumpkin 2005 Fifth Estate Publishing

The Gnostic Gospel of Thomas: Wholeness, Enlightenment, and Individuation by Joseph Lumpkin 2012 Fifth Estate Publishing

The Scholars' Translation of the Gospel of Thomas
by Stephen Patterson and Marvin Meyer

The Complete Gospels: Annotated Scholars Version.* Copyright 1992, 1994 by Polebridge Press

The Other Gospels: Non-Canonical Texts. Philadelphia: Westminster, 1982.

The New Testament and Other Early Christian Writings: A Reader. New York: Oxford University Press, 1998.

The Apocryphal New Testament. Oxford: Clarendon, 1993.

The Gospel of Thomas: The Hidden Sayings of Jesus. San Fransisco: HarperCollins, 1992.

Vol. 1 of New Testament Apocrypha. Westminster/John Knox, 1991.

Lectures of Stephen Hoeller through Gnosis.org

Nag Hammadi Library In English. San Fransisco: HarperCollins, 1988.

Nag Hammadi Codex II,2-7 Together With XIII,2*, BRIT. LIB. OR. 4926(1), and P.OXY. 1, 654, 655. Vol. 1. New York: Brill, 1989.

The Greek Fragments.Nag Hammadi Codex II,2-7
Edited by Bentley Layton. Vol. 1. New York: Brill, 1989.
Critical Greek Text.

The Oxyrhynchus Logoi of Jesus and the Coptic Gospel According to Thomas. London: Geoffrey Chapman, 1971.

The Sayings of Jesus From Oxyrhynchus. Cambridge: Cambridge University Press, 1920.

New Sayings of Jesus. The Oxyrhynchus Papyri. London: Egypt Exploration Fund, 1904.

Amundsen, Insights from the Secret Teachings of Jesus.

Blatz, B., The Coptic Gospel of Thomas, W. Schneemelcher, ed, New Testament Apocrypha, English translation by R. McL. Wilson, James Clarke & Co. Ltd.; Westminster/John Knox Press, Cambridge; Louisville, 1991, 110-133.

Bruce, F.F., Jesus and Christian Origins Outside the New Testament.

Crossan, The Birth of Christianity.

Crossan, Four Other Gospels.

Crossan, In Fragments.

Crossan, The Historical Jesus.

Doresse, J., The secret books of the Egyptian Gnostics: An introduction to the Gnostic Coptic manuscripts discovered at

Chenoboskion, Viking/Hollis & Carter, New York/London, 1960.

Fitzmyer, J.A., The Oxyrhynchus logoi of Jesus and the Coptic Gospel according to Thomas, J.A. Fitzmyer, Essays on the Semitic background of the New Testament, Scholar's Press, Missoula, 1974, 355-433.

Funk, New Gospel Parallels.

Funk and Hoover, The Five Gospels.

Grant, R.M., Gnosticism and Early Christianity.

Grant, R.M., and Freedman, D.N., The secret sayings of Jesus, Garden City/Doubleday Collins, New York/London, 1960.

Jeremias, J., The Parables of Jesus.

Kloppenborg, et al., Q-Thomas Reader.

Koester, H., Ancient Christian Gospels.

Layton, B., Nag Hammadi codex II,2-7 together with XIII,2*, Brit. Lib. Or.4926(1), and P. Oxy. 1, 654, 655, E.J. Brill, Leiden, 1989.

Layton, B., The Gnostic Scriptures: Ancient Wisdom for the New Age, Doubleday, New York/London, 1987.

Gartner, The Theology of the Gospel According to Thomas.

Gerd Ludemann, Jesus After 2000 Years.

Morrice, Hidden Sayings of Jesus.

Patterson, The Fifth Gospel.

Robinson, J.M., ed., The Nag Hammadi Library.

Robinson, J.M., and Koester, H., Trajectories through early Christianity, Fortress, Philadelphia, 1968.

Rudolph, K., Gnosis.

Theissen, G. and A. Merz, The Historical Jesus: A Comprehensive Guide.

Valantasis, The Gospel of Thomas.

Wilson, R.M., Studies in the Gospel of Thomas, A.R. Mowbray & Co., London, 1960.

Earlychristianwritings.com/ thomas

Look for other fine books by Joseph Lumpkin.

For a complete catalog of books go to:

http://apocryphalbooks.org/

or

http://www.fifthestatepub.com

The Books of Enoch: The Angels, The Watchers and The Nephilim: (With Extensive Commentary on the Three Books of Enoch, the Fallen Angels, the Calendar of Enoch, and Daniel's Prophecy)

The Book of Giants: The Watchers, Nephilim, and The Book of Enoch

The Encyclopedia of Lost and Rejected Scriptures: The Pseudepigrapha and Apocrypha

The Book of Jubilees; The Little Genesis, The Apocalypse of Moses

The Book Of Jasher
The J. H. Parry Text in Modern English

Fallen Angels, The Watchers, and the Origins of Evil:
A Problem of Choice

End of Days: The Apocalyptic Writings

The Apocalypse of Abraham, The Apocalypse of Thomas, or The Revelation of Thomas, 4 Ezra, also referred to as 2 Esdras or the Apocalypse of Ezra, 2 Baruch, also known as the Syriac. Apocalypse of Baruch

For audio interviews by Joseph Lumpkin go to:

http://fifthestatepub.com/feinterviews/

For video interviews go to:

http://fifthestatepub.com/media/video/

Don't forget to watch all of the segments on Youtube, and other video caching sites.

Made in United States
North Haven, CT
02 April 2022

17766035R00212